ADULT AND NON FORMAL EDUCATION

ADULT AND NON FORMAL EDUCATION

Editor

Dr. Rameshwari Pandya

Adult and Non Formal Education

Rs. 875

ISBN: 978-81-7835-837-6

Published in 2010 in India by
Gyan Publishing House
23, Main Ansari Road, Darya Ganj
New Delhi-110002
Phones : 23282060, 23261060
Fax : 011-23285914
E-mail: books@gyanbooks.com
Website: www.gyanbooks.com

Laser Type Setting by: Rudra Computer Graphics, Delhi
Printed at : Chawla Offset Printers, Delhi

Dedicated to

Development Managers

Contents

Preface

"Adult and Non Formal Education: ***Different Perspectives*****"** is very interesting as well as informative book. The editor has put in all the hues, shades and color of Life Long education. This book describes, explains, evaluates and even theorizes, wherever necessary the important issues of Adult Education and Non-formal Education. The new and innovative teaching methods which were used over the years for action projects and community outreach programmes are discussed in detail. Combination of teaching strategies, charts, posters, flash cards, mobiles, dramas, bhavai, role plays, street plays, puppets, focus group discussions can be used for for imparting Education to the people of deprived section of community living under adverse conditions. The book is based upon belief that the education has a larger canvas than literacy and the action itself can and should be used as a medium of education. The important issues like Capacity building of rural women through self help groups, Vocational education, Functional Literacy, Health education, The development goals, Environmental education, Gender mainstreaming and Empowerment of women, Training the disabled and Leadership training are covered in the book. The entire book shows how these content areas can be addressed through action programs. This book will be useful to development workers, people working in GO's and NGO's, graduates and postgraduates students of home science and women's polytechnics in universities and institutes of higher education. It will also serve the needs of activists, academicians, practioners, policymakers and planners engaged in development management as they will also find this book stimulating and useful.

Introduction

In Chapter 1 **"Effective Teaching Strategies"** the editor Rameshwari Pandya and Poonam Tewari explains that it is important that teachers should have practical knowledge about instruction. Of late teachers are finding it very difficult to manage the over crowded classrooms single handed, particularly school level. Teachers need support or help either from within the school or from outside. The frame work involves different steps like the context and a-contextual approach. The context based approach is typified by the "school to work". At the other extreme, the acontextual approach is not goal oriented and is based on the premise that education is an end in itself. The emphasis in the a-contextual approach to education is on the development of values that would make students better human beings. The delivery of a-contextual elements calls for advanced learning methodoliges. The popular teaching strategies like discussion, seminar, and problem based assigments, groupwork, face to face contact, role playing. These methods have many advantages as they are learner oriented, democratic and help in logical and rational thinking capacity. It is important that we help in the capacity building of the teachers. We know that if teacher's performance does not improve neither will student-learning achievement. Incentive programs need not center on monetary rewards. They could include a range of intrinsic rewards, such as special recognition, more authority over decision making at school level, or greater opportunities for travel or training. The effectiveness of education is dependent on the effectiveness of a teacher. Most of the Indian classes are still teacher-dominated hence we should pay greater attention to teacher's effectiveness to improve the teaching learning situation so that the future generation is adequately prepared to face the changing times.

In **Chapter 2** Sushil Kumar Goel writes **"Techinical Vocational Education and Training in India: Challenges and Emerging Concerns"** The National goal of Vocationalization of Education is to fulfill the manpower requirement for national development and social requirement of providing employment to the youths. The Revised National Policy on Education (1986) and its Programme of Action (1992) while emphasizing the need for strengthening Vocational Education Programme, set a target to divert 10% of secondary students by 1995 and 25% by 2000 to vocational stream. Vocational courses at +2 levels have been designed and developed keeping in view the state of employment in the organized and unorganized sectors. Emphasis is being given on developing entrepreneurship skills to enhance self-employment and employment in unorganized sector. In spite of the fact that a large percentage of graduates from schools and degree holders are unemployed or underemployed, the response of students with reference to seeking admission in vocational stream has been low. Today, we are at a crucial point at which the economic, social, political, technological and physical environment throughout the world is changing very fast. Technical and Vocational Education and Training (TVET) should be accessible with equal opportunities to all without any discrimination rooted in caste, creed, gender, age or color. The learner, teacher, industry/employer, society and the government are the key stakeholders in planning, managing and delivering TVET. The need and concept of vertical mobility as well as emerging issues are presented in the Chapter. The position of TVET in India is in a state of flux due to lack of proper coordination among the various concerned departments and institutions. Vocational education can play an important role in achieving a vital instrument for Human Resource Development and to improve quality of life of people in general.

Niyati Pandya and Rachana Bhangaokar have titled **Chapter 3** as **"Power in Education: Influences on Children's Reasoning Capacities"** The Chapter draws from ethnographic observations made as part of a study that aimed at understanding moral development among children. Participants (N=80) belonged to four urban slum communities of Baroda city. Based on experiences and insights, the Chapter presents a critique of the teaching-learning process in educational settings and its debilitating effect on the development of basic capacities and life long skills (e.g. interpersonal communication, confidence and independent thought) crucial for future adjustment in life and society. In doing so, the paper discusses on-field challenges for a researcher utilizing a qualitative approach and underscores the importance of using child-centered strategies in education and research.

Chapter 4 by Rameshwari Pandya,Varsha Parikh and Anuradha Mathu is **"Reaching the Development Goals by Life Long Education"** Literacy is the basic need and condition for improving the capabilities and empowering an individual to be efficient in various fields. It is a potential instrument of individual well being as well as social development. It is closely related with productivity and quality of life. Literacy is an outcome of knowledge and information skills that are essential and useful for ensuring efficiency and effectiveness in our day to day life. Mere information is not so useful unless it is processed and well organized and also readily available for a particular purpose. The information with understanding and application becomes true knowledge. Life long education as an idea evolved in the context of the third world countries struggling to liberate themselves from the oppressive conditions of mass poverty.

"Life long education is based on the view that learning occurs throughout life as a normal and natural process, in the same way as physical and personal development continues".

Literacy is not only a part of the development of national resources, but a basic requisite for basic human development. Progress of one cannot be achieved without the other. Both are mutually interactive and beneficial. Therefore, both go hand in hand to achieve the target of total human development. Human Development and the quality of life and citizens are central to any development planning. The application of computer software and hardware can be rightly termed as explosion studies infer that 90% of the technology that we would have to use in 21st century is yet to be discovered as the lion's share of is ought to be credited from the bank of computer. In the beginning it is necessary that the people are sensitized to the problem of environmental hazards. The approach to implement the aforesaid programme should be instructions and training programmers. The course content may vary from place to place according to regional needs. Land degradation, deforestation and desertification, may be due to problems of over population, poor soils, use of marginal lands and fuel wood harvesting.

It is rightly said that self-sufficiency is the "key to stronger woman". Many of the problems, which are faced by women, existed because they were either illiterate or economically dependent on others. For Life Long Education programme we need to collaborate with other institutions and organizations working with similar objectives .The modern world is flooded with resources and opportunities for learning. New media and methods are now available for making learning more effective and efficient; various self-learning techniques are increasingly being available. A large number of agencies, materials and individuals, factories, farm museums, libraries, books, journals, religious groups, and political parties are playing their role in providing learning facilities. Proper environment and favorable conditions have to be created for self-learning and life-long education. Adequate planning for co-coordinated and collaborative efforts should be promoted through different agencies, individual situations and resources.

Chapter 5 "Tap The Untapped: A Project on Functional Literacy" by Rameshwari Pandya and Dimple Saluja. They write that Educational system is a Sub-system of the society. The student community is a vast reservoir of human energy waiting to be harnessed for useful purposes, they need clarity of vision, direction and opportunities that will capture and arrest their imagination, tap the power, unlock the talents and develop their potential, Youth constitute the most crucial asset of the community. Education should be closely related to the social life situation in a concrete manner for the development of social efficiency and responsibility. Education should be geared to be in tune with social demands, cultural imperatives and national requirements. Integration between an educational institution and society has to be there because the ultimate objective of the educational institution is to produce socially efficient members of the society. The Adult and non Formal education is one of main features of our Department of Extension and communication, Faculty of Family and Community Sciences. This time the department got the chance to carry out functional literacy project with coolies of Vadodara Railway Division. In total fifteen employees of Railway were given functional literacy. The main emphasis was given on Non formal way of teaching. At the end employee learnt to read as well as they were able to write simple words and sentences in Hindi and Gujarati language. Overall it was fruitful experience to teach the Class IV employees of Western Railway Division.

V. K. Rai and R. P. Rai in **Chapter 6 "Environmental Education to Environmental Ethics Education: Need of**

A Paradigm Shift for Sustainable Development" explains that Nature is a wonderful book authored by God and it does not belong to man rather man belongs to it. The Sun, the Moon, the rivers, the forests, the land the animals themselves are gifts of nature. They need to be cultivated, not desecrated, they need to be preserved, not polluted, they need to be conserved, not wasted, and there are central teachings of our religions. Moreover, it is an unadulterated truth that we are not using our resources we are abusing them and overlooking the dire need of conservation of resources and environmental protection. Hence the need of the hour is thus adopting sustainable strategies for an environmentally benign and socially forward looking development process. Sustainability thus implies meeting current human needs while preserving the environment and natural resources need by future generation. The field of environment ethics concerns human beings ethical relationship with the natural environment. Ethics is related to the moral principles that govern a person's behavior. While numerous philosophers have written on this topic, environmental ethics only developed into a specific philosophical discipline in the 1970's. Mahatma Gandhi also warned mankind against this catastrophe, saying that nature can satisfy human needs and not their greed. In order to tackle this menace there has been paradigm shift from economic centric approach to social centric recently. All said and done efforts should be made to simultaneously address development and environmental imperatives for realizing the concept of sustainable development as coined by Brundtland commission of 1987.

Chapter 7 by Varsha Parikh and Sheetal Onkar writes **"Enhancing Elementary Education Through Teaching Learning Materials (TLMs)"** A key to excellence in teaching is an acceptance and understanding of all children and their individual differences. The essence of best teaching is that the subject matter has to be communicated effectively to the students to make them understand the basic ideas. Effective communication can no longer be possible with words alone. Our traditional "chalk and talk" method finds it difficult to motivate learners. The teacher often understands the difficulty of conveying ideas and information without using resources beyond words. Teachers play very important role in raising standard of education. Informed teachers know there is rich mine of inexpensive materials like pamphlets, pictures, charts, posters, from discarded school books and exhibits of various types. To enable learners to keep pace with these widening frontiers of knowledge our teaching has to be geared up. Looking at the present scenario, there is vast difference in the teaching performance of private and government schools. Talking about elementary and primary schools of Nagar Prathmik Shikshan Samiti (NPSS), situation is quite different. Here, teacher can't ignore the fact that children coming in these classrooms are socially and economically deprived. These children display hostility, differences or withdrawals. Here, teacher is all the more taxed in finding out new ways of presenting the same information, because these students need to get more interested and more able to work with concrete, perceptual experiences. The NPSS school teachers, who are rarely exposed to in–service training programme and who always does everything else first and teaching at the last, need to be trained in proper preparation and use of TLM tricks of trade. This will make learning quicker and interesting. Hence, the need of conceptualizing this project emerged. Through present study the an attempt has been made to start resource cell of teaching learning material for one of the Cluster Resource Center (CRC-2) of Nagar Prathmik Shikshan Samiti (NPSS) of Baroda, Gujarat.

In **Chapter 8**, O.P Mishra and A.K Singh writes about importance of "**Leadership Trainirg**" and explains that the Leadership training is ultimately about creating a way for people to contribute in the development of the society. Leaders are recognized by their capacity for caring for others, clear communication and a commitment to persist. A person who is given a particular powerful authoritative position has the right to command and enforce obedience by virtue of authority of his position. There are various types of leaders present in the society. Some of the important types of leaders are operational leaders, popularity leaders, assumed representative type, prominent talent, professional leaders, lay leader, autocratic leaders, democratic leader, laissez-fair leader, monomorphic leader, polymorphic leader etc. Leaders play many roles for the development of society. Some of the important roles of a leader are spokesman, harmonizer, resource allocator, planner, executive, symbol, disseminator, entrepreneur, goal setter etc. Identification of local leaders is a difficult task. However, one can use discussion method, workshop method, group observer, questionnaire or socio-metric method, election method, reputational method, self designating technique, tracer method, social participation method etc. for locating and identifying leaders in the social system. Selected or identified leaders should be trained and used for extension work. Major objectives of leadership training can be mastering fundamental concept, learning method of identifying and analyzing problems to develop competence in group processes, and acquiring necessary technical skills for up-liftmen of the society. Informal training methods like observation, reading and talking should be used by those who are willing to develop their own leadership quality. Formal training methods like lecture, discussion, symposium, field trips, training groups, buzz groups etc. should be used by training agencies or institutions for developing leadership abilities of the selected local leaders. Trained local leaders should be used for development work in their own society.

Aparna Rao in **Chapter 9** writes **"Transparency in Leadership Communication: The Need of The Hour"** it aims to identify an interesting correlation between transparency in leaders' communication and team success. The main objective of this Chapter is to prove that team performance, goal achievement and organizational growth are directly proportionate to transparent leadership. The Chapter also aims to highlight the correlation between employer-employee trust and performance. The Chapter is based mainly on secondary data from cases/examples of successful/unsuccessful projects and companies. Communication techniques of leaders who moved away from the 'beaten track' of traditional autocratic systems, to a highly empowered team that enabled quicker decisions, responsibility, credit and ownership for the outcome, are highlighted. The researcher attempts to bring out the relationship between leadership communication methods; team loyalty and organizational performance of some companies in India and the U.S. Interviews of employees of some organizations in Mumbai were also conducted. The case studies compare between four leaders for their democratic leadership approach, and four examples of a lack of this approach. Cases include the ISRO SLV-3 project in 1973, Marbury Engineering, a civil engineering firm, the partnership between Wal-Mart and Procter & Gamble, and Stu Reed, Motorola. It can be concluded safely that a direct and democratic approach to communication is an effective tool to increase trust, credibility and enhance performance.

Chapter 10 "Reproductive Health Awareness Among Tribal Women Through Folk Ways" By Jagrati Vadnerkar and Rameshwari Pandya highlights that Tribals display a far less health and modernity as compared to the rest of the population. Their own beliefs, illiteracy, poverty, non-access to scientific information contribute to this low Health Modernity status. Obviously it might lead to maternal as well as child mortality. Similar crude births practices were found to exist in other tribal groups. The tribal women are suffering from the overall burden of three fold responsibilities' and affected with reproductive health problems. Pregnant women, women giving birth, and nursing mothers are also depicted. This perhaps indicates that the women represented fertility, motherhood and were the progenitors of the tribe. Female disadvantage in mortality attributed as the cause for the low sex ratio. Maternal mortality was reported to be high among various tribal groups but no exact data could be collected. The main causes of maternal mortality were found to be unhygienic and primitive practices for parturition. There is a common myth that home is the safest place to conduct deliveries and are afraid of using contraceptives and don't get their children immunized. This leads to the poor level of health care among women in the region. Tribal people, however, are diffident about new programmes because they have been exploited by politicians in the past." In the recent days the government run health delivery system does not function properly and so tribal women are still in the need to cope up with their reproductive health concerns. This is the challenging and emerging issue to take a step forward regarding creating awareness among reproductive health of tribal women. Their Health status can be improved significantly by scientifically executed intervention with target-appropriate educational material and techniques. In most of the tribal communities, there is a wealth of folklore related to their culture. Documentation of this folklore available in different socio-cultural systems can be modified and it may be very rewarding and could provide a model for appropriate health and sanitary practices in a given eco-system. As with the culture they also have their own folklore, folk songs, dances etc. Almost all tribal communities possess rich mythologies, folk tales, stories .which illustrate their affinity and relationship with tradition and traditional characters. Hence the folk media that includes role plays dramas; nautanki etc. will be the more convenient and effective way to create awareness among them.

Jagdish Solanki writes about **"Non-formal Education Through Red Ribbon Club"** in **chapter 11** and insists that we cannot live our life, unless we educate ourselves in non-formal, formal or informal ways. The term formal education refers to the structured educational system provided by the state for children. Non-formal education refers to education which takes place outside of the formally organized school. The very purpose of Non formal education is to produce individuals who are effective members of the society to which they belong and to develop intellect, character, appreciation and physical wellbeing of each individual. In this Chapter an attempt is made to describe RED REBION CLUB (RRC) as one of the process oriented programme, initiated by a SVADES (Society for Village Development in Petrochemical Area) which is a collective endeavor that binds the industry and rural community together towards effective socio-economic development in the rural areas surrounding industry. It is indeed a unique example of unified action in the corporate sector to contribute to the progress of rural community, their development and social upliftment. Svades is registered under the Societies Act, 1860, as a voluntary organization set up by the giant public and private sector industries in the Nandesari area of Vadodara Taluka, in the state of Gujarat, India. The flow of the chapter includes the objectives, Basis Strategies, Role of principals, programme officers, In charge, peer leaders, in forming of RRC. Further the chapter highlights five important Health issues for Health promotion and describes how health issues of youth influence the overall development of an individual.

In **Chapter 12** by Anjali Dewan **"Spirulina As A Nutritional Supplement for Adolescent Girls Health"** it deals with 200 adolescent girls in the age group of 13-15 years from two Govt. Schools of Shimla belonging to low income group. The subjects were equally divided into Experimental (E) and Control groups (C). The respondents of group E were supplemented with 2 capsules (1gm.) of spirulina after mixing with one serving (40 gm.) of wheat besan ladoo daily for six days a week for a period of two months while the group C was given a placebo for the same period. The dietary survey was conducted for three consecutive days by 24 hour recall method before and after supplementation. The results of the study showed that the mean daily intake of cereals, pulses, green leafy vegetables, sugar and jaggery was inadequate in both the groups. The intake of roots and tubers, visible fat exceeded the recommended allowances. Paleness of skin and conjunctiva, dental caries, fatigue were most prevalent among the clinical signs. The prevalence of common ailments was more marked in group C when compared with group E after introducing spirulina in the ladoos. Thus, better nutritional status and health could be attributed to spirulina supplementation. The adolescent girls were encouraged to eat a balanced diet.

Chapter 13 "Gender Mainstreaming and Empowerment of Women" by Sudha Rani explains that the development of women has always been the central focus of planning since Independence. Empowerment is a major step in this direction but is has to be seen in a relational context. The discrepancy in the ideology and practice of the empowerment policy of women in India constitutes its continued social, economic and political backwardness. Women make up 52% of our country's population. Hence there can be no progress unless their needs and interests are fully met. Empowerment would not hold any meaning unless they are made strong, alert and aware of their equal status in the society. Mere legislation and constitutional provision are not enough, but true emancipation is required through gender mainstreaming, gender analysis and empowerment of women in the various administrative, political and economic perspectives only then the all-round development of society and the nation is possible. A clear vision is needed to remove the obstacles to the path of women's emancipation both from the government and women themselves. Empowerment would become more relevant if women are educated, better informed and can take rational decisions. It is also necessary to sensitize the other sex towards women. It is important to usher in changes in societal attitudes and perceptions with regard to the role of women in different spheres of life. Adjustments have to be made in traditional gender specific performance of tasks. Change in basic attitude is required which will make people welcome the birth of a daughter. A change should give priority to the education, health, protection and empowerment of women as a matter of pride. Efforts should be directed towards all round development of each and every section of Indians women by giving them their due share. Effective gender analysis leads to better definition of human resource need and capabilities and to rectify the gender imbalance that exists. It results in a more equitable allocation of resources and benefits.

Parimal H Vyas and Priti Nigam in **Chapter 14** writes that India is a multifaceted society where no generalization could apply to the entire nation's various regional, religious, social and economic groups. Nevertheless, certain broad circumstances in which Indian women live affect the ways they participate in the economy. The Constitution of India provides legal equality for men and women of this country, however, social and economic equality is yet to be achieved. The position of Indian women has considerably changed from the birds in a cage situation. Attempts have been made to empower women in India and she has made significant strides in all fields, although their number remains insignificant. The literacy drive coupled with Information and Communication Technology (ICT) access has made Indian women to attain certain degree of cultural and economic independence to take their own decisions. The chapter **"Women and Information Technology: A Critique"** is written, keeping inmind women's empowerment as a key objective, with the use technology to successfully build personal confidence and self-esteem that has had wider implications in women's lives. Social attitudes and cultural biases are mainly identified as crucial factors discriminating against women and holding them back from attaining higher level jobs. Though women are better represented in the IT sector, they have not assumed significant role and status. We need to make effective use of complementary strategies in management, covering areas such as training, networking, mentoring, review of recruitment and promotion, family friendly policies, awareness raising, positive action, recognition of women's increasing economic role and contribution

The **Chapter 15** titled as **"Capacity Building of Rural Women Through Self Help Groups"** by Anu Kathuria, Savita Singal and Shashi Varma explains how income generation activities can lead to women empowerment. Keeping in view women's immense contribution to family and rural community, a pilot project of linking self help groups (SHGs) with banks has been introduced in Haryana to encourage thrift and savings amongst rural women and to supplement their credit needs for income generating activities. An exploratory study was conducted in Sirsa district of Haryana to study the formation, existence and nature of SHGs in rural areas. One village from each of the seven blocks of Sirsa district was selected randomly and the list of SHGs formed in these villages was obtained from the District Rural Development Agency (DRDA) of Sirsa. A total of 28 SHGs were formed out of which the composition of 24 SHGs was 'female only', having a size of 10 members each. Six Shgs had discontinued their income generating activities due to lack of cooperation among members and marketing problems. Maximum SHGs were involved in dairy agri-business, had undergone training. SHGs conducted their meeting once a month with more than ninety percent attendance of members in meetings. They were saving Rs. 50/- per month and had their accounts in Haryana Gramin Bank and State Bank of India. Internal loaning among members was practiced to meet emergencies and financial records were maintained by the group secretary. Majority of the SHGs (19) had also been sanctioned loans between Rs. 3.0 to 3.2 lacs for starting income generating activities. Out of these, 11 SHGs had also received this amount in their account while 8 SHGs had received only half of the sanctioned loan as first installment of loan. The findings on the whole have important implications for the policy makers and field functionaries

In **Chapter 16** Anjali Patnaik explains **"Assessment of Information Level of Adult Women"** India is no more considered as poor in food production. Despite of increased food production the tribal, rural and slum communities are suffering from malnutrition due to their ignorance and illiteracy. In this context this project has been carried out with the objectives of assessing the information level, practice behavior and media habits of the tribal and rural communities by developing low-cost media messages to impart education in respect of food and health care during pregnancy. Thus, 200 numbers of samples (adult women – mothers and would-be mothers) were chosen at random. With the help of social animators nutrition education was imparted by using low-cost messages. The base-line study and end-line study were conducted for pre and post evaluation purposes respectively. Focus group meeting and interaction with the social animators made the message comprehensible and easier. The comparison between baseline and end line study proved the effectiveness of low-cost messages in educating, motivating and creating awareness among the tribal and rural communities.

In **Chapter 17 "Vocational Education, Training and Rehabilitation of Persons with the Disabilities in a Technological Era"** by Sushil Kumar Goel explains that the Persons with Disabilities (PWDs) in India form the largest disadvantaged group like in most countries of the world. They are generally neglected, isolated, deprived and starved of the facilities and services which are available to the general public. They do not get their due share and also media coverage of their struggles is almost negligible. Physical accessibility, communication and social integration are the major obstacles to education and training for PWDs. There is a direct correlation between education and employment. The problem is a very complicated one because most of the PWDs do not have any formal education, three – fourth of the handicapped population living in the rural areas is completely illiterate and most of them happen to be adults. Thus imparting technical training and employment of PWDs is a serious challenge for the society. The issue of disability directly pertains to the human rights and it has been the result of long struggle. An unequal society lives in a constant fear of disaster and it would be unstable. The PWDs expect an active participation in all activities of their living. It has to be realized by all members of the society that PWDs definitely deserve some range of vocational choices and life styles like any other citizen. In a developing country like India where nearly 100 million population of People with Disabilities (PWDs) live and three – fourth of this population lives in the rural areas, it is a very challenging job to provide vocational training to PWDS . They face tremendous problems due to lack of awareness and unhealthy attitudes of the society. They need suitable vocational training, support services and necessary help for placement. Children lack vocational options and they do not have appropriate vocational choice due to incompatibility between their socio-economic status and range of abilities. The capabilities, interest and skills required for a particular trade are more important rather than having higher expectations for white collar jobs for their children with disabilities. It may also not be possible for many persons with disabilities to find open competitive employment. Under such circumstances, it may be beneficial for them to think of self-employment. Following the enactment of PWDs Act, 1995, more emphasis has been laid down for the integration of PWDs into the mainstream of life. It implies that PWDs get equal opportunities for training in their field of choice. The professionals and community members must ensure that they provide their whole – hearted support to PWDs in this direction.Vocational Education and Training will not only empower PWDs to enhance their productivity, but will also ensure job security, social equity and inclusion in the community.

Chapter 18 Training of 'Adobe Photoshop' to Differentlyabled People by Rameshwari Pandya and Pooja Mistry highlights that the computer technology is spreading all over the world and have become an integral part of the education system also. The physically handicapped is a valuable human resource which is often left untapped. This reservoir of human capabilities should be viewed from the perspective of employability if we are to help them achieve any measure of self- reliance. Computer knowledge coupled with certain other job skills increases one's chances of getting a job. Computer education is an eligibility criterion for almost all of the modern-day jobs. The differentlyabled persons have limitation of walking, standing but for computer work they are fit as they can perform their work in sitting posture. Adobe Photoshop, or simply Photoshop, is a graphics editing program developed and published by Adobe Systems. It is image manipulation software is the flagship product of Adobe Systems. It has been described as "an industry standard for graphics professionals" A project was carried out to develop understanding regarding computer 'Adobe Photoshop' amongst selected Differentlyabled people of Vadodara city. Importance of computer 'Adobe Photoshop'.Uses of Computer 'Adobe Photoshop'. Uses of Different toolbar. Uses of Different Menu bar. Small Animation was taught with proper planning and Teaching Aids. The society for the physically handicapped helps them in discovering their ability, exposing their potentials and equipping them accordingly to achieve a new identify. Simultaneously it assists them to cross the world of the disability to a different ability and from sympathy to empathy. There were 53% of handicapped between 15-30 year of age where as 35% were between 31-45 years where as 12% between 46-60 years. 100% of handicapped people had disability of legs, 47% of them were handicap from the birth & 35% were because of polio and12% were having any other reason and 6% of people were disablled because of accident. 82% of people reported that they were provided government facility and only 18% of people reported that they did not get any facility.

List of Contributors

Dr. Rameshwari Pandya
Senior Lecturer
Dept. of Extension and Communication
Faculty of Family and Community Sciences
The M.S. University of Baroda
Vadodara Gujarat

Dr. Poonam Tewari
Faculty of Home Science
G.B. Pant University
Agriculture and Technology
Pantnagar, Uttaranchal
Uddam Singh Nagar

Prof. Sushil Kumar Goel
Head & Dean of Instructions
Department of Education
Regional Institute of Education (NCERT)
Bhopal, Madhya Pradesh

Dr. AK Singh
Professor
Department of Extension Education,
Institute of Agricultural Sciences
Banaras Hindu University,
Varanasi, Uttar Pradesh

Prof. Parimal H Vyas
Head
Department of Commerce
Including Business Administration,
Ex-Dean Faculty of Commerce,
The M S University of Baroda, Vadodara

Ms. Priti Nigam
Lecturer
Department of Commerce Including
Business Administration,
The M S University of Baroda, Vadodara.

Dr. Anu Kathuria
Lecturer in Home Science
CMK PG National Girls College
Sirsa, Haryana

Prof. Savita Singal
Family Resource Management
CCS Haryana Agricultural University
Hisar, Haryana

Prof . Shashi Varma
Family Resource Management
CCS Haryana Agricultural University
Hisar, Haryana

Dr. Anjali Pattanaik
Reader
P.G. Department of Home Science
Berhampur University
Berhampur, Orissa

Dr. Anuradha Mathu
Senior Lecturer
Dept. of Extension and Communication
Faculty of Family and Community Sciences
The M.S. University of Baroda
Vadodara, Gujarat

Ms. Jagrati Vadnerkar
Research Scholar
Dept. of Extension and Communication
Faculty of Family and Community Sciences
The M.S. University of Baroda
Vadodara, Gujarat

Ms. Dimple Saluja
Lecturer
Dept. of Extension and Communication
Faculty of Family and Community Sciences
The M.S. University of Baroda
Vadodara, Gujarat

Ms. Varsha Parikh
Lecturer
Dept. of Extension and Communication
Faculty of Family and Community Sciences
The M.S. University of Baroda
Vadodara, Gujarat

Ms. Pooja Mistry
Research Scholar
Dept. of Extension and Communication

Faculty of Family and Community Sciences
The M.S. University of Baroda
Vadodara, Gujarat

Ms. Sheetal Onkar
Research Scholar
Dept. of Extension and Communication
Faculty of Family and Community Sciences
The M. S. University of Baroda
Vadodara, Gujarat

Dr. Anjali Dewan
Head
Department of Home Science
St. Bede's College
Shimla, Himachal Pradesh

Dr. Jagdish Solanki
Reader
Faculty of Social Work
The M S University of Baroda
Vadodara, Gujarat

Ms. Niyati Pandya
Research Assistant
Department of Human Development and Family Studies
Faculty of Family and Community Sciences
The M. S. University of Baroda
Vadodara, Gujarat

Dr. Rachana Bhangaokar
Lecturer
Department of Human Development and Family Studies
Faculty of Family and Community Sciences
The M. S. University of Baroda
Vadodara, Gujarat

Dr. V.K. Rai
Ex-Dean of Education
V.B.S. Purvanchal University
Jaunpur, Uttar Pradesh

Dr. R.P. Rai
Amghat New Colony
Ghazipur, Uttar Pradesh

Dr. OP Mishra
Reader
Department of Extension Education,
Institute of Agricultural Sciences
Banaras Hindu University,
Varanasi, Uttar Pradesh

Prof. Aparna Rao
Chetana's Institute of Management and Research,
Bandra, Mumbai

Dr. Shobha Rani
Scientist (Home Science),
KVK, Harnaut,
Nalanda,
R.A.U., PUSA, Bihar

1

Effective Teaching Strategies

Dr. Rameshwari Pandya
Dr. Poonam Tewari

Teaching is not a theoretical act that has universal application, but a very practical act that takes place in specific classrooms with unique students. Teachers may draw upon theories of instruction as inspiration in an eclectic way, but success in the classroom depends on the decisions teachers make based on their practical knowledge about teaching. Therefore, the topic "Teaching Strategies" must not be taken out of context and treated as a universal to follow. Instead, "Teaching Strategies" must be contextualized as one part of a teacher's practical knowledge about instruction. On the other hand, teaching can be seen as an act of cultural transmission (Spindler, 1987). The conventions of culture can greatly simplify choices that teachers make. For instance, the assignment to read and memorize the language of science is a cultural convention in many countries were a thin walls between resource-poor classrooms of 70 or more students require silence, because the teachers in the adjacent classrooms should not be disturbed. Instructional innovations (such as requiring students to interact) that are developed in more affluent countries may seem foreign to the culture of the less affluent school. Interactive teaching strategies, therefore, cannot be misconstrued as being universals for teaching science.

The conventions of culture can also explain why changing teaching strategies involves more than technical training to manage, for example, interactive students Reforming teaching strategies certainly causes changes in the micro culture of a classroom, which is embedded in a micro culture of a educational setting, which in turn is a living social icon of the culture of the community or nation. Rampal (1994) describes the tension and fear that ensued after inquiry was successfully introduced into a school in India. Even when this scientific inquiry solved a local puzzle for the community, students had to learn to cope with the community's backlash. The point is not to dismiss inquiry or other teaching strategies associated with reform. Rather, the point is that we need to recognize that teaching strategies must be discussed in the cultural context of culture transmission in a particular school or college or even in the non-formal education setup.

Of late teachers are finding it very difficult to manage the overcrowded classrooms single handed, particularly at primary school level. Teachers need support or help either from outside the institute or from within the institute. Support from within the school is the best. This type of support is possible for the teacher from the school children. The teacher's can take the help of the school children themselves to manage the other children.The students selected to assist the teacher can be otherwise called as group leaders. The class teachers should take care in identifying or selecting the group leaders, either from the same class or from higher classes. Both types of selections are recommended as per the needs of the children.

Children are the future of the nation and that basic school education is the foundation on which the intellectual capital of any nation rests. Scratch the surface just a little and a plethora of issues crop up that are fraught with on-going and deep-seated disagreement. These issues range from the meaning of education itself through issues related to the content of education and the technology of its delivery to issues concerning assessment and learning atmosphere. Often, critiques of educational systems address one or more of these issues in isolation. Here, we propose a broad framework within which the tricky issues related to education can be posed and discussed. This framework involves the following three steps, which is outlined in greater detail in the following paragraphs.

The context-based approach is typified by the "school-to-work" (STW), the approach that has gained currency in the developed countries. Proponents of this approach argue that education must be relevant to the real world, the world of work, and should be in the context of the demands made by this world. At the other extreme, the a-contextual approach is not goal oriented and is based on the premise that education is an end in itself. The emphasis in the a-contextual approach to education is on the development of values that would make students better human beings. Emphasis is also placed on unlocking the hidden potential in every human being for discovery and knowledge creation.

The implementation of a strategic posture that balances context-based and a- contextual learning requires design of aligned delivery mechanisms, besides appropriate content. Indeed, where the concern is about the student "learning to learn", process overrides content as the vital enabler - how the student is learning decides whether he / she learns how to learn rather than what he/she is learning. With the advent of computers and the Internet, attention has now come to be focused on the use of information and communication technology in education. So much so that the term "educational technology" has come to be widely (mis) used to mean "technology in education". We however use the term to denote the tools that are employed to accomplish the educational objective. True, advances in ICT need to be fully exploited but educational technology involves much more than cables, hardware and software. It requires strategic teaching - the choice of educational tools that fit the educational objective and the individual student. Delivering the right blend of context-based and a-contextual elements requires the right blend of several pedagogical methods.

While transfer of knowledge and development of lower order skills can be achieved by instructional methods, the delivery of a-contextual elements calls for advanced learning methodologies among which can be cited the following:

(a) Generative learning methodologies where students become investigators and teachers become facilitators.
(b) Cooperative learning methodologies that involve students working together in small groups to collaboratively resolve an issue.
(c) Student centered learning methods, which encourage questioning, reflection and cognition,
(d) Problem-based learning that confronts students with unstructured situations and requires them to identify the problem and recommend a solution.

What are the Teaching Strategies?
Guide to Teaching Strategies

Strategies to promote effective teaching are as diverse and numerous as the students entering a classroom. There is no "right" strategy for all teachers and all students. However, there are many "best fit" strategies that suit the teacher's personality and the students' learning style. Many states and school districts emphasize specific teaching strategies to help attain state goals and assessments. To view the strategies advocated in your district, visit your state's education department Web site.

Popular Teaching Strategies

Facilitator I Discussion

Effective discussion requires interaction between the teacher and students in a safe no-fault environment. This strategy requires:

- Positive classroom climate, in which every student has equal opportunities and is encouraged to participate in discussions.
- Lessons that can be discussed with open-ended questions and contain no single "right answer".
- Teaching students listening as well as speaking skills.
- A teacher / facilitator to control the discussion by keeping students on topic, questioning for clarity, and controlling domination by one or more students

Socratic Seminar

Students discuss the ideas and qualities of literature, a piece of music, a work of art, or historical documents within a small group seminar. Teachers act as facilitators and co-learners as well as organizers of the seminar. This strategy requires:

- Formal staff development on designing and leading seminars.
- Teaching communication skills as well as literary and visual analysis techniques.
- Small class sizes and blocked time periods for the seminar.

Problem-Based Learning or Active Learning

Students demonstrate knowledge and understanding by actively solving real world problems related to the lesson. Real world problems refer to projects and/or assignments related to current problems in today's society. This strategy require :

- Extensive unit preparation combining academic curriculum with a "real world problem".
- Teaching teamwork, research, and presentation skills.

- Student use of the Internet and other varieties of reference materials for research.

Cooperative Learning

This category contains a variety of teaching strategies that assist students in learning academic content by working in structured collaborative groups. Cooperative teaming is not simply "group work". This strategy requires:

- Teacher training in cooperative learning techniques.
- Teaching students roles and responsibilities of individuals in the cooperative group.
- Careful planning of academic assignments for the cooperative groups
- Classroom organization and structures that enable students to work in small cooperative groups effectively.

Classroom Strategies

Teacher working with diverse student populations and related issues of diversity should carefully balance academic content with instructional processes

- Use visuals
- Build on what studentsalready know
- Use group work
- Use lecture outlines andOverheads
- Involve parents
- Connect lessons with Examples from the "real world"

Small Group Teaching Strategies

The statement throws light on the importance of the place called 'classroom' in a formal system of education. It is really the place where the mature personality of the teacher influences the immature personality of the student. Clearly speaking, the way by which the teacher-student interaction that flourishes in the classroom decides the nature of the excepted behavioral outcome. The achievements of students in today's classrooms are really crunched by overcrowded classrooms, insufficient classrooms facilities, outdated teaching-learning strategies etc.

the small group teaching strategies may be most rewarding experience, which now-a-days gains popularity in secondary and tertiary levels of education.

Characteristics of Small Group Teaching Strategies

Active Participation: The first and foremost nature of a small group teaching strategy is that it must lead the members to a process of learning by active involvement of all the participants. Many recent researches in this area suggest that a tutorial atmosphere is highly essential to ensure effective teaching and learning in small group. If so, the members must range between 10 and 15. But in India a group up to 20 can be considered as a small group.

***Face-to-Face Contact*:** A thickly packed lecture or lecture-cum-demonstration class suffers a major setback from the absence of face-to-face contact, which is an essential condition for teacher to learner and learner-to-learner communication. So the second characteristic that a small group teaching strategy must possess is face-to-face contact.

Purposeful Activity: The third characteristic of small group teaching is that the session must have a purpose and must develop in an orderly way. The purpose must be the development of various faculties of all the domains - Cognitive, Affective and Psychomotor (B.S. Bloom 1967). So the selection of instructional objectives is a major factor in fixing the purpose of small group teaching strategies.

Why Small Group Strategies?

The small group provides an important atmosphere referred to as the social ecology. The development of such social ethos and values is the very determinant of the overall educational objectiveness. Development of higher level intellectual, affective and manipulative skills such as reasoning, problem solving, valuing, analyzing and synthesis, accepting feelings, development of attitudes, acquisition of interpersonal interaction ability, use of language and comprehensive ability, group dynamics and leadership qualities etc.

Modes of Small Group Teaching Techniques

One to One discussion: It finds use as an "ice-breaker" when the group meets first and helps in enhancing the listening skills.

Buzz Groups. The Buzz groups encourages maximum participation of students in the small groups at times. Here the group is divided in to further small groups of 3 - 4 students. Discussion is held for a few minutes. The process of "buzz" occurs due to active verbal interaction.

Brainstorming. Brainstorming is highly useful to elicit creative thinking to solve a problem. A continuous practice on brainstorming develops divergent thinking capacities amongst students. In brainstorming the major thrust is on the development of novel ideas and not on the quality and applicability of the thought originated. Ideas of any nature and extreme are welcomed. Quantities of ideas are given preference.

Role-playing. A role-play is very valuable in teaching interpersonal communication both verbal and nonverbal skills, particularly in areas with a high emotional content. Role-playing was found to be useful in modifying perceptions and to bring about and an empathic attitude. Evaluation and feedback regarding various roles is important for improvement.

Evaluation Discussion. This is a mode used to identify the merits and demerits of the small group teaching itself. Teacher themselves review the progress of the method and the materials in use. Each member is free to make a written statement on the performance of the small growth including the teacher.

Advantages of Small Group Teaching Strategies

- Learner oriented,
- Brings a democratic classroom climate,

- Individualization of learning, Training to adapt to various situation,
- Development of a logical and rational thinking capacity,
- Flourishing of creativity and interpersonal communication skills
- Development of higher order faculties of various domains,
- Life orientation by taking various responsibilities by students.

OTHER STRATEGIES

- Decentralized planning and implementation of local solutions to fit local problems
- Strengthening community-based mechanisms for school management Improve government schools to create a "Lokshala" model of "community school"
- In-service training programme for teachers with distance education element Cluster level strengthening of training/ developing cluster resource center
- Incentive package for performing teachers in multi-grade classrooms
- Block as unit of implementation, participation and accountability
- Locally relevant pedagogy and curriculum using "joyful learning / teaching methods"
- Coordination of UN agencies to develop, monitor and use child / school / community indicators leading to quality education
- Promoting policy dialogue on decentralization, community participation and school effectiveness.

TYPES OF TEACHING STRATEGIES

The Lively Lecture-8 Variations

- The Exquisite Oral Essay
- The Participatory Lecture
- Problem Solving : Demonstrations, Proofs, and Stories
- Energy Shifts: Alternating Mini-Lectures and Discussions

- Cutting Large Classes in Half Without Losing Control : Debates
- Smaller Groups in Large Classes : Simulations and Role Playing
- "Bells and Whistles" - The Affective, Emotional Media Presentation.

The Exquisite Oral Essay

The oral essay is a final polished work that skillfully treats a single intellectual question or problem, it has unity, the topic is introduced, illustrated, and concluded within a course period. This essay provides an "intellectual experience" for the students as they are treated to the teacher's thinking on a specific topic. Oral essays, although inspirationally, reduce students to passive observers, who are engaged at best in an internal dialogue.

The Participatory Lecture

The participatory lecture is best described as orderly brainstorming in which students generate ideas that are then organized in some rational, coherent pattern on the chalkboard. The only rule of brainstorming is to acknowledge every idea offered by writing it down. Once the board is filled, students can suggest categories and position the ideas in some coherent structure. At the end of class, the instructor or one student can be given the charge of copying the "concept map" and making copies for all the students in the class.

Problem Solving: Demonstrations, Proofs, and Stories

This lecture begins with a question, or a paradox, or an enigma, or a compelling unfinished human story; In essence, a problem that inspires student interest and require resolving. Solving the problem, depending on the discipline, may require a scientific demonstration, a mathematical proof, an economic model, the outcome of the novel's plot, or an historical narrative. While the instructor presents the problem, the students are asked to supply suggestions for the solution. These offerings can be discussed, debated, and even voted upon.

Energy Shifts: Alternating Mini-Lectures and Discussions

The following variation recognizes the conclusions of attention span studies by making clearly delineated 15-20 minute shifts in energy from the teacher to students and back again. Generally, the session begins with a 15-20 minute mini-lecture that sets the stage for an issue or topic, followed by 10-15 minutes of class discussion of implications and effects, followed by another mini-lecture that wraps up the topic or issue. This mini-lecture may provide ideas not offered in the discussion, put the discussion in a disciplinary perspective, or provide the instructor's unique insight on the topic.

Cutting Large Classes in Half without Losing Control: Debates

A structured debate can achieve more student participation and engagement without changing the instructor's central and vital role in the classroom. Students can either be assigned a side of an issue to support, or they can come to class prepared to take a seat on one particular side of an issue. The instructor can serve as the moderator and mediator, guiding the debate process such that each side gets equal time for presentation.

Smaller Groups in Large Classes: Simulations and Role Playing

The following variation is guaranteed to add energy, participation, and interaction to classes, and is adaptable to political science, economics, sociology, and other disciplines. Simulations generally begin with a mini-lecture that clearly establishes the context and setting for the role playing. Then the class is divided into a number of small groups, each representing a clearly designated role. Each group is assigned a specific, concrete task; usually to propose a position and course of action. The proposals emanating from the different groups will inevitably conflict with each other in same way; ideologically, tactically, racially, regionally, or over scarce resources.

"Bells and Whistles": The Affective, Emotional Media Presentation

An audio-visual presentation, whether it's a slide show, a video, or another uniquely-created program, has the potential to evoke affective, emotional learning by students. These presentations, especially ones with music, are designed to hook student emotions in order to arouse their interest, but there is also extensive content inherent in the visual images and lyrics. Class discussion can follow.

SUGGESTIONS

Strategies for Improving Teacher Performance

India's strategy for improving the quality of primary teaching focuses principally on providing in-service teacher training through DIETS, capacity-building at the national, state, and district levels, and pilot programs supported by NGOs and donors. This is a first step, but systematic reform is needed. It could begin with a re-evaluation of the need for lengthy pre-service teacher training in the light of higher general education among prospective teachers. It could also address the crucial issues of increasing teachers' performance incentives in small, widely scattered rural schools and improving teachers' working conditions. And it could consider ways to increase the representativeness of the teaching without reducing quality.

Improving Teachers' Preparation and Skills

Five strategies could be considered for improving teachers' preparation and skills. The first is to sustain the trend toward 12 years of pre-training general education for primary teachers. This program of general education could be made more rigorous, and entrance into teacher training institutes could be based on a standards-based screening process.

A second strategy is to concentrate both pre-service and in-service teacher training on improving teachers' repertoire of teaching skills. This will require strengthening the capacity of primary teacher training institutions to provide this training. The faculty of these institutions typically lack experience in primary education, whether as teachers or researchers. Teacher educators typically hold secondary rather than primary teaching degrees and therefore have taught only at the secondary level. And the research tradition in India has not supported the concentrated study of primary education, particularly research on classroom practices.

Without primary-level teaching or research experience, particularly in rural schools, Non formal education teacher educators are poorly prepared to educate. Moreover, they do not use a full range of active learning approaches even though research has shown that student teachers learn effective pedagogical approaches only when these approaches are demonstrated and used during their training (Jangira and Ahuja 1994, Ainscow 1994; Jangira 1995a, 1995b). The reorganization of the NCERT and the recent initiative by some university departments to produce graduates specializing in education could help overcome this deficiency in research and practical experience among teacher educators.

A third strategy is to shorten the duration of pre-service teacher training to take into account teachers' higher level of general education. Offering one year of intensive training in primary pedagogy instead would increase the number of trained teachers available.

A fourth strategy is to shorten the time between a teacher's completion of pre-service training and his or her posting to a position, as a way to improve the quality of teaching and learning and to minimize waste. In several states - Gujarat. Karnataka, Kerala, Maharashtra, Tamilnadu, and Uttar Pradesh - the yearly output of teachers from elementary teacher training institutes far exceeds the number of available positions. In some of these states teachers wait 8 to 10 years for a job. often forgetting what they learned during pre-service training. The resources spent on their training are wasted.

Some Indian educators argue that the entire policy on pre-service teacher training needs to be reconsidered to take into account the imbalance between supply and demand in some states. They suggest recruiting grade 12 graduates from the national open market (where supply exceeds demand by about 10 percent), posting them to the schools where they will be required to work to expose them to the socio cultural milieu, and then sending them for training to DIETS and other elementary teacher training institutes. The National Council for Teacher Education, established through an act of Parliament in 1993, is reviewing teacher education in India (National Council for Teacher Education, 1996). This review should cover these issues, particularly the quality of training, its alignment with requirements of teachers in actual school conditions, and its compliance with standards for physical facilities and staff.

Improving Teachers' Motivation through Performance Incentives and Better Working Conditions

The present system of teacher compensation and supervision, coupled with poor working conditions and weak inservice training, provides few incentives for teachers to improve their performance. And if teacher performance does not improve, neither will student-learning achievement. Incentive programs need not center on monetary rewards. They could include a range of intrinsic rewards, such as special recognition, more authority over decision-making at the school level, or greater opportunities for travel or training. The key is to reward effective teaching and to discourage "defective" teaching (Hanushek 1994).

Implementing incentive systems is not easy. Internationally, as well as in India, developing and employing incentive structures requires both extensive experimentation and evaluation of the results. Failures and mistakes are inevitable, given the lack of experience with such schemes. The full advantages may come only after a substantial number of new teachers and school personnel, with skills different from those currently plentiful in the schools, have been induced to enter teaching. Nonetheless, performance incentives remain the best hope for getting on a path of long-run improvement (Hanushek 1994).

One way to attract and retain good teachers might be to expand opportunities for career development, possibly by creating positions for master teachers and making these master teachers eligible for promotion to DIETS on the basis of performance. Teacher compensation policy is the responsibility of the national and state pay commissions and is beyond the scope of this study. But other strategies for introducing performance incentives could be explored, including strategies that rely-on village education committees and *Panchayati Raj* institutions. These local institutions could monitor teachers' attendance and provide recommendations for recognition or training opportunities.State and centrally sponsored schemes have begun to address working conditions for teachers. Operation Blackboard, which focused on eliminating single-teacher, single-classroom schools, addressed teachers' isolation. The consolidation of multiple small schools, which is being planned as school mapping exercises begin to identify opportunities, should also help. Continuation of the DPEP's efforts in support of the repair of school buildings, construction of toilets, and other improvements in facilities could improve teachers' perceptions of their working conditions.

Matching Teachers with Students

Teachers often are more effective with students who share their characteristics. Female teachers are more effective with female students the gender gap in learning achievement is smaller in schools with a higher share of female teachers. And teachers who share the ethnic background and language of their students are more effective than teachers who do not.

Recruiting female teachers for rural area is a particular need; fewer women are interested in rural teaching assignments than in urban assignments because of concerns about harassment and lack of facilities. Improving facilities and working conditions is thus necessary to increase the attractiveness of primary school teaching to women, especially in rural areas.The issue of harassment as a deterrent for female teachers considering rural positions also needs to be addressed. One possible solution is to employ educated married couples as teachers in small rural schools. Most teachers in low-literacy districts are married men, and about 13 percent are married to women with more than 10 years of education. Recruiting these women as teachers could increase the percentage of female teachers in low-literacy districts.

CONCLUSION

The effectiveness of education is dependent on the effectiveness of a teacher. Most of the Indian classes are still teacher-dominated hence we should pay greater attention to teacher's effectiveness to improve the teaching learning situation if the future generations are to be adequately prepared to face the changing times.

Effectiveness may be taken as one's hold on the situation and it is related to the power of influencing the environment. It is accepted prevalence of one's personality by his co-worker and subordinates. An important educational concern is the identification of able and effective teaching personnel. Attractive school buildings, well-equipped laboratory and library, efficient administrative staff, correct policies and progressive curriculum are not adequate for the effectiveness of the teacher is vital for the attainment of successful educational goals.

Teacher's effectiveness is nebulous concept as no universally acceptable formula can be given to define an effective teacher. Barr explains, "Teachers effectiveness as a relationship between teachers, pupils, and other persons concerned with the educational understanding".

Gupta and Kapoor have defined Teachers effectiveness as a repertoire of efficacy exhibited by a teacher in: Instructional strategies

- Classroom management
- Personal disposition, temperament
- Evaluation and feedback
- Interpersonal relations
- Initiative and enthusiasm
- Professional values
- Innovations in the everyday teaching-learning situations.

The teachers are willing to change their role and take up the crucial role and define themselves against all the teaching media by accepting those tasks that machine cannot do developing attitude, motivation, discovery, creativity, development of feelings and other subtle outcomes of learning and teaching.

Teachers must learn to communicate about the work together to solve common educational problems. Teachers must work towards establishing themselves as professionals. Teachers are required to engage in official assessments, typically formal tests, solely because they are members of bureautic organization. Teachers need to perceive themselves as members of large profession.

Effective teachers have the ability of approachability, cheerfulness, dependability, intelligence, enthusiasm, fairness, honesty, morality, and patience. At the same time effective teachers possess those characteristics that we have valued in teachers for generations they know their subjects well enough and with the changing time using different strategies for becoming effective teacher.

References

- **Benedict K.Y,** (1998) Small Group Teaching Strategy, University News, Association of Indian Universities, 25 May 1998, Vol. 38, No. 21.

- Computers in Class XI from Current Academic Session. Times of India, Ahmedabad, 31st August 2002.
- **Dhupker Dutta Gitika,** (1992) Teaching - An Overrated and Outdated Activity, University News, Association of Indian Universities, Vol. XXX, No. 15.
- **Hiral Dholakia,** (2002) Making Learning Exciting, Times News Network, Baroda Times, 24th July.
- **Manu Patrick,** (2002) What Makes Teacher a Professional, University News, Association of Indian Universities, 3-9 June, Vol. 40, No. 22.
- **Pandey Saroj,** (1991) Changing Roles of Teachers, University News, Association of Indian Universities.
- **Reddy Venkata K,** (1995) The Importance of Being a Teacher, UGC Professional Competency in Higher Education, Centre for Professional Development in Higher Education, University of Delhi.
- **Santawani Sarla, S,** (1986) Perception of MSU Students about their Teachers, M.Ed. Dissertation, Faculty of Education and Psychology, M.S. University, Baroda.
- **Singh L.C, Jaimini Nirupama T.S,** (1988-92) Fifth Survey of Educational Research, Trend Report, NCERT, Vol 1.
- **Soundrya K.K ,** (1997) Importance of Teachers, The Educational Review, Triplicane, Madras, January 1997, Vol. Ill, No. 1.
- Website : www.google.com.

2

Techinical Vocational Education and Training in India: Challenges and Emerging Concerns

Prof. Sushil Kumar Goel

Despite the recommendations of many Committees and Commissions and also latest announcement by the Prime Minister of India on 15th August, 2006 to establish Mission on Vocational Education, Technical Vocational Education and Training is yet to get a proper recognition in the education system of the country. The state Governments have made many pious pronouncements for its expansion, but substantial actions are yet to be initiated. With the challenges of emerging technology, market and job opportunities, and changing vocations and skill requirements, Technical Vocational Education and Training has now become a matter of utmost importance. Lack of Vocational Teachers with adequate preparation, professional training and competence is a major constraint in the successful implementation of the Technical Vocational Education and Training at the senior secondary level. The content, practicum and the objectives of teacher education for vocational stream, therefore, demand serious consideration for starting a pre-service training programme.

A vocational teacher has to be professionally competent both in his/her specific discipline (content) as well as in transacting the knowledge and skills (pedagogy) to his/her students making them competent to perform a job effectively and efficiently. Therefore, in addition to the objectives given in the teacher education for the vocational stream has to achieve the following objectives for development of competencies in student teachers:

- To integrate academic and vocational curricula so the student teacher can acquire a variety of skills.
- To prepare them to develop competency based curricula and plan course content and methods of instruction.
- To develop teaching aids such as instructional software, multimedia visual aids or study materials.
- To provide pedagogical skills for individualized instruction and tutorial and or remedial instruction.
- To prepare them to conduct training sessions, on-the-job training, to teach and demonstrate principles, techniques, procedures and/or methods of designated vocational subjects.
- To prepare them to assess students on competencies, work to determine progress, provide feedback and make suggestions for improvement.
- To prepare them to provide vocational guidance and counseling to students on course selection, career decisions, and other academic and vocational concerns.
- To prepare them to inculcate dignity, values and work ethics among the students.

Career planning at the stage of entering adulthood is a very serious concern among youths and their parents also, because the entire base of life is dependent at this crucial function of life. Raina & Bhargava (2001) discussed some essential considerations for choosing a right career for happy life. The career planning should be done keeping in view of the physical limitations and potentials of the individual, his cognitive, personality and temperamental characteristics be studied as per the need of the career, his interest and aptitude be assessed and on the above all his personality and family conditions may also permit him for choosing his career, only then successful career planning be made.

TVET For Human Development

Human Development is a vital ingredient for building a nation. It may be appreciated that the purpose of all development is to bring happiness in the lives of the people by improving their quality of life and standard of living. Thus, human development by itself is the end of all developmental activities; at the same time it accelerates the process of development. There are different dimensions of human development, such as poverty elimination, health care, employment, wage and income generation, reducing child mortality, reducing maternal mortality, empowering women, enhancing enrolment in schools, reducing gender gap, availability of water, long and healthy life, decent standard of living, decent work to do for earning livelihood, etc. These aspects are concerned with individuals' growth, society's development and finally with national development.At individual level, what is needed is developing capabilities for ensuring a happy and healthy living. Dimension of this development may vary from individual to individual, depending upon what makes one happy. However, some dimensions related at individual level are: (i) a good income base (ii) self-respect (iii) security, status and recognition in society (iv) supportive family (v) a sense of belongingness to a group or society. At society/community level, the developmental aspects may include cohesive society, peaceful living, general prosperity amongst its members, good living conditions and comfortable environment, availability of water, electricity, transport, health services, housing, roads, educational institutions and safety and security of all its members Other aspects may include availability of work opportunities for its members as per their potential and capabilities without any discrimination because of gender, caste, religion; enabling them earn wages or generate income, etc. At national level, development means economic development, wealth generation, prosperity of the people, enhancing employment, conducive environment for people of the country to live together happily, free of disease and hunger, have sense of belongingness, have pride and participate in their own destinies, etc.

Every aspect of the societal or national development requires human force to manage and implement it. For example, for health care and health services, doctors, nurses and other paramedical personnel are required to manage hospitals, nursing homes, pathological services, etc. For providing water, electricity, housing, roads, transport, etc. a large number of professionals and persons with relevant skills and knowledge are needed to maintain and manage the services. Similar is the case with other sectors. Thus for the overall development what is required is development of individuals' capabilities as per his/her potential, and application of these capabilities for his/her own benefit and for the benefit of others, resulting in the development of society, and finally the development of nation. This suggests that there should be some mechanism for developing individuals' capabilities and a system to provide them opportunities to use their capabilities for the prosperity of the society and building of the nation. This is dynamic processes, where individuals' capabilities are developed, which contribute to the economic growth and the benefit of the economic growth provides further developmental opportunities to individuals. This process can continue till a dynamic equilibrium is achieved based on the availability of resources and capability of resource generation. There are obviously some restrictive factors within the system as well as outside the system, which do affect this process.

The importance of education for development is not a new realization. It has always been recognized. The point, which requires consideration, is "What form of education should be provided - which help individuals to do, to improve living standard to acquire skills and knowledge necessary for gainful employment, to live and work with dignity, to participate fully in development and to improve the quality of their lives. The form of education imparted should be relevant to achieve the above goals and must be available to all children, youth and adults. There is a general agreement that basic education is essential for improving upon the standard of living; as also higher education, especially in science and technology. These are the two extremes. At one end, all children of school going age should have the right for basic education; on the other a small percentage of youth get the opportunity to acquire higher education in science and technology. In between there are a large number of children and youth who are left in a state, where they do not get opportunities to acquire the skills and knowledge to enhance their potential enabling them to live and work with dignity and participate fully in development process. It is here that Vocational Education and Training is required for a large number of people, covering various socio-economic sectors, and covering local occupations as well as those where global competition is required. The vocational education, thus, should be comprehensive and 'inclusive', i.e. any and every one desirous to acquire skills and competencies in any vocation should be given an opportunity to acquire and develop them. It should be a part of life long education programme.

Keeping school children as the target group initially, and using the already existing policy framework, efforts are needed to strengthen the implementation of work education, pre-vocational education and vocational education programme in school system. Various strategies and methodologies should be adopted based on location and resources available. An integrated and comprehensive work education and vocational education programmes for the youths, is essentially needed especially when a large percentage of children leave school at different stages. More over, large number of children enter the world of work during their school age; either by choice or by the force of circumstances. This group of young people over the years will be making the large workforce whose services will be used in different sectors of economy. Being unskilled, they remain unemployed or get only casual appointment and remain on low wages. This affects their whole behavior and is vulnerable to be exploited by undesirable people. On the other hand, if employed, the quality of goods produced and services provided by them are of low standard. The quality of services to people provided by them being poor, adversely affect the overall quality of life of general public. The problem has to be seen in the perspective of human development. Providing this target group with skills and competencies, which may create opportunities for their employment (wage or self) and in turn improve their quality of life as well as that of others is a major concern. This should, therefore, be seen in the perspective of human development issue within the overall concept of 'Technical Vocational Education and Training (TVET) for All'.

Sustainability And Economic Progress

Sustainability of man and environment is the principal goal of development in this millennium. This can be achieved locally, nationally and globally by promoting harmony within humanity and between humanity and nature. The concept of human development, defined and understood in various ways, is much broader than the HDI. It is impossible to come up with a comprehensive measure or even a comprehensive set of indicators - because many vital dimensions of human development are non-quantifiable. The Indian way of life has an inherent system of development of human resources through which our artisans, artists, cooks, tribal and ayurvedic medicine practitioners and a host of others learn their craft including their science and technology and skills. During the six decades of growth after independence, India has attained multifaceted economic progress. However, millions of India's peasants starve for want of a supplementary occupation. Over 80% of its population has more than a quarter of their time lying idle. The problem is how to utilize these billions of hours of the nation. Carrying out sustainable development activities through development of a skilled manpower base in the country is the main objective of vocational education. The skilled manpower required in rural areas for sustainable development can be developed block-wise through coordination of various formal and non-formal programmes already running for different target groups by establishing a Block Level Vocational Institution (BLVI) with adequate infrastructure.

Challenges To TVET In Twenty-first Century

Today, we are at a crucial point at which the economic, social, political, technological and physical environment throughout the world is changing very fast. Globalization of economics is the foremost important factor leading to changes in the world of technical and vocational education. The adoption of the policies of liberalization and globalization is exaggerating the problem of unemployment in the developing nations. For developing world, sustainability and ecological aspects should determine the educational model for skills and competence. The approach to vocational education programme in the early years of the new millennium should be such that the skills and competencies developed through it should be environmentally sound and developmentally justifiable. Globalization is also likely to bring in greater opportunities in the service sector which is expanding very fast. Countries should develop suitable strategies so that the skilled manpower in the upcoming field is prepared.

Education And Training In A Technological Era

With the explosion in knowledge and advent of globalization and liberalization of economic policies and at the same time realizing the concept of "Compulsory Elementary

Education", it is perceived that education has a fundamental role to play both in personal as well as social development. In a rapidly changing technological society, one has to keep learning even after the formal education is over to keep abreast of latest developments. It therefore, emerges that the concept of 'learning throughout life' will be greatly accepted in the new millennium. Thus, the society in the new millennium will be a learning society founded on the acquisition, renewal and use of knowledge. Also, the rapidly changing technologies give rise to consideration for a generic vocational preparation of the learner, since in a highly technology oriented world, one could not predict with any degree of accuracy as to what the skill requirement would be after 10 years or so. Thus, a package of core skills may be given to all students in order to make them more trainable and consequently more employable in diverse situations. This would provide the knowledge base for non-occupation specific vocational education on which one could build further academic base for higher level occupation or an immediate vocational specialization through enterprise based training, apprenticeship or more specialized vocational training in institutions. It is not just enough to establish integration between the prevailing technology and the indigenous knowledge. It is equally important to base our entire educational dynamics on the traditional knowledge and technology. The so called traditional system of science and technology should be coupled with the formal system. Learning through life has become an essential component and as such, vocational education should be in the main stream of educational channel and provide competencies to students to deal with many situations and work in teams. In the presence of several systems providing education and training in a variety of programmes both in the formal and non-formal sectors in vocational education; it is quite evident that there is a need for a central authority to coordinate education and training programmes prevalent in the country. The proposed central authority shall coordinate the education and training programmes so as to optimize the use of resources on one hand and avoid duplication of efforts on the other.

In order to counter the pressure of changing scientific scenario on education and training programmes, some processes call for innovation. One of these is devising new methods in initial training of teachers and trainers and facilitating continuous up gradation of their competencies. Teacher preparation programme for pre-employment and self-employment specific vocational courses would require a separate system than that for general education and the same has to be large enough to meet the needs of such teachers in the country. The system has to maintain closer links with the industry to reduce wastage. Also, future teacher preparation would include new innovative methods like distance learning, tele-conferencing and video conferencing, etc. In order to make learning more realistic, joyful, useful and rewarding in our life, the present day cognitive learning should derive strength from the surrounding world of work. Such learning would call for reorganization of teacher preparation curricula in collaboration with stakeholders in industry curriculum developers and vocational teachers with sound school-industry linkages as part of the curriculum transaction method. It is essential that each and every TVET curriculum/programme should compulsorily include environmental issues on one hand and the concept of sustainable development on the other. Also learning of foreign language(s) may become inevitable for those who wish to migrate with their skills. In view of this, the TVET curricula should be reorganized in such a way that foreign language(s) and certain aspects of culture could be incorporated wherever necessary. Also, in future, there should be a strong component or weightage to entrepreneurial skills in all technical and vocational education and training curricula irrespective of the target group.

Vocational education and training (VET) systems throughout the world have undergone unprecedented change over the last 20 years (Chappell, 2003). The policies of new vocationalization together with the emergence of new economic times have transformed VET. As a result many traditional VET policies and practices have undergone major changes in terms of their organization and purpose. These changes are often spoken of as one response to the changing nature of work brought on by the impact of new technologies and globalization on national economies. More VET research has also occurred as a response to the changes in VET. However, given the unprecedented nature of VET change it is perhaps timely to consider whether VET research itself has responded sufficiently to the challenges presented by these changes.

TVET For All

In times to come, no country would remain in isolation from others and the world would transform into a single huge market wherein the nations would compete for hold and superior skilled human resource and technology would dictate terms, this in effect would set the stage for "TVET for all". TVET should be accessible with equal opportunities to all without any discrimination rooted in caste, creed, gender, age or color. Universality could be used as an instrument to eliminate disparities and build social order. So far, universalisation of vocational education has been a bottleneck which must be rectified at the earliest. Thus "to do" must be taken as an integral part of meaningful education and vital to the education system. It could be given a fixed, compulsory weightage as in case of language(s) or it could be optional, free for all to choose from a wide range such that a person studying medicine might as well offer a course in handicrafts. Also, it is desirable that the distinction between academic and vocational education, if at all, should be more fluid and the students should be able to interchange between the two at any stage or age. While planning to achieve universalisation of vocational education, improved and ensured access of girls/women and marginalized youth need focused attention.

Changing Roles Of Government And Other Stakeholders In TVET

The learner, teacher, industry/employer, society and the government are the key stakeholders in planning, managing and delivering TVET. The learner of vocational education benefits the society, by virtue of being a creative and productive member of the society later on. With the kind of innovations taking place in learning process, a learner is likely to prefer "self-learning" in this millennium. Teachers occupy the pivotal position in the system of vocational education. The teacher is expected to play a role of manager and promoter of vocational education in the changed scenario. The industry must be proactive in extending its cooperation and collaboration for Vocational Education Programme (VEP). It should realize that its investments in vocational education will, in turn, result in providing required work force which will contribute towards enhanced productivity of the industry itself. Vocational education also contributes in developmental process of the society by giving it many more skilled and gainfully employed individuals. Government by providing vocational education is benefited in the form of increased GDP, enhanced employment, increased efficiency and meeting the diversified human resources requirement. Community participation along with the role of industry and enterprises is well recognized for success of VEP. The partnership needed between government, private enterprises and vocational education institutions with large scale employers who have sufficient opportunities for vocational education students to gain work experience is very important. Equally important are the small scale employers who are the main source of employment and therefore, education for employment is of much significance in such enterprises. However, it remains that the government has a primary responsibility to its citizens to provide education, including vocational education. Legislative support is also required for better implementation of VEP. The Delors Commission felt that it is not only justifiable but also desirable to raise money from private sources in order to ease the pressure on national budgets. Though the state funding remains of prime importance in the developing countries, private funding can come from a variety of sources. Cost could also be shared by the state and the enterprise. Besides, international donor assistance could also be sought. Internal resource generation by vocational education institutions should be pursued as a major policy decision in the next millennium. The Production-cum-Training Centers (PCTC) should be established and strengthened so as to provide an educational experience which links the world of work with the teaching learning process and also provides hands on experience to students to use skill in producing goods and services.

Excerpts From "Learning: The Treasure Within"

The Delors Commission states that diversification of the types of study available is imperative in order to make the most of all forms of talents so as to reduce academic failure and prevent the far too-widespread feeling among young people that they are excluded, left with no prospects. This should include both conventional education, which focuses more on abstraction and conceptualization and approaches that alternate school with work experience in a way that brings out additional abilities and inclinations. The Commission also believes that the prospect of being able to go back to education or training would alter the general climate by assuring young people that their fate is not sealed forever between the ages of 14 and 20.

In developing countries, it is incumbent on the universities to provide the vocational and technological training of the future leaders and the higher and middle level education required if their countries are to escape from their present treadmills of poverty and under development. The main parties contributing to the success of educational reforms are first of all the local community including parents, school heads and teachers, secondary, the pubic authorities and thirdly, the international community. Education system can no longer be expected to train a labor force for stable industrial jobs, they must instead train individuals to be innovative, capable of evolving, adapting rapidly changing world and assimilating change.Education must transmit, efficiently and on a massive scale, an increasing amount of constantly evolving knowledge and know-how adapted to a knowledge driven civilization because this forms the basis of the skills in the future.

Four Levels of TVET

Under the Technical Vocational Education and Training (TVET) programme, there are four levels – graduate/post graduate courses in the Engineering and Technology Institutions/ Colleges, diploma courses in polytechnics, vocational training courses at Industrial Training Institutes (ITIs) and Vocational Education courses at the 11th and 12th years of schooling (vocational stream in general schools). Below degree level, there are: diploma courses in polytechnics, crafts training courses and apprenticeship training courses in ITIs; and vocational education courses at 10+ level in schools offered under separate vocational stream. At the National level, it is under the Ministry of Labor that programmes offered under ITIs are looked after, while the diploma courses in Polytechnics and vocational courses at +2 level are being governed by the Department of Education of Ministry of Human Development (MHRD). However, both these systems are managed by the State Governments. That the Central Government ministries of Human Resource Development or Labor still retain significant influence is partly because education now falls under concurrent list (Central as well as State Government control) and partly because of financial support provided by the Central Government in managing this system.

The Industrial Training Institutes (ITIs) require minimum qualification of Class VIII passed for a few courses and class X passed for the rest. On the other hand for most of the diploma courses offered in polytechnics the minimum qualification is X pass. The vocational courses are offered in Classes XI and XII; after successful completion of Class X in general schools. While polytechnics are established to supply middle level technical manpower (supervisory level) for industries, ITIs are required to provide skilled and semi skilled personnel for the industries. Both these sub-systems are, thus, directly related to industrial development in the country and are required to meet the manpower requirement of the industries. A close linkage between these institutions and industries has always been a major issue in order that manpower produced is as per market requirement; to enhance their employability in industries.

Curriculum For Senior Secondary Schools

Considering the varied roles of a vocational teacher, the pre-service training programme would prepare student teachers in different aspects, such as pedagogy, philosophy of Education, concept of Vocational Education and Training, content-cum-methodology, human resource management, information and communication technology, entrepreneurship development.

The areas to be included in the curriculum of the pre-service training programme for vocational stream are as follows:

A. General

- Emerging Indian Society (emphasis on science, technology, electronics, trade, commerce, industrialization and economy, etc.)
- Philosophy of Education, Sociology, Cultural Anthropology and their bearing on Vocational Education and Training
- Educational Laws and Acts (including Apprenticeship Training Act, etc.)

- Development and Usage of Learning Resources (audio-visual aids, multimedia learning packages, etc.)
- Pedagogy of Vocational Education and Training (Development of Competency based curricula and learning materials/modules, competency based training, etc.)
- Occupational and Industrial Psychology
- Psychology of Adolescence and Learning
- Economic and Commercial Geography
- Life Skills/Employability skills (Communication skills, Numeracy skills, Interpersonal skills, Team work, etc.)
- Entrepreneurship Development
- Business and Human Resource Management
- Elementary Labor Laws, Labor Welfare and Labor Problems
- Schemes and Programmes of Vocational Education and Training (Challenges, Status, Problems, Issues, etc.)
- Vocational Guidance, Counseling and Work Ethics
- Contemporary issues such as Environmental Education, ICT, Human Rights, HIV/AIDS, Intellectual Property Rights, etc.
- Any other region specific issues.

B. Specific

All vocational courses recognized by CBSE/State Boards of Sec. & Hr. Sec. Education / Central Board of Vocational Education and Training

For Example:

- Advertising
- Auto Mechanic
- Carpentry
- Catering and Cooking
- Computer Hardware
- Electrician
- Fashion Designing
- Financial Marketing and Management
- Food and Fruit Preservation

- Hotel Management
- Interior Decoration
- Spinning and Weaving

C. Practical Exercises

- Competency bases teaching and training (individualized instruction, problem solving approach, remedial instruction, etc.)
- Designing flexible and short cycles of training schemes that directly respond to training needs
- Development of tools for competency based assessment
- Preparing students portfolios
- Workshop Techniques
- Internship (developing and transacting lesson plans)/On-the-Job Training
- Market survey and reporting
- Practical Accountancy (tax laws, maintenance of accounts, payment procedures, etc.)

Curriculum Transaction and Evaluation

The theoretical components will be transacted as it is done in the general academic stream with more emphasis on skill development. But practicum will be conducted in actual work situation (on-the-job training) for adequate duration. Visits to work place (enterprises, industries, factories, farms, workshops, etc.), market, vocational establishments and laboratory work, will get priority. Student teachers will learn to organize apprenticeship, on-the-job training and workshop practices. Formulation of projects, their evaluation, market survey and reporting, accountancy and auditing etc. will be the integral part of practical work. However, management, organizational behavior, marketing, salesmanship, advertising, etc. would be used as strategies for inculcating specific competencies.

For the theoretical components, the methods of assessing the achievement of student teachers will almost be the same as in the general academic stream with appropriate modifications. But for the practicum and practice of vocational education and training a different approach will have to be adopted. The actual work performed during the apprenticeship, projects prepared, market surveys conducted, materials and goods actually produced will have to be evaluated continuously. It will be evaluated whether the suggestions given by workshop superintendent and the supervisor have been duly incorporated. Gradual improvement in performance skills need to be taken into consideration. Viva-voce examination for the teachers of vocational education and training have to be given due importance. The performance should only be graded and not marked.

Palanivel, Urwin & Murphy (2006) conducted a comparison of business graduates' labour force destinations following post-secondary vocational education and training in three Indian states. The Higher Secondary Vocational Education programme in India was introduced in 1976-77, to boost the supply of manpower trained to an intermediate skill level. This paper uses data collected during a study of the impact of vocational business courses in the three states of Kerala, Goa and Haryana. The study collected information on a range of indicators of student background, their views on the vocational education programmes, their employment status following completion, as well as some idea of their reasons for enrolling. The study considers the findings from the three states and places this in context by drawing on the extensive literature in this area. As with many studies of this nature, there are limitations placed on our interpretation of the data. However, the main findings do support the view that a destination of *continued education and training* may act as a form of hidden unemployment for the most disadvantaged who graduate from vocational education and training programmes; reflecting a wider need for policies that ensure buoyant local labor markets, with sufficient and appropriate demand for labor, alongside vocational education and training programmes.

Desai & Whiteside (2000) studied vocational higher secondary education graduates in the state of Gujarat. The Indian Government remains committed to the policy of diversification of the secondary curriculum, despite considerable evidence that vocational secondary education is struggling to establish itself. This article provides detailed information on the experiences and views of the limited number of successful graduates from secondary vocational courses who have entered the world of work. It draws on evidence from a large survey, conducted in Gujarat in 1996, of the views of students and ex-students of such courses. The evidence confirms the findings of previous studies that participation in vocational secondary education is linked to the students' socio-economic status, caste background and parental educational level, but also indicates that poorer students, driven by economic necessity, and with fewer private and familial resources, are the most likely to accept entry into the world of work at the end of their vocational schooling.For making the pre-service training programme more effective and meaningful, expertise form leading institutions like National Institutes of Technical Teachers' Training and Research (NITTTR), National Institutes of Technology (NITs), Pandit Sunderlal Sharma Central Institute of Vocational Education (PSSCIVE), National Council for Educational Research and Training (NCERT) and other agencies including NGOs may be utilized.

Vertical Mobiity

Vocational education and training in India is being offered through formal and non-formal mode by various government and non-government organizations. There is lack of coordination between such organizations. The Vocational Education Programme (VEP) at the +2 level has emerged as the single largest programme of technical and vocational education and training in the country. However, due to the terminal character of the VEP at the +2 level, there is a problem for those vocational pass outs who want to pursue higher education for better learning or employability. Vertical mobility for vocational graduates has been recommended in several National Seminars/working groups organized in the past. The need and concept of vertical mobility as well as emerging issues are presented in the paper.

Need for New Vocational Subjects with Emphasis On Skill Component

New vocational subjects should be identified and introduced at the first degree level in line with the vocational courses being offered at the +2 level. This is required to facilitate admission and to strengthen the vocational skills and competencies already acquired by the students at the +2 level. Changes in the contents of existing vocational subjects will also be required to make skill component of higher order and not the same as learnt at the +2 level. At present, in terms of skills, the UGC courses are of lower order than those at the +2 level.

This would entail opening new faculties of vocational fields and a graded programme of study with higher competence and confidence. It would be the forerunner of a vocational education system parallel to the present academic degrees.

Emerging Issues

The following issues need to be discussed and resolved for higher academic pursuit of vocational graduates both in general and professional education courses:

- What is the desired type of vertical mobility?
- Should there be a full-fledged vocational stream like humanities, science, commerce, engineering and technology system at the tertiary level to provide vocational graduates an opportunity for further enrichment (as recommended by Kulandaiswamy Committee)?
- Should the students of vocational education have direct entry into existing vocational courses offered by different

universities under UGC programme of Vocationalisation of first degree education?

- Should there be a parallel system of vocational education from school to university level to facilitate life long learning process?
- Should bridge courses/remedial courses/pre-requisite courses based on the deficiencies identified by the higher education system be offered by the boards/ universities/ open learning system?
- Is there a need for amendment of norms in the formal higher education/professional education to admit vocational stream students? Entrance test for various professional courses would have to be redesigned in order to provide adequate assessment of the prior learning (+2 or otherwise)?
- Should the students of vocational education be allowed in the competitive tests for entrance in different professional courses such as engineering and medical? However, the ability to compete will be the responsibility of the students.
- Should students of vocational stream be allowed entry in polytechnics in 2nd year wherever applicable without appearing in any entrance test?
- What percentage of students will be allowed to go for higher education?
    - to be admitted for vocational subjects
    - to be admitted for general higher education
- What should be the eligibility and testing procedure for admission?
- How the life long learning process be facilitated through open universities or by other courses being offered by specialized institutions?
- What types of linkages are required to be established between various institutions/organizations/agencies to facilitate vertical mobility?

- What would be the role of professional bodies which offer higher level professional courses concerned with different vocational areas (Health and Paramedical, Engineering, Business and Commerce, etc.)?

Position of TVET In India

The position of Technical and Vocational Education and Training (TVET) in India is in a state of flux due to lack of proper coordination among the various concerned departments and institutions. There is a need to introduce a National Vocational Qualification (NVQ) system in the country to integrate the various TVET programmes to optimize utilization of resources and time and to minimize wastage of human and capital resource. A management structure has been proposed for operationalzing the NVQ system. It would involve setting up a National Vocational Authority (NVA), a Qualification and Curriculum Development Agency (QCDA) and a National Competency Testing Agency (NCTA) for planning, curricula and training materials development and testing and certification of competencies. The QCDA would function through Training Boards (TBs) in different economic sectors, Training Needs Assessors (TNAs), and Training Providers and Assessors (TPAs) for setting skill standards and implementing training and retraining programmes based on specified skill standards.

The TVET programme has to be evaluated right from its inception. Continuous feedback about the performance of the programme related to the implementation of various activities, preparation of training packages, institutions selected for running the programme, training conducted and certificates issued, etc. should be maintained and updated to monitor the programme effectively. A database should be developed and updated on various aspects related to the implementation of the NVQ framework. The information should be utilized to assess performance, modify practices, redefine skill standards, and identify potential problems and to make specific recommendations for remedial measures and operational improvements. A quarterly progress report on the implementation of the NVQ system should be published by the NVA.

NCFSE And VET in Schools

The National Curriculum Framework for School Education (NCFSE, 2000, 2005) gives some components of Vocational Education and Training in the document, but in view of certain developments in the field during the recent past, some comments/suggestions/observations are given below on NCFSE.

- There are two basic approaches to vocational education and training: the infusion approach and the separate programming approach.
- The infusion approach integrates vocational education and the existing curriculum.
- Separate programming can involve (i) developing a separate curriculum devoted to vocational education, and (ii) developing separate vocational education classes.
- Students are in fact, served best through the use of a combination of the infusion and separate programming approaches. The combination approach permits a balance between academic skills and vocational education skills, providing a unique opportunity to tie together the two sets of competencies.
- The method of infusing vocational education involves stressing the relevance of regular subjects to the problems of earning a living and other aspects of life. Here is a list of suggestions for ways that this type of instruction might be implemented.

Maths: Emphasis the kinds of information communicated by numbers: age, weight, height, sizes of clothing, addresses, phone numbers, social security numbers, license numbers and so on. Demonstrate practical applications of mathematical processes as in measuring, money management, construction plans and computing wages and deductions. Have student interview adults to discover how they use maths in their jobs and at home. Investigate how mathematics is used in the school cafeteria – altering recipes, determining the prices that should be charged, ordering food and tallying receipts.

Language Arts: The children can be acquainted with how people use language in different occupations through activities involving role-playing. Application blanks, classified advertising, resumes and tax forms can be examined. Students can practice writing business and thank you letters and using the telephone. The psychology of advertising can be studied.

Social Studies: Study the history and future of a particular job, business or industry. Examine the variety of jobs and services available in a community. Teach map reading as an aid to student mobility and explain how it can be useful in occupations such as delivery man or taxi driver. In the study of history or of different cultures, needs common to all people can be emphasized.

Health, Physical Education and Fine Arts: Jobs and other pursuits that require strength, dexterity and endurance can be discussed. The relationship between nutrition and exercise, and good health can be studied. Oral hygiene, cleanliness and appropriate dress can be emphasized. The appreciation of the arts and of aesthetics can be taught as a leisure-time activity.

The experience unit is probably the most appropriate for infusing vocational educational concepts in to the total instructional programme. The core areas are arithmetic, social competencies, communication skills, safety, health and vocational information. A particular unit might emphasize one core area more than the others, depending on the topic, but experiences in all the core areas should be planned for each unit. For example, a unit on manufacturing could cover mathematics, science, health and safety, language arts and other academic subjects. Mathematical skills could be related to wages, salaries, prices and hours worked. Scientific principles could be explained in terms of machinery observed on a field trip. Health and safety could be approached through a discussion of special clothing worn by workers, company safety rules, health services available at a factory. Interviewing, reading, films, socio-drama and role-playing could be related to language arts. A unit devoted to vocational education could focus exclusively on that subject (such as community helpers) or it could be designed to help students meet other educational objectives as well. It could include such topics as community services, good work habits and self- awareness. The unit approach is especially helpful to teachers on the children with special needs, because it permits the children to learn information and develop concepts by means other than reading, and it provides many opportunities for remediation.

A number of techniques and activities can be used in vocational education. One of the best is to invite family members and persons from business, industry and social groups to visit the classroom and discuss their work and social activities. A panel of several persons is an interesting forum for such discussions. Field trips to places of employment, community service agencies and recreation facilities can also be effective. Field trips should be carefully planned around a set of objectives, and they should be integrated with activities in the classroom. Within the classroom, role-playing, socio-dramas and simulation are excellent methods of developing specific vocational education concepts. Students can practice for situations such as riding a bus, making a date, or interviewing for a job and they can develop socio-dramas for acting out various social or occupational situations. Simulation can provide a realistic opportunity to learn about a particular occupation, business or community agency. In special education settings, assembly lines, stores, banks, corporations and restaurants can be simulated successfully. Employment situations can be simulated through the use of time clocks, by designating work areas and by assigning workers roles on a rotating basis. Class discussions, demonstrations and inquiry or problem solving techniques can be used effectively at both the elementary and secondary levels.

An Overview

We still blame Macaulay for the kind of education in India. This is even after 62 years of our independence. Should we continue with it further or should we have an honest introspection and analyze the whole situation in right perspective? Sixty two years is not a small period in the history of an independent nation for establishing its own indigenous educational system as per its requirements. It is high time to get rid of Macaulay and to have a fresh look at what we have today and what we should have for better tomorrow? While undertaking this exercise, we have to take an account of our national efforts particularly during post-independence period. Even before independence, the great Indian thinkers and philosophers had contributed in visioning the type of education, which India should have for its development. Our Father of the Nation, Mahatma Gandhi had visualized as early as in the late thirties, the Basic Education (*Buniyadi Shiksha* or *Nai Talim)* seeking to harmonize intellectual and manual work and to develop desirable work values.

In the post-independence period several Commissions and Committees were formed which made many significant recommendations to improve the educational system in India including vocational education. Radhakrishnan Commission (1948) recommended a vocational bias in intermediate courses. Mudaliar Commission (1952) recommended diversification of secondary education by creating multipurpose schools to enable students to take up different vocations.

Education Commission (1964-66) under the Chairmanship of Dr. D.S. Kothari took a very comprehensive view of the educational system in the country. It emphasized the need to strengthen the vocational education programme in the country, finally diverting fifty percent of students to vocational stream after 10+. Its recommendations included setting up vocational institutions and Agriculture Polytechnics and strengthening other institutions like ITIs, Polytechnics, Technical Schools, etc. which were offering vocational courses. One of the major recommendations of the Commission was vocationalisation of higher secondary education at 10+ providing distinct academic and vocational streams. It also recommended provision for vocational courses for about 20 percent of students after class VIII. The Commission recommended liberal funding by Central Government to have the necessary impact of vocationalisation of education and to emphasize its point gave example of American education system where enough funds were provided by the Federal Government which brought in a major change in the educational scenario of the country. The Kulandaiswamy Committee report (1985) on Vocationalisation of Education reemphasized the same point again.

The National Policy on Education (1968) while taking into consideration the recommendations of the Education Commission made two significant recommendations; adoption of the 10+2+3 pattern of education and the institution of two distinct streams – academic and vocational, at the +2 stage. The National Policy on Education, 1986 (as modified in 1992) accorded high priority to the programme of vocationalisation of education and also provided scope for starting vocational courses after class VIII. Emphasis on development of attitudes, knowledge and skills for entrepreneurship and self-employment was given in the Policy.

A Centrally Sponsored Scheme (CSS) of Vocationalization of Secondary Education was launched in 1988 for providing financial support to states for implementing vocational education programme. The Ramamurti Committee (1990) while reviewing the National Policy on Education recommended "Vocational Education for All" for the secondary school students from Classes IX to XII covering 4 years with a curricular mix of academic and vocational subjects.

A critical study of the recommendations made; What were implemented; What were NOT implemented; How were they implemented; and finally what happened, as a result of these half-hearted attempts – we are still continuing with Macaulay system. What is therefore, required is to reconsider and have a fresh look on vocationalisation of education in its totality. In this context, a few points for consideration are presented below:

- Concept of rural schools for a cluster of villages so elaborately discussed and recommended by Radhakrishnan Commission.
- Vocational courses on a large scale to enhance employability of school children emphasized by Mudaliar Commission and Kothari Commission.
- The liberal central funding recommended by Kothari Commission and Kulandaiswamy Committee, when took the shape as Centrally Sponsored Scheme (CSS) for Vocationalisation of Secondary Education was interrupted twice in a span of 15 years [and the actual amount disbursed on an average comes to Rs. 10 lakhs per school over a period of 12 to 13 years].

National Curriculum Framework for School Education NCFSE, 2000, 2005 developed by NCERT has given enough emphasis on vocational education. It has emphasized the need for introducing vocational education at different stages of school and treated work education and vocational education as part of the same continuum. At the same time it has shown concern for the vocational needs of the total population in general and recommended 'Vocational Education for All'. The recommendations of the NCFSE may be treated as multi-pronged strategy for developing skills and competencies in people to enhance their employability, increase in productivity and improve the quality of life and develop self-esteem in individuals. This is obvious from its recommendation to have: work education from primary education onwards; pre-vocational courses along with the general academic courses for class IX and X; generic vocational course for academic stream in class XI and XII; and separate vocational stream at +2 stage for those who need an alternative to higher academic education and desire to enter the world of work at an early age. Provision of vocational courses at the age of 14+ in class IX or X can be used to develop some skills in the students, to enable them to enter the world of work at least with some skills thereby making a smooth transition from school to the world of work, if they so desire at an early stage.

While keeping focus on the formal education system, the NCFSE has also considered the vocational training of a large number of weaker and deprived segments of society-women, minorities, backward communities; disadvantaged groups; traditional artisans and craftsmen etc. In view of needs of such a large target group who should be provided employable skills, but might not be in a position to spare full-time and long years for the acquisition of these skills, the Framework has recommended flexible, modular vocational courses with provision for multi-entry and multi-exit. Inadvertently it has recommended that after universal elementary education if a child wants alternative to formal academic courses, then vocational courses in modular form may be provided. The courses in this case may meet the needs of the learner and relate to his/her environment. Contextualization of vocational courses thus may help in the retention of the students, and work as dropout intervention strategy. Such modular courses can also help in developing multi-skilled persons.

On the basis of above stated rationale and recommendations of Education Commission, Policy and Committees as well as National Curriculum Framework for School Education it is desirable to introduce relevant, locally need based vocational courses at secondary and higher secondary level and also through flexible and non-formal mode. The need to vocationalise education should be perceived in terms of the developmental paradigm of the country or the state. It is only then that better appreciation of vocationalisation of education can be developed. Viewed from this point, one can identify a variety of socio-economic sectors requiring vocationally skilled personnel who can take up the jobs to be performed effectively and efficiently. Preparing youths for specific employment in organized sector and government jobs cannot be the main objective of vocationalisation in the present situation where employment opportunities are diminishing. On the other hand, there are jobs to be performed in the unorganized sector as well as many other opportunities exist which can be exploited by a properly educated and trained person having some entrepreneurial skills. Proper guidance and support system may, however, be needed to make use of these opportunities. Some of the areas where such opportunities can be created are related to sustainability (food production, food preservation, water management, utilization of non-conventional sources of energy), transport and transport related jobs, marketing of products, finance management and accounts related jobs at different levels, business and trade related and large number of jobs in service sector – in the rural areas as well as urban and semi-urban areas such as maintenance and repair, health needs and services, providing comforts and some luxury and entertainment to people at large. Of course, agriculture in our country is one area which should never be forgotten. More than 60 per cent workforce is engaged in agriculture and agriculture related activities; and 70 per cent population still live in rural areas. To ensure that young people from rural areas do not migrate to cities in large number and swell the slums in metros and big cities, it is necessary that vocational courses in agriculture, forestry, agro-based industry, rural marketing, etc. be offered to them, to enhance their productivity, income generating capacity, thereby improve the quality life. The need to provide education for the cognitive development has been recognized by one and all; but overemphasized in the school curriculum – may be a fall out of Macaulay's policies.

However, the issues like – large number of children dropping out from school education at different stages, only less than 10% joining higher education; more than 25% of people still living below poverty line, economic empowerment of girls/ women; poor socio-economic conditions of different groups of people – SC/ST, minorities, rehabilitation of people with special needs; require a rethinking on the kind of education that need to be provided which can redress these issues in a comprehensive way – and within a span of ten to fifteen years, prepare a strong foundation for future development and progress in which each and every person may contribute significantly and feel proud of it. In return, he/she should live with dignity and respect and have self-confidence and self-respect. Vocational education can play an important role in achieving it; if considered as a vital instrument for Human Development or Human Resource Development and to improve quality of life of people in general.

References

- **Chappell, Clive,** (2003) Researching vocational education and training: Where to from here? *Journal of Vocational Education and Training,* 55 (1), 21 – 32.
- **Delors, Jacques,** (Commission Chair) (1996) *Learning: The Treasure Within, Report to UNESCO of the International Commission on Education for the Twenty-First Century*, Paris: UNESCO.
- **Desai, G & Whiteside, T,** (2000) Vocational higher secondary graduates on Gujarat, *Journal of Vocational Education and Training,* 52 (1), 49-61.
- **Government of India,** (1985) *Vocationalisation of Education: Report of the National Working Group constituted by the Chairman,* New Delhi: *AICTE,* Ministry of Education, Govt. of India.
- **MHRD,** (1986) *National Policy on Education (NPE),* New Delhi: MHRD, Govt. of India.
- **MHRD,** (1988) *Scheme of Vocationalisation of Secondary Education,* Department of Education, New Delhi: MHRD, Govt. of India.

- **MHRD,** (1992) *Programme of Action on National Policy on Education,* Department of Education, New Delhi: MHRD, Govt. of India.
- **Mishra, A K,** (1994) *The Development of Technical and Vocational Education in India - A Case Study in Quality Improvement: Case Studies on Technical and Vocational Education in Asia and the Pacific,* Melbourne, Victoria: UNESCO-UNEVOC, RMIT.
- **Mishra, C K & Verma, A P,** (1990) Quick Appraisal of Implementation of the Centrally Sponsored Schemes on Vocationalisation of Secondary Education – Uttar Pradesh (Publ. No. 193: *in Hindi*). Department of Vocationalisation of Education, New Delhi, NCERT.
- **Mishra, C K & Verma, A P,** (1991) *Vocationalization for All: Report of the National Seminar on Work Experience, New Delhi: NCERT.*
- **NCERT,** (1970) *Education and National Development: Report of the Education Commission* (Kothari Commission, 1964-66), New Delhi: NCERT.
- **NCERT,** (1976) *Higher Secondary Education and its Vocationalisation,* New Delhi: NCERT.
- **NCERT,** (1986) *Report of National Seminar of Vocationalisation of Education,* New Delhi: NCERT.
- **NCERT,** (1998) *Vocational Education Programme - Issues and Imperatives for Future Planning: A report of the Working Group on the Revision of the CSS of Vocationalisation of Secondary Education,* New Delhi: NCERT.
- **NCERT,** (2000) *National Curriculum Framework for School Education,* New Delhi: NCERT.
- **NCERT,**(1983) *Learning to Earn: Report of the National Seminar on Vocationalisation of Education,* New Delhi: NCERT.
- **NCERT,**(1985) *Vocationalisation of Education - Profile and Directions: Report of National Seminar on Vocationalisation of Education,* New Delhi, NCERT.
- **NCERT,**(2005) *National Curriculum Framework for School Education,* New Delhi: NCERT.

- **Palanivel, A; Urwin, Peter & Murphy, Richard** ,(2006), A comparison of business graduates' labour force destinations following post-secondary vocational education and training in three Indian states, *Journal of Vocational Education and Training,* 58 (3), 271 – 282.
- **PSSCIVE** (1998) *Report of the D S Kothari Seminar on Linking Vocational Education at +2 Level with Higher Education,* Bhopal: PSS Central Institute of Vocational Education.
- **PSSCIVE** (2000) *Report of the National Seminar on Vocational Education Programme: Present Status and Future Directions in the New Millennium,* Bhopal: PSS Central Institute of Vocational Education.
- **Raina, Reeta & Bhargava, Rajshree** (2001) Essentials for career planning, *Indian Journal of Psychometry and Education,* 32 (1), 143-144.
- **UGC** (1999) University Grants Commission: A Comprehensive Note on the Scheme of Vocationalisation (Career Orientation) of Education at the First Degree Level, New Delhi: University Grants Commission.

3

Power in Education: Influences On Children's Reasoning Capacities

Ms. Niyati Pandya
Dr. Rachana Bhangaokar

Two incidents from an urban, slum setting....

Scene I: Kailash in class at the community learning centre

Kailash (11 years) entered the class with his friend. They greeted the teacher and me (researcher) as they took their places on the floor. As the teacher took attendance, Kailash emptied his bag, preparing for the class. While the teacher instructed children to rote memorise their texts and simultaneously questioned students one at a time about what they had studied, Kailash looked straight into his book as if trying to avoid being noticed by the teacher. He dreaded the series of grueling questions and answers with the teacher. Soon it was his turn and he was summoned by the teacher. As the teacher asked him questions from the text, he tried to answer "correctly" though haltingly- fear, hesitation and disinterest writ large on his face. The teacher sarcastically reprimanded him for not being prompt and confident. She seemed unaware of the fact that such humiliation before classmates and friends may further increase his diffidence.

Scene II: Kailash outside the class

As I (researcher) entered the community, I saw a group of children playing a game of 'satodiyu'. Among them was Kailash, engrossed in the game. Accompanied by a couple of children from the community, I sat down to watch the game while we waited for children to return home from the afternoon shift of school. Though he saw me and showed recognition, he seemed uninhibited, quite unlike what he was in the class. I was pleasantly surprised to see him actively interact with friends, laugh at jokes and also argue when fights broke out whenever a rule was broken. He also accompanied one of his friends for the research interview and actively participated in a discussion that I initiated with the group towards the end.

I made these observations during the course of my Masters' research with children from the lower socio-economic class, in urban slum communities of Vadodara city. They reflect contrasting forms of behavior in two separate contexts- a classroom where the authority of teachers and fear of being humiliated augments submissiveness as against the play situation where the child feels free, openly expresses opinions and enjoys greater levels of comfort and confidence.

This raised several questions in my mind-What compels a generally happy, confident and bright child to revert to a rather submissive and passive state? Why is the class room experience (in school or otherwise) so threatening for children? Are schools doing enough, other than imparting education? Are the schools, in any way, nurturing potentials, building capacities and preparing children to face the world with confidence?

The present Chapter discusses challenges of working with children in community settings and how these could be dealt with by devising strategies for capacity building, essential for basic interaction with children and more importantly, for giving them opportunities so their voices be heard.

Purpose in the Community Settings and Research Overview

I entered the communities as a first time researcher interested in understanding how children distinguish between "right" and "wrong". My research area, the development of morality in children, was a challenging one. The research was a part of a larger research project at the Department of Human Development and Family Studies and funded by the Indian Council of Social Science Research (ICSSR), New Delhi.

The sample for my study comprised 80 children (aged 8 and 11 years) from the lower socio-economic group. To come in contact with them, I approached a local non-governmental organization which provides educational assistance through community learning centers to children in several urban slum communities of Vadodara. The central aim of these learning centers was to bring every child in the age range of 6-14 years in the education net and to provide need based academic support, to facilitate their learning, performance and retention in schools. Majority of these children attended municipal schools while some attended private vernacular medium schools catering to children belonging to the lower socio-economic group. Their parents were either engaged in some form of skilled labor, domestic labor or were self employed (e.g. vegetable vendors). Many were either unemployed or had no stable means of income. Thus, survival was a daily struggle for these families. With limited or no exposure to formal education, most of these parents wanted their children to do well in school. They heavily depended on schools and community learning centers with the hope that their children would do well in studies and gain employment, thereby paving the way to a better standard of living.

As mentioned earlier, my research area was the development of morality in children. Moral orientation of an individual is greatly influenced by culture (Shweder & Much, 1991). It intersects with several other spheres of development and is reflected in thoughts, behavior as well as interactions. To study these subtle and interwoven aspects of morality make the task of a researcher very challenging. Ethnography was used as a qualitative method to understand children's morality. Weisner (1996) proposed ethnography as an important method because it brings the "cultural place" into the study of development. Thus, data was collected using qualitative methods including in depth interviews, observations and field notes (Miles & Huberman, 1994). Such triangulation of methods created scope to capture subtleties of the context, underlying indigenous concepts and contextualised responses. Moreover, the method brought me closer to reality, as understood by people of a particular culture or context.

The tool for the study included five hypothetical scenarios, each of which presented a social-moral dilemma before the child participant. These scenarios were developed through a series of detailed discussion, brainstorming and pilot tests. They were developed around everyday experiences of children such as lying, stealing, helping others and so forth, such that they would pose relevant social-moral dilemmas before them. Efforts were made to make these scenarios interesting and story-like in easily comprehensible language. Care was also taken to ensure that scenarios were developmentally appropriate and ecologically valid.

In order to gather rich and authentic data, children's responses have to be well articulated. After initial rapport building, I expected children to reason with conviction and express their independent views. However, my regular interactions with children at the learning centre proved otherwise. On many occasions, children did not participate in the research interview wholeheartedly. Their responses were hesitant and brief. The context of learning at the centre made children behave submissively. I wondered if children perceived me as a 'teacher' because I interacted with them through the community learning centre. Schools and other institutions of formal learning can play a very important role in building capacities of children and instilling confidence. But, in reality the restrictive teaching-learning practices I observed did not seem to foster this crucial development in children. After discussions with my advisor, we concluded that my association with the centre was becoming a barrier to the research goals. We thought that the site for conducting the interviews had to be a more relaxed, child-friendly place. At the same time, some homework and change in approach on our part was required before children actually participated in the research interview of this nature.

With this background, let us understand the features of schooling and education in India. A broad understanding of education for everyone implies better opportunities and upward mobility on the social ladder. Schooling is valued universally but the transaction of education in classrooms in India is inherently complex.

The Context of Schooling and Education in India

Traditional concepts of education in Indian society are based in its *Guru-Sishya Parampara*, which roughly translates as the traditional relationship between the teacher and the taught. The word *guru* has several meanings- important, great, venerable, respectable, best, excellent, teacher and preceptor, thereby suggesting not only educational and spiritual importance but also a teacher's hierarchical supremacy. A teacher therefore commands and naturally gets unquestioning faith and respect from all. The teacher-taught relationship is based on the assumption that each has a different relation to the body of knowledge comprising the school curriculum- the teacher is the one who already knows and the student "comes to know" from the teacher in the process of learning (Sarangapani,1999).

In the Indian social fabric, respect for elders is ingrained in children from early years- whether in the context of family, classrooms or the society at large. In an ethnographic study by Sarangapani (1999), children of a village school drew parallels between parents and teachers, asserting that they extended the same unquestioning faith and respect to teachers as they would to parents and that complete obedience was their foremost duty. Therefore, this authority of adults over children in the home context automatically extends to the teacher-student relationship, and results in children being easily conditioned to obey. Unfortunately, more often than not, in this process they receive information passively, without actively engaging in thought, raising questions or discussing concepts independently. The depressing physical space, demoralized teaching force and the absence of hands-on experience, contact with nature and other forms of learning make school an unexciting experience for learning (Kumar, 2008).

All hopes of parents who have had no exposure to formal education seem tied to their children's education as a means to escape the stigma of being illiterate and thus fulfill their desire for a better life and income (Sarangapani, 1999). In contrast, majority parents who have attained some level of education seem to have lost all hope due to their own negative experiences and memories of schooling and the inability to gain employment in spite of being educated. Hence, dropout rates are high and child labor persists, especially due to lack of faith in the educational system. This is further compounded by the absence of teachers from classrooms and a greater tendency towards corporal punishment, creating immense fear among children.

These features of the state of education in India were also reflected in my ethnographic observations of the community learning centers, as discussed in the following section.

The Teacher-Taught Relationship: Observations from the Field

Each learning centre had a Head who took the role of a teacher. On an average, 25 children occupied the cramped premises of the centres, with generally inadequate light and ventilation. As in a typical school setting, here too teachers held a position of absolute authority, which was to be respected and feared. Children were expected to show complete obedience and in the name of discipline the teacher exerted a lot of control.

Children would generally be silent unless ordered to speak by the teacher. In a commanding and sharp- toned voice teachers ordered children to rote memorise answers from their texts and issued other instructions. Most children wore bored looks on their faces; others looked around or were busy rote learning from their texts diligently. Enormous emphasis was given on rote memorizing content from text books. Classroom discussions were limited only to what was mentioned in these texts, with no activity-based learning or other spontaneous discussion on related topics and sharing of ideas. Children took turns to be 'questioned' by the teacher, and were expected to have memorized the answers in a way that was identical in every respect to the standard "correct" answer. Teachers did not seem to completely pay attention to or show interest in what children actually said, unless they were unable to give the "correct answer" or when they took some time to think before answering. Being unable to answer the teacher's question implied that they were not trying hard enough to memorise and repeated "failure" in doing so could result in being punished or even humiliated before other children. During my visits I came across several instances of children being either pinched, slapped or humiliated in other ways, on such occasions. Following is an example that illustrates this situation:

The teacher reads out a question from Manish's book.

Manish (shy, quiet)

Teacher: "Speak out loud. Didn't your mother give you any breakfast before coming here?"

Manish (hesitant, mumbles answer)

Teacher: "I can't hear you, can anyone hear what he's saying (asks everyone in class, some kids laugh, others reply "no" in chorus). Speak up loud!"

Manish (in a soft voice, answers "correctly")

Teacher (slapping Manish): "I can't hear you. Who else has come prepared with answers for chapter 8?"

(Rekha instantly raises her hand and answers 'perfectly')

Teacher to Manish: "Did you listen carefully? (pinches him) Speak like her next time or I will not let you come for class".

Such instances made children aware of power relations created between themselves, other children and the teacher. Children who succeeded in doing well in studies, which meant memorizing and reproducing exactly from the text, were praised and projected as ideal students while those who couldn't were labeled as poor students. Often, being a "good student" had its own drawbacks, as the teacher wouldn't give them a chance to answer, assuming that they would be able to answer well.

In the process of schooling, students had imbibed similar ideas about learning- that rote learning was an assured way of performing well in exams, textbooks were true sources of knowledge, the teacher expected unquestioning faith/obedience and had the authority to punish, in order to discipline those who did not comply. The following informal conversation between a group of girls and me illustrates their views regarding punishment. All these girls wished to be school teachers in the future:

Me: "Should there be punishments in schools?"

Jaishree: "Yes, it is important to punish sometimes."

(Other girls nod in agreement)

Me: "What kind of punishment?"

Mansi: "Touching toes, beating, hitting with the scale on the palm, standing outside the class the entire day...."

Payal: "... sitting on the floor to complete the homework, not letting them go home without completing homework..."

Me: "Will you punish children like this when you become teachers?"

Mansi: "Yes, only then will children learn."

Jaishree: "There are some children in our class who do not do their homework ever, and they never learn. To make such children work hard, the teacher has to punish them. Only then will children make an effort to do better."

Me: "How do you feel if you get punished?"

(Quiet)

Mansi: "We feel bad, but it is for our own good that the teacher punishes us. She wants us to work harder and do well in exams, so it is alright."

Their experiences in such an educational set up not only narrowed down their approach to learning and repressed their originality but also seemed to threaten their perceptions about themselves, their abilities and the outer world. Thereby putting forth a challenge for all those like me, who wanted to interact with children, and make attempts to understand their thought processes.

Even though I went with an open mind, I realised after a few initial visits that there were many surprises in store for me and that there will be a lot to learn as well as unlearn while I interacted with them.

Interviewing Children: Barriers and Challenges

I encountered my first few challenges as I started interviewing children by narrating hypothetical scenarios which presented before them social-moral dilemmas. These dilemmas were developed keeping in mind moral dilemmas that children could experience in their daily lives. They were based on social-moral concepts such as stealing, lying, cheating in exams to help a needy friend, helping an injured kitten and the like. Children had to solve the dilemmas and give justifications for the same. Depending upon how children chose to resolve the dilemmas, I administered some pre defined as well as spontaneous probes. However initially most children showed difficulty expressing their thought and in sustained reasoning. They could only tell me what would be 'right' to do and thus, make a decision to resolve the dilemma but could not respond to 'why' the decision would be correct. Following is a response to a scenario which poses before the child (11 years) a dilemma of choosing between helping an injured kitten and proceeding to a football ground where his team is waiting for him for a crucial match -

Me: "What should Rahul do? Should he help the kitten or go for the match?"

(Quite, no eye contact, respondent fidgeting with her dress nervously)

Me: "Should Rahul go for the match?"

(Moves her head to indicate 'no' in reply)

Me: "What should Rahul do then?"

Mita: "He should save the kitten."

Me: "Why should he save the kitten?"

(Quiet, staring at the recorder)

Me: "Would you have saved the kitten even if you would have to miss the match?"

(Nods in reply)

Me: "Why is it so important to save the kitten?"

(Quiet)

Many were reluctant to participate because they feared the interview was a testing situation and that they would be expected to give "correct answers" like in school or the learning centre. This fear was perpetuated by adults who accompanied children while I interviewed them. Parents, teachers and neighbours reflected the tendency to devalue independent thought and pressurized children repeatedly to be attentive, listen to me carefully, learn whatever I told them and give "correct answers" to my questions. They also probed children or answered for them as if underestimating their potential to express themselves. Adults drew parallels between school performance and general ability to reason or interact. Parents and other significant adults would tell me from the very beginning that their child did not perform well in school and thus, would not be able to discuss anything with me. School performance was indeed central to adults in estimating their children's overall ability.

Thus, interacting with children and engaging in informal interaction in itself became a challenge for me. As a researcher several questions came to my mind- Should I accept the cryptic responses and limited views from children? Was my approach or method of inquiry unsuitable? Were the dilemmas irrelevant, difficult or was the language a problem? I realized it was important for me to engage in discussions and help children open up if I wanted to do a good qualitative study.

Several questions came to my mind- What made children unable to reason and express their views? Was it that they considered me a stranger or an authority figure as I was introduced to them by their teacher at the centre who apparently held a position of authority? Did children not have opinions at all or were they not given enough opportunities to develop the ability to engage in debate, discussion and expression of thoughts?

Through previous experiences in working with people belonging to the lower socio-economic groups I was prepared for the hesitation respondents might have in openly expressing their views. However, I was struck by how aggravated this hesitation was and their unpreparedness for informal interaction. Thus, I had to improvise on my approach and shift gears from being an interviewer from outside the community, introduced by teachers, to being a non-threatening friend eager to engage in informal discussions. Fortunately my training in human development and research helped me devise strategies to deal with the barriers emanating from my conviction that they did possess the basic capability to express individual thought.

Becoming a Friend: Rapport Building Activities

I began with rapport building sessions with a focus on encouraging children to share ideas in a group. The duration of each rapport session was approximately 20 minutes. These were conducted in groups of four. Through these sessions, efforts were made to encourage children to engage in informal discussions, sharing of opinions and the process of reasoning. We began with a game where all of us took turns to introduce ourselves. This activity helped initiate informal discussions about their likes, dislikes, interests, routines, family and friends. While some children showed enthusiasm, others took their time to open up. Care was taken that each child was given equal opportunities to share ideas, with the understanding that every child may reason at a different pace. This was followed by group discussions and activities where children had to complete stories based on their thoughts or take a stand and give reasons for the same. The following example illustrates a story and the lively discussion that ensued.

The story was about a village where people lived together happily. One day, a young man belonging to the village returns from the city and realizing the importance of education, asserts the need to build a school for them. Everyone in the community agrees and they begin to look for a suitable place where the school can be built. They come to the conclusion that the land at the centre of the village would be ideal. However, there is one difficulty- the chosen piece of land has about fifteen full-grown mango trees laden with fruit and is the only open land that children could play in. The villagers are in a fix. What do you think will happen next?

(Silence)

Me: "What do you think the villagers will do?"

Jaya: "They will cut the trees."

Me: "Will that be a good thing to do?"

Akash: "They should not cut trees. Trees are very important, they help us in many ways, we have read in our chapter." (Some nod in agreement)

Me: "How do trees help us?"

Akash: "They give us fruits and vegetables and are home to squirrels, monkeys, and birds also."

Me: "How do trees help us when we have played for a long time and need to rest?"

Jaya and Imran (excitedly): "We can sit under the trees, they gives us cool shade."

Jagruti: "We have also read in science that when we breathe we take in oxygen and exhale carbon dioxide gas. The trees take in this carbon dioxide and give us oxygen in return. So if there are no trees, we will die."

Imran: "Trees also bring cool breeze and rains. I also read that tall trees have long roots which hold the soil and don't let it flow away with water during floods."

Me: "So should the trees be cut to clear the land for a school?"

Imran: "They should not cut the trees. They should find another place to build the school because it is important to go to school, they can get a good job when they grow up."

Me: "This is the only land available, what should they do then?"

(Quiet)

Jagruti: "They should cut only those trees that cannot be kept. The school can be made with the trees in its compound and around it."

Akash: "They should cut the trees. But if they cut fifteen trees, they should immediately plant fifteen new trees around the school and take care of them every day." (All of them agreed).

Thus, children enthusiastically engaged in discussion. Although schools seemed to give them factual information, their teaching learning techniques and the environment created in classrooms did not seem to create opportunities for children to engage in independent thought and expression of ideas. Therefore, this exercise was in no way related to my study on morality but was more to facilitate the reasoning process in general, such that children could articulate themselves more confidently and with conviction.

I also observed that children were distracted by the tape recorder I used during interviews. In an attempt to familiarise children with the recorder, I introduced it to the group towards the end of each session. This again was done in the form of an activity where children took turns to record a few lines about what they liked about their discussions and enjoyed listening to each other's voices in the recorder excitedly. Apart from reducing children's unfamiliarity and fear towards the recorder, this also made them realise the need to speak up loud and clear during interviews. Thus, through these sessions a general increase in children's comfort levels was observed, which reflected in their interactions and eagerness to be participants in the study.

Children as Peer Leaders

Gradually, after the rapport sessions an enthusiastic group of children, who now considered me as their friend expressed their desire to help me and took initiative to be peer leaders in my research. Thus, as I proceeded with data collection in each community I was assisted by peer leaders from the communities who showed willingness to snowball participants as I conducted interviews in each *"gali"* or *"fadiya"* of the communities. These peer leaders helped me build rapport with other children, their families and other community members who were curious to know about my study. They introduced me to their friends, cousins and neighbors as a friend and encouraged them to take the interview. I visited their homes, met their families and neighbors and had informal interactions. Children shared with me their pictures, school projects and art work. I also played with them and their younger siblings. In this process, I not only got to know more about them but also got to be known and trusted by them. This helped reduce children's levels of anxiety as they perceived it less as a testing situation but more like a fun activity. I realized that the peer leaders also mentioned that the interview was not in any way associated with the centre or school and that I was not going to share any information with the teachers. While I interacted with adults, I made it a point to convey to them the same, and that I was not looking for "correct answers" from their children, but only wanted to know their views.

The Process of Interviewing Children

During the interviews, attempts were made to ensure that all the children thought of all possible options to resolve the dilemmas. This was done through probe questions, for example:

Me: "Should Rahul help the kitten or go for the match?

Seema (3 years): "Rahul should go for the match."

Me: "Why?"

Seema: "So that he can win the match for his school and get a prize."

Me: "If Rahul decides to go for the match, he won't be able to help the kitten, will that be alright?

Seema: "No, Rahul should quickly remove the kitten's leg and then ride his cycle fast and go to play the match."

Me: "Suppose you were in Rahul's place and had to decide between playing the match and helping the kitten, what would you have done?"

Seema: "I will help the kitten."

Me: "Why?"

Seema: "Because life is precious and we will feel good that we have done good in our life, our day will go well."

Me: "If you help the kitten, you won't be able to play the match, will that be alright?"

Seema: "Yes, because even if I go for the match without helping the kitten, I will feel guilty and won't be able to concentrate on the match. I will lose the match".

Such probe questions also helped children to respond by making realistic decisions and justifications.

This experience of interacting closely with children made me realise the need to be patient, flexible and sensitive to individual differences among children. Every day and every child provided scope to learn and improvise on my approach. Sometimes I needed to spontaneously administer probes, substitute terms with those which were more familiar to the child, or give them time to think. At other times, I had to answer their questions, give examples to ensure that the child has understood the scenario as intended by me, or even listen to their real life examples that they shared with me while expressing their opinions. I realised that every child was different and that there was no one standard way by which children would either understand or express their thoughts. On the whole, such a flexible, child centred approach greatly contributed in making their responses more realistic and believable thereby ensuring validity of their responses.

The rapport building sessions and other strategies ensured children's full participation in the research process. This not only enhanced the quality of the overall research but also explained how different the lives of these children and families were, in comparison to other social classes of society. Their contexts of everyday interaction explained the distinct nature of children's responses, most replete with their concerns for avoiding punishment from others or God to resolve the dilemmas posed. This reiterates the importance of paying attention to the larger picture in which human development occurs.

Some Reflections...

Quality education entails two basic goals- to foster keen interest in acquiring basic knowledge and to develop life- long skills such as analytical thought, confidence, effective communication, leadership and moral responsibility. It is every child's right to get quality education, dignity and support for harmonious development. While academic learning may be crucial for better prospects of employment, this alone does not suffice. Interpersonal skills, originality of ideas and the motivation to excel go a long way in helping children realise their true potential and leading a meaningful life. Parents of children belonging to the lower socio-economic groups, who have limited exposure to formal education, struggle to earn just enough to meet the needs of daily living. Yet, they invest their hard earned money in children's education and have aspirations for their children's success. Unfortunately these parents have little say in matters relating to their children's education. Additionally, structured educational settings (schools, tuition classes and community learning centers) provide very few opportunities to involve parents in their children's education. The home-school linkage in most settings is very poor.

Parents feel formal education can create the possibility of a better future for their children. They show complete faith in the educational system and reinforce the same among children, who have no other source of support for education. However, their hopes are thwarted by educational settings that focus merely on academic performance, and fail to ensure the development of major life skills. They propagate rote memorization as the ultimate means to learn and perform well in exams. Rather than providing children opportunities to develop capacities, many school practices stunt children's psychosocial development in unimaginable ways.

In most cases, physical punishment is used as the primary means of disciplining children. This not only creates immense fear in their minds but has fails to ensure that children internalize the right behavior or develop a genuine interest in learning. Thus, the main motivation to study is to avoid punishment rather than gain knowledge, build capacities for analytical thought, discussion and a general sense of confidence, all of which will help them in different spheres of life. Such a system of education may not only suppress their potentials but also make them ill equipped to develop leadership in life, explore opportunities, become self-reliant, make choices and shape a healthy future for themselves and their families. This further creates dependence on fate, thereby creating an external locus of control which has implications on their personalities, school performance, employment opportunities and wellbeing in future.

We must not forget that if strict corporal punishment can bring about temporary behavioral change among children, it also has the capacity to leave a permanent scar of humiliation and insecurity in their personalities which adversely affect future adjustment in life and society.

Let us not forget, that the burden of adult roles is shouldered much earlier by children from the lower socioeconomic class than their middle, upper middle class counterparts. Developmentally, during adolescence they may experience greater control over their lives. However, this newly acquired sense of freedom can also result in expression of defiance towards any form of authority, rebellion and vulnerability to engage in anti-social activities. Conversely, they may withdraw completely from responsibilities towards themselves, their family as well as society. An early glimpse of this can be seen in children who are defiant even in school, those considered extremely 'notorious' in class and on whom punishment no longer has any impact. This trajectory of development from childhood to the onset of adulthood shows a pessimistic picture of where our youth may end up.

This calls for specific interventions. There is an urgent need to take a closer look at the educational system in these communities and its impact on children and families. These interventions could be in the form of staff training in schools for retaining children's interest in education, reducing the use of corporal punishment and thereby, creating a more pleasant perception of authority among children. These measures will equip children with skills as well as motivation to do well in life. We are well past the time to ask children what kind of teachers they would like to have. Rather, their unheard voices need quick answers, those from sensitive teachers and adults around them.

References

- **Kumar, K.** (Ed.) (2008) *A Pedagogue's Romance: Reflections on Schooling.* Oxford University Press.

- **Miles, M. & Huberman, A.** (1994). *Qualitative Data Analysis (2nd ed.).* New Delhi: Sage Publications.
- **Pandya, N.** (2009). Social-Moral Development of Children in the Indian Context: A Cultural-Developmental Analysis using the "Big Three" Ethics Framework. Unpublished Masters Dissertation, The Maharaja Sayajirao University of Baroda,
- **Shweder, R. & Much, N.** (1991). Determinants of meaning: Discourse and moral socialization. In R. Shweder (Ed.), *Thinking through Cultures: Expeditions in Cultural Psychology* (pp. 186-240). Cambridge, MA: Harvard University Press.
- **Weisner, T. S.** (1996). Why ethnography should be the most important method in the study of human development. In R. Jessor, A. Colby, & R. Shweder (Eds.) *Ethnography and Human Development: Context and Meaning in Social Inquiry* (pp. 305-324). Chicago, IL: University of Chicago Press.

4

Reaching The Development Goals By Life Long Education

Dr. Rameshwari Pandya
Ms. Varsha Parikh
Dr. Anuradha Mathu

Literacy is the basic need and condition for improving the capabilities and empowering an individual to be efficient in various fields. It is a potential instrument of individual well being as well as social development. It is closely related with productivity and quality of life. It enables an individual to realize himself / herself, to achieve his / her worth, to know and discharge his / her rights and responsibilities properly. In India like all civilized countries literacy as well as education was given priority as the most valuable asset in the human life. It was given not only a place of pride, but, also regarded as a very potential instrument of individual development, social upliftment and national reconstruction. It was taken as a means of liberation individuals from all kinds of bondages and as a means of improving one's life. Literacy whether defined narrowly or broadly is a fundamental need of an individual or a society in general. Other fundamental needs are food, habitat, clothes, health and education at its minimum conceived of as literacy. Literacy is also instrumental to the satisfaction of these needs, like for example, reading a note or a receipt, signing a contract, clearly understanding the advertisements or reading the instructions of hygiene from any publicity material. Thus, generally literacy has become synonymous with minimum of education and has been broadened to cover all meaningful operations that are undertaken by an individual in his everyday life. Literacy in its broader concept has rather taken the place of education and has been taken as a basic human need.

According to Education Commission of India "we do not equate literacy with the mere ability to read and write. Literacy is to be worth while, must be functional. It should enable the literate not only to acquire sufficient mastery over the tolls of literacy, but also to acquire relevant knowledge which will able him / her to pursue his / her own interest and needs". So it means that it is not only reading and writing but also they should understand their need, interest, problems which they are facing in their life like for example if a person is literate but he / she can not judge or not able to identify his / her need like good food for healthy living, good transportation facility for our community or keep his / her self up to date with having information about new technology and its uses in day to day life.

Life Long Education and literacy

Literacy is an outcome of knowledge and information skills that are essential and useful for ensuring efficiency and effectiveness in our day to day life. Literacy is a prerequisite an essential condition for acquiring and applying knowledge for taking decisions and for solving problems. In short, it is necessary for successful living and for improving the quality of life.

Mere information is not so useful unless it is processed and well organized and also readily available for a particular purpose. The information with understanding and application becomes true knowledge. As man grows he grows in knowledge. That is why learning is living and living is learning. Therefore the UNESCO has emphasized life long education and pleaded for learning society. Life long education as an idea evolved in the context of the third world countries struggling to liberate themselves from the oppressive conditions of mass poverty. This idea throws up a challenge to the intellectuals to integrate and synthesize desperate knowledge into a coherent whole and suggest what should be done humanistically as well as, what can be done scientifically and technically. As it is, we are still at the stage of popularizing the concept of life long education. To put this idea into practice we have to translate it into a working system. No educational system is invented they have to evolve according to socio-historical conditions.

Life long education as a concept brought into focus the realization that knowledge reform is a crucial and critical programme as important as land reforms though not more important to enable the poor to participate in the process of development and to share fruits of development. "The spread of education, touching those at the bottom equally with those in control is the true power house of economic development". Knowledge is to be continually recreated and rediscovered as man's needs and aspirations change. "Educational system itself to form a whole it must provide mobility on the vertical and horizontal planes as well as a far wider range of options. It is also necessary to do way with certain types of differentiation and segregation".Life long education is based on the view that learning occurs throughout life as a normal and natural process, in the same way as physical and personal development continues.The concept of lifelong education as an educational strategy emerged some three decades ago, through the efforts of the OECD, UNESCO and the Council of Europe. It was a response to the anomaly that while individuals learn throughout life, the provision of education opportunities was limited largely to the early phase of life, dominated by formal education. Like for example in school or formal system we have very restricted learning which is needed and curriculum based but in today's world we have to make a human being competitive so he / she has to have knowledge regarding all areas like about new technologies, globally what is going on, in politics, about constitution, environment, gender empowerment, etc.

Literacy Programme (Under the Five Years Plans)

Eradication of illiteracy has been one of the major national concerns of the Government of India since independence. During the first Five Year Plan, the programme of Social Education, inclusive of literacy, was introduced as part of the Community Development Programme (1952). New implementation machinery comprising male and female Social Education Organizers at grass-roots level and a Chief Social Education organizer at the project level was created. A comprehensive training support was provided through the establishment of Social Education Organizers' Training Centers (SEOTCs). Model community centers, rural libraries, Janata Colleges, youth clubs, mahila mandals and folk schools were encouraged. Folk schools on Danish High pattern called Vidyapeeths in Karnataka and Jagriti Vihars in Bihar provided a variety of skill-oriented education programmes to the rural youth. Government of India established a Council for Rural Higher Education for promoting the provision of graduate-level manpower through the scheme of Rural Institutes. These gave fillip to rural development including literacy programmes. A Standing Committee of the CABE on Social Education was constituted in 1956. A National Fundamental Education Centre was started to provide high-level training facilities and undertake researches related to adult education. Efforts of varied types were made by the States for the spread of literacy. Among these, the Gram Shikshan Mohim initiated the Satara district of Maharashtra in 1959 was one of the successful mass campaigns. It aimed at completing literacy work village by village within a short period of 3 to 6 months, through the honorary services of primary teachers and middle-school and high school student, supported by the entire community. It achieved a good deal of success but suffered from the lack to follow-up due to financial constraints and some of its good work was lost as a consequence.

In spite of these varied initiatives the programmes of adult literacy did not take much headway. The Community Development Programme got weakened as was soon abandoned. It was assumed that adult literacy would automatically become universal as soon as the universal and compulsory elementary education became a reality. The literacy rate in India, therefore, increased only from 18.37 per cent in 1951 to 24.02 per cent in 1961. But the Kothari Commission (1964-66) took up the threads again and emphasized the importance of spreading literacy as fast as possible. It suggested the following measures.

- Expansion of universal schooling of five-year duration for the age group 6-11.
- Provision of part-time, education for those children of age group 11-14 who had either missed schooling or dropped out of school prematurely.
- Provision of part-time general and vocational education to the younger adults of age group 15-30
- Use of mass media as a powerful tool of environment building for literacy.
- Setting up of libraries.
- Need for follow up programme.
- Active role of universities and voluntary organization at the State and district levels.

It was hoped that with the help of these measures, the national percentage of literacy could be raised to 60 by 1971 and 80 by 1976. The Resolution on NPE 1968 not only endorsed the recommendations of the Education Commission but also reiterated the significance of universal literacy and developing adult and continuing education as matters of priority.The Education Commission had observed that "literacy if it is to be worth while, must be functional". Literacy in 1967-68 aimed at popularization of high yielding varieties of seeds through adult education was a step in this direction. The programme covered 144 districts where nearly 8640 classes were organized for about 2.6 lakh farmer-adults by

1977-78 but in this programme, the clientele remained selective and several largely illiterate group viz. artisans, landless labor, SCs, STs and women got neglected.

The Central Advisory Board of Education at its meetings held in 1974 and 1975 lent strong support to non-formal education programmes for adults with emphasis on functionality dimension. The scheme of Functional Literacy for Adult Women (FLAW) started in 1975-76 in the experimental ICDS project areas was gradually expanded in 1981-82. The FLAW aimed at enabling illiterate adult women to acquire functional skills along with literacy to promote better awareness of health, hygiene and childcare.

Similarly, the Tenth Five Year Plan recognized education as a critical input in human resource development and in the country's economic growth. It also reiterated the fact that though the major indicators of socio-economic development growth rate of the economy, birth rate, death rate, infant and maternal mortality rates and literacy rate - are interlinked, the literacy rate is a major determinant of the rise and fall of other indicators.

It was in recognition of this that three of the 11 monitorable targets of the Tenth Plan focused on elementary education and literacy:

- All children in schools by 2003, all children to complete five years of schooling by 2007.
- Reduction in the gender gap in literacy by at least 50 percent by 2007.
- Increase in literacy rates to 75 percent within the Plan Period.

Importance of Literacy and Life Long Education for Development

Literacy is not only a part of the development of national resources, but a basic requisite for basic human development. We all know that literacy and development are very much interrelated and inter dependent. Progress of one cannot be achieved without the other. Both are mutually interactive and beneficial. Therefore, both go hand in hand to achieve the target of total human development. It is the common experience in most of the developing societies that wells dug are concerted to compost pits and public latrines lie unused, and then left to collapse. Roads and bridges developed are allowed to deteriorate and even hospitals are not attended. Schools are established, but children do not go or droop out, and adult education centers are opened but not adult is found there. In today's scenario those who are illiterates we have to make them aware or educate about basic literacy and even with that as many people are facing problem of poverty they need to have good vocational training and market to sustain so they can survive and can have good standard of living and also they can participate in developmental programmes.

Lack of literacy is a great deprivation which leads to so many deprivations and deficiencies. Illiterate people generally have low income and their living conditions are extremely miserable. Social services for them are practically non existent and wherever these are available are not utilized properly. The high levels of illiteracy are positively related correlated to the high rate of fertility and high rate of mortality. Among the illiterate people, mortality rates are higher and life expectancy is shorter. The highest incidence of malnutrition and starvation occur in the areas where illiteracy is the highest. For development of nation we have to remove illiteracy and with that we also have to give life long education as supplementary education on nutritive food, clean surroundings, health and hygiene etc. Literacy and life long education can also bring about social changes in making the deprived sections of the society more assertive and conscious of their rights and duties. They after getting themselves literate are empowered to demand for their basic needs and fight out the social injustice and oppressions like violence, dowry, drugs, gender discrimination etc.

Thus, the primary aim of literacy programme is not only to provide with the skills to cope with the written words in everyday life, but to enable them, to gain greater freedom, to make choice to have a better grasp of real life, to enhance personal liberty and to have other sources of knowledge. What is fundamental in the literacy process is to invite people to discover their importance for them is not to read alienated history but to make history.Reading and writing leads to training for work, increases productivity, a great participation in civil life and a better understanding of the surrounding world. Literacy ultimately opens the way to basic human culture. Literacy help an individual to acquire a new pair of eyes which activates him to improve upon his own lots as well as that of his community, and thereby his nation.

Literacy and Human Development

Investment potential on human capital has now been recognized. Economists had long assumed that the main component of a country's productive wealth in physical assets ("produced assets"). But according to World Bank's assessment for 192 countries, physical capital on average accounts only for 16% of total wealth. More important is natural wealth, which accounts for 20%. And more important still is human capital, which accounts for 64%. Literacy is now part of the Human Development Index. Government of India has also accepted this position, and one of the important components in the National Human Development initiative announced in the Union Budget 1999-2000 is education, forming also a component in the Prime

Minister's 'Special Action Plan'.By improving people's ability to acquire and use information, education deepens their understanding of themselves and the world, enriches their minds by broadening their experiences, and improves the choices they make as consumers, producers and citizens. Education strengthens their ability to meet their wants and those of their family by increasing their productivity and their potential to achieve a higher standard of living. By improving people's confidence and their ability to create and innovate, it multiplies their opportunities for personal and social achievement.

In the field of Development Economics, literacy holds an important place as a parameter to measure development. It has been recognized that the "Human Development Index" (HDI) developed by UN is a measure of the overall development of the country. One of the three components used in the calculation of HDI is "Literacy" as it is a cumulative measure of several factors that contribute to human development. As per UN Development Report, 2000, India's ranking in HDI is 128, with education index registering a low .55 due to a low adult literacy rate of 55.7 and combined primary, secondary and tertiary gross enrolment of 54. In their book, "Development Reconsidered", Owens and Shaw have stated: "It is self-evident that literacy is a basic element of a nationwide knowledge system. The most important element of a literacy program is not the program itself, but the incentive to become and remain literacy." When people are able to believe that they can improve their lives through their own efforts, when they realize that some newly created opportunity is denied to them because of illiteracy, then only they will learn how to read, write and count".

Education is thus viewed as an integral part of national development. Development is not only 'economic growth'; rather, it 'comprehended opportunities to all people for better life' with 'man as end of development and instrument'. Education and development are linked in a variety of ways. First, education, as stated earlier, is a human right, the exercise of which is essential for individual development and fulfillment. The capacity of an individual to contribute to societal development is made possible and enhanced by his or her development as an individual. In this light, education is also a basic need. It is also a means by which other needs, both collective and individual, development and fulfillment. The capacity of an individual to contribute to societal development is made possible and enhanced by his or her development as an individual. In this light, education is also a basic need. It is also a means by which other needs, both collective and individual, are realized. Thus, education is the instrument by which the skills and productive capacities are developed and endowed. All these interrelationships of education and development are inseparable from the conception of educational policies. It is in the second order of 'action' that problems arise. The problems of illiteracy will not solve by itself in the flux of time. Without organized literacy action, illiteracy will continue to stagnate indefinitely along with the associated ills of poverty and underdevelopment. Experience has shown that determined literacy action is the exception and that more often, literacy campaigns are 'turned on' and 'turned off' in line with short-term policy changes. In the light of the discussions earlier, Literacy and Education have overlapping connotations both as an engine of socio-economic progress as well as for individual growth. An attempt at serious semantic distinction is not followed here in the discussions.

Human Development and the quality of life and citizens are central to any development planning. Human Development indicators such as access to basic education and health services have a strong linkage with eradication of poverty and economic progress. The strong focus on universal basic education and health in the 10th plan, which laid down specific monitorable targets in these arms, shows a visible shift in the approach to development planning. For improving the quality of life the use of new technologies and scientific knowledge in the delivery of education and health services and promotion of scientific and technological interventions in these social sectors is likely to have a significant impact not only on the quality of health and education services but also on their accessibility to the urban and rural poor and the disadvantaged sections.

Clear policies to improve programmes and their delivery in social sectors like education and health, supported by increased public sector spending in these areas, as also efficient use of new technologies such as ICT, is essential for development of Human Capital.

To bridge the divide between the "haves" and "have nots" and to ensure economic progress of the latter, access to quality basic education and health care is imperative not only to reduce social and regional disparities, but also to achieve balanced growth and development. States, which have given high priority to investment in the education and health sectors, have shown greater economic progress in recent years. For overall development different thrust areas are needed.

Thus, literacy is needed for

- Human rights
- Environment Education
- Personal development
- Vocational Education
- Computer Education
- Women Empowerment
- Consumer Education
- Population Education

Human Rights

The Human Rights Act 1998 gives legal effect to certain fundamental rights and freedoms. There are 16 basic rights taken from the Human Rights. These rights not only affect matters of life and death like freedom from torture and killing but also affect your rights in everyday life: what you can say and do, your beliefs, your right to a fair trial and many other similar basic entitlements. The rights include:

- Right to life
- Prohibition of torture
- Prohibition of slavery and forced labor
- Right to liberty and security
- Right to a fair trial

- No punishment without law
- Right to respect for private and family life
- Freedom of thought, conscience and religion
- Freedom of expression
- Freedom of assembly and association
- Right to marry
- Prohibition of discrimination
- Protection of property
- Right to education
- Right to free elections
- Abolition of the death penalty

It is important for people to be aware of their rights so that they are not exploited. The chance of being exploited is more in case of illiterate masses. This is an important component to be incorporated in Life Long Education in case we want real development of People.

Computer Literacy

The novel idea that sparked from the mind of Charles Babbage would not have thought to conquer this world in such a short span of time. The application of computer software and hardware can be rightly termed as explosion studies infer that 90% of the technology that we would have to use in 21st century is get to be discovered an the lion's share of is ought to be credited from the bank of computer. The 21st century man would be in in-complete without computer literacy as a part of social education and to boost it up with adult education programme.

Mass Approach to a Computer Friendly Society

General awareness about computer such as what they are, their scope and significance and how they will influence the people like in the days ahead, has to be developed in very simple term and integrated with the second and their phases of literacy programme.

- Mass media, print media and special films on the computer related topic should be used in creating computer awareness.

- Above all personal commitment by the computer professionals to create an awareness in his fellow men and women who are ignorant about computer and create a computer friendly environment which will be fertile enough to boost up the computer aptitude in our forth coming generation so as to scale greater heights in computer technology are necessary.

Modes of Spreading Computer Awareness

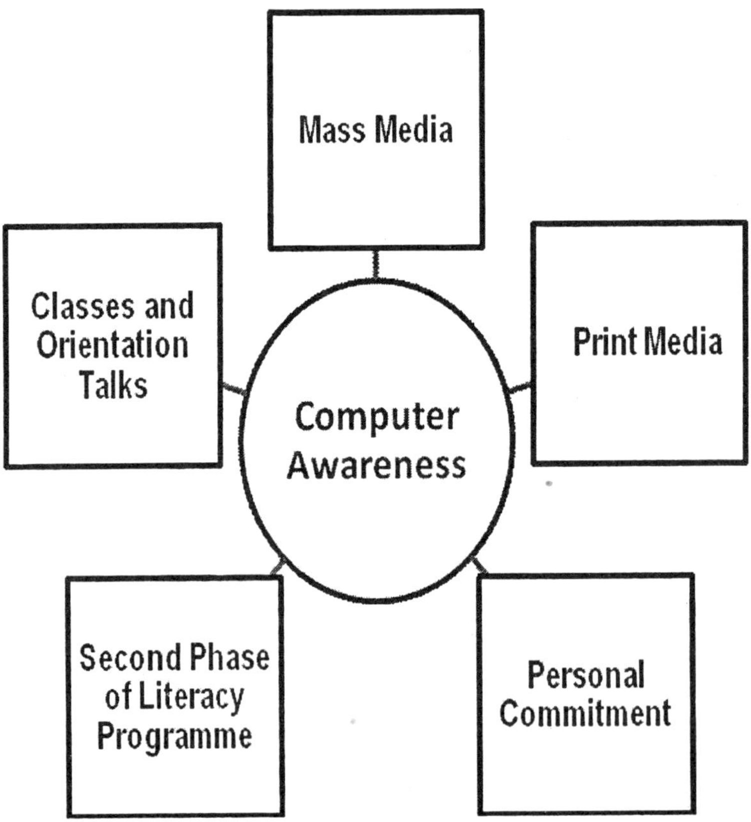

Environment Education

One of the most glaring problems the world faces today is the environmental pollution. Man has exploited nature excessively at the cost of the environment. There is an immediate need to make people aware about environmental degradation, pollution, ecological imbalance and it's after effects. The message "Save our Planet" can effectively be given to the masses through adult education programme. Day to day problems of environmental pollution need to be focused upon and clear understanding, especially to the village folks should be explained.

The strategy should be

(a) Detailed and practical uses of environment information.

(b) General information covering wide range of environmental issues.

In the beginning it is necessary that the people are sensitized to the problem of environmental hazards. The growth of population and increasing pressure on the natural resources-air, water and land resulting in poılution, pose new challenge to the welfare of not only the present, but also the future generations.The approach to implement the aforesaid programme should be instructions and training programmes. The course content may vary from place to place according to regional needs. Land degradation, deforestation and desertification, may be due to problems of over population, poor soils, use of marginal lands and fuel wood harvesting. The environmental strategy should be able to identify basic knowledge on where, when, how and whom to contact for guidance in respect of environmental needs.

Environment Education

Objectives

In UNESCO document (1981) the goal of environmental education is to develop a world population that is aware of and concerned about the environment and its associated problems and which has the knowledge, skills, attitudes, motivations and commitment to work individually and collectively towards solutions of current problems and the preservation of new ones the objectives basically are :-

(1) **Awareness**

To help individuals and social groups acquire an awareness of the sensitivity to the total environment and its allied problems.

(2) **Knowledge**

To help individuals and social groups acquire basic understanding of the total environmental, its associated problems, humanity's critically responsible pressure and role in it.

(3) **Attitude**

To help individuals and social groups acquire Social values, strong feelings of concern for the environment and the motivation for actively participating in its protection and improvement.

(4) **Skills**

To help individuals and social groups acquire environmental problems.

(5) **Environmental ability**

To help individuals and social groups evaluate environmental measures and education programmes in terms of ecological, political, economical, social aesthetic and educational factors.

(6) **Participation**

To help individuals and social groups develop a sense of responsibility and urgency regarding environmental problems to ensure appropriate action to solve these problems.

Necessary steps of Environmental Literacy

For general information, following may from the subject content for educating adults to become environmentally literate.

- Plastic pouches after use should not be thrown on farm lands because these pollute the soils.
- The water of wells, ponds and rivers should not be polluted by bathing animals or dumping garbage in them.

- The dead animals should be removed before the decomposing.
- Solar energy should be encouraged for light and cooking purposes.
- Fertilizers should be used in appropriate quantities to avoid its bad effects on the soil or use organic farming.
- Tree plantation should be encouraged in and around villages.
- Smoke inhaling through bidi or tobacco should be discouraged.
- Bio-gas plant should be encouraged to minimize the use of wood fuel.
- People should be encouraged to abandon unscientific beliefs.
- Waste recycling should be organized.
- Lesson for disaster management should be taught.
- Environmental training should be multidisciplinary focusing on interaction between environmental phenomenon and human activity and its impact on development.

Women Empowerment

It is rightly said that self-sufficiency is the "key to stronger woman". Many of the problems, which are faced by women, existed because they were either illiterate or economically dependent on others.The constitution confers on women equal rights and equal opportunities-political, social and economic. In practice however, by and large, women have not been able to take adequate advantage to their rights and opportunities for a variety of reasons. The ultimate goal of the programmes for women's education has been total involvement of women in the mainstream of national activities. This cannot be achieved as long as a large majority of women in the country remains illiterate and ignorant. Education and illiteracy and bringing about certain attitudinal changes constitute matters of prime concern to all of us.It is therefore essential that the programmes of literacy among girls and women are taken up with much greater vigor. Primary education for the girls of school-going age and functional literacy for out of school young girls and women assume much significance in this context.

Relations in respect of female literacy rates for women aged 15 and over with other socio-economic and demographic indices

- Female literacy rate is strongly and positively related with mean age at marriage i.e. the higher the literacy percentage, the higher the mean age at marriage.
- Female literacy rate is strongly and positively related to the percentage using contraception i.e. the higher the literacy percentage, the higher the rate of use of contraception.
- Female literacy rate is strongly and negatively related with infant mortality rate, crude birth rate and total fertility rate i.e. the lower the literacy rate, the higher the infant mortality rate, birth rate and fertility rate.
- Female literacy rate is weakly and positively related with the percentage urban and female work participation rate.
- Progress in raising literacy enhances the progress of the family welfare programmes in India.

Main aims of programmes for women empowerment

The aims are as follows

- Making women and men more conscious of their rights and responsibilities, the implications of the laws governing women's status in society and developing an understanding about the various manifest and concealed ways, which cause women's oppression.
- Assisting women to achieve economic viability, through acquisition of literacy and other necessary skills and resources.

- Providing women access to knowledge in other areas, particularly in health, child care, nutrition, family planning etc. and
- Assisting women to form their own groups for learning and productive activity, and to strengthen their participation and voice in the developmental process.

The importance of women's education has been well recognized by our planners. Schemes such as, 'Condensed Courses for Women' organized by the Central Social Welfare Board has been in operation in country. All the five-year plans document stipulated that priority should be given to women in need of care and protection and women with dependent children. Provision was also made in the plan for a programme of functional literacy for women, which would endow them with necessary knowledge and skills to perform the functions of a housewife, such as child care, nutrition, health care and home economics.

Obstacles to participation of Women in adult Education Programmes

- Social attitude in the home and society do not allow women to go and attend adult education centers.
- Husbands, mother-in-law, father-in-law and certain persons in the community do not want their women to go out of the home, especially at odd hour to attend adult education centers.
- In certain areas and communities the veil system is prevalent, under which women cannot move around unveiled before elders.
- Most of the rural women - especially the poor are overworked in the sense that they do double work, in the field and at home, and therefore do not have the time and energy to participate in adult education.
- Since there are no arrangement of crèches attached to AEC's as small children hinder purposeful participation.

- Regards scheduled caste women, certain sections of the community are reluctant to sit with them under the same roof for participation in the programme, because age-old tradition of untouchability is still prevalent in certain parts of rural areas.
- They don't appear to have the inner urge to go to the AEC's because they have molded themselves to lives with these disadvantages and they believe in karma (deeds) and Kismat (fate) which govern their lives.

Role of Home Scientist and Extension Worker as Development Manager

Role of extension worker is shown in model that how he / she can help in providing literacy and life long education.

One can see this model of literacy and life long education it is divided into three educational systems that is :

- Formal education system
- Non formal education system (Children)
- Adult education system (Adults)

• Formal education system is about education which is imparted in formal system and with that we should also include some extra education for them which is useful in their life like in primary moral education, in secondary family education, sex education etc. so according to age they should be provided with this education.

• Non formal education system is for those who are not going to schools or those who are dropouts. We have to provide them basic literacy and also with that we have to give them good life long education like as "gyan sathe gammat" so they can be motivated and also can have good education for their life.

• Adult education system is for adult age from 15-35 years can have good education programmes with good basic literacy and to sustain their interest their need and interest based programmes like vocational training, consumer education etc.

Model of Literacy and Life Long Education
Literacy and life long education

Formal Education	*Non-Formal Education*	*Adult Education / Life long education*
Primary Section	**Basic Literacy**	**Basic Literacy**
- Education in the areas of moral values	**Extra Curricular Activities**	**Vocational Training**
- Consumer education	- Gyan Sathe Gammat	**Awareness** in the areas like consumer education, health, environment etc.
- Environment education	- Moral Values	**Teaching them newer technologies**
Secondary Section	- Environment Education	- Non Conventional Sources
- Family education	- Traffic Rules	
- Sex education	- Competitions : Such as Drawing, Games etc.	
- Gender equality	**Vocational Training**	
- Vocational Guidance		
Higher Education		
- Disaster Management		- Human Rights
- Marriage and Family life		- Computer Education
		- Women Empowerment
		- Environment Education

↓

For all these three Educational Systems

←
- ❖ Publicity
- ❖ Teaching aids and Literature

→
- ❖ Well Educated Professional
- ❖ Proper Training

↓

Collaboration with other Organizations and Institutions

↓

Proper Evaluation Systems

↓

Documentation and Research

so they can use the education in their day to day daily life and can have better life.

Now for all these three educational systems we need to have good educated employees those who have proper training in particular field like for example for giving sex education one need to have good expert who has thorough knowledge about it.Good publicity of the programme is important so that people are made aware about it and they can take benefit out of it. And we should have proper literature and teaching materials for each subject like for computer education, environment education women empowerment and human rights etc. we should have flash cards, charts, posters, slides and films.

For Life Long Education programme we need to collaborate with other institutions and organizations working with similar objectives like for women's health education one can collaborate with NGO's like Olakh, Sahiyar etc. then we need to have proper evaluation programmes in between and at the end of the programme and at last we should have proper research and documentation for future use.Each one can teach one if it is made possible then also literacy goals can be achieved and with that this life long education is here then we can achieve all HDI, GNP, GDI, all Index and we can be developed nation but for that we have to take immediate action with this concept of literacy and life long education because if literacy is not there to make people understand about life related education is not possible so this both are interrelated and government should take this into consideration.

Home Science and Life Long Education

The major objective of Home Science is to lead satisfying personal, family and community life. The major five areas of Home Science have ample scope for co-coordinating with the existing development programme for Life Long Education. Following are activities carried out under the Home Science extension which show relevance of Home Science to the programmes.

1. Home Science extension workers contact women individually and in groups, to encourage them to articulate their need, plan a developmental activity for them and motivate them to participate in those activities.
2. Home Science colleges and their departments organize training progrmmes for various categories of personnel working in the adult education programmes, such as health workers, Gram Sevikas, extension officers, persons involved in women welfare activities and so on, and help the programme in terms of personal contacts, materials and methodology to be adopted.
3. Home Science Extension worker also enable beneficiaries to fully benefit from the schemes offered by the government and voluntary organizations by collaborating with them in their activities. They make people aware of the benefits of the various schemes and encourage them to fully utilize it.
4. Home Science Extension workers develop strategies for communicating with the target group effectively.
5. Home Science Extension departments organize literacy classes under the course of Adult education and suitable teaching and learning materials are developed.
6. Home Science colleges conduct researches which contribute to the effectiveness and improvement in the adult education programmes such as need assessment surveys and evaluation of various stages of various development programmes on the basis of the beneficiaries opinion. On the basis of these research findings home scientists modify or change their programme strategy and also give suggestions to the respective agencies for improvement in their programmes.

Life Long Education is a basic human right. It is an opportunity provided to the open society to its members for learning and continuously practicing the art of discussion of all issues and problems that confront the society. It begins with literacy and numeracy an through the acquisition of literacy and numeracy in relatively less structured situations and through informal techniques it not only makes the members aware of issues and problems in certain soft areas of individual and social life such as those of nutrition, health, hygiene, population, environment, etc. but also extends to critical issues in economy, society and polity such as those of land reforms.

Suggestions

The deschooling society, non-formal education, open schools / universities, distance learning system and teaching / learning process supported with educational technology. All these concepts aim at making learning imaginative and enjoyable, reducing rigidity and irrelevance in the organization and curriculum, providing learning facilities through various agencies, making use of various media and methods in the teaching-learning process, etc.

Now attempts are being made to identify the dimension of life-long education in our present life-situations and to see life-long education in an overall perspective. Life-long education has to be understood not merely as a "starting" and "promising" concept, but as an effort to concretize, elaborate and implement the "global approach to education". This is to be regarded as an organizing principle of the "whole" education from the individual and societal view point and from school and out-of-school standpoint.Life-long education should not be interpreted as an extension of schooling or college education, an equivalent to continuing education or a set of complementary educational activities after regular education. It also does not mean a life-long schooling or a new fashioned name for adult education. Deleon (1976) has aptly remarked, "While all these trends are more or less present and cannot be discarded, the contemporary thinking about life-long education has much more complex overtone".

On the whole, there should not be monopoly of any organization in providing education or learning experiences.

Education will be multi-dimensional, multi-media and multi-source so that closed teaching systems can be transformed into open learning systems and the once-for-all educational pattern into life-long pattern of learning. Freedom and flexibility are to be ensured in the learning system. Education will be co-extensive and co-terminus with life.The modern world is flooded with resources and opportunities for learning. New media and methods are now available for making learning more effective and efficient, various self-learning techniques are increasingly being available. A large number of agencies, materials and individuals, factories, farm museums, libraries, workmates and playmates, books, journals, religious groups, and political parties are playing their role in providing learning facilities. Proper environment and favorable conditions have to be created for self-learning and life-long education. Adequate planning for co-coordinated and collaborative efforts should be promoted through these multi-farious agencies, individuals situations and resources. So that we are able to reach the Development Goals.

References

- **Akth N. and Bheem D.M,** .(2003) Adult Education through University system of India : A Brief Comment, Indian Journal of Adult Education, Oct.-Dec.
- **Ansari, N.A.**(1984). Adult education in India, S. Chand and Co. Ltd., New Delhi.
- **Bhatia, S.C. Patil, B.R,** (1982) Research in adult education, Proceedings of National Seminar, India, New Delhi.
- **Bhatia, S.C,**(1980). Some Critical considerations in adult education, University of Delhi.
- **Chaudry K.C. and Sachdere J,** (1996.) Total Literacy by 2000 Indian Adult Education Association, Indraprasth Estate, New Delhi Division of Field Studies and Training Extension Section. U.S. Department, Pamphlet.
- **Dutta S.C,** From Literacy to Liberation, Zakir Husain Memorial Lectures from 1970-1985 Vol. I, Indian Adult Education Association.

- India. Ministry of education and social welfare, (1978) Directorate of Adult Education, Monitoring the NAEP, Report of the All India Seminar August. New Delhi.
- **Khandai H,** (2003) Sustaining literacy skill among neo-literates through library, Indian Journal of Adult Education, Oct.-Dec
- **Kundu, C.L,** (1978). Adult Education, Sterling Publishers Pvt. Ltd., New Delhi.
- **L. Bello Pollard**, Adult Education for Home Making, Teaching Adults.
- **Mohsini, S.R,** (1973). Adult and community education. Indian Adult Education Association, New Delhi.
- **Rahi A.L.** Adult Education Trends and Issues, The University and literacy by George Tohme, Indian Publications.
- **Shah S.Y,** An encyclopedia of Indian Adult Education, National Literacy Mission - Directorate of Adult Education, Jawaharlal Nehru University.

5

Tap The Untapped : A Project On Functional Literacy

Dr Rameshwari Pandya
Ms. Dimple Saluja

India is a country with tremendous vitality. India and her people are committed to secularism, socialism and democracy. This commitment, however, will remain unfulfilled till we achieve the development of human resources in terms of skills, attitudes and values, to battle on all fronts: economic, social and political: at all levels, regional, national and international; to free people from hunger, poverty and disease; to have "RESPONSIBLE INDIVIDUALS WHO SHALL BE EAGER TO WORK, HELP AND COOPERATE FOR THE BETTERMENT OF SOCIETY",

Educational system is the sub-system of the society. The student community is a vast reservoir of human energy waiting to be harnessed for useful purposes, They need clarity of vision, direction and opportunities that will capture and arrest their imagination, tap the power, unlock the talents and develop their potential, Youth constitute the most crucial asset of the community. They should be utilized fully in the process of modernizing the traditional rural society through the transfer of science and technology. This would be possible only when education is related to the solution of the personal and community problems and a close association between the curricula, colleges and the community is established. But this is a task of great magnitude requiring a gigantic effort. A multi-pronged approach is necessary to achieve this aim considering India's vast geographical limits, her regional economic imbalances, and frequent national calamities, the diversified cultural ethnic groups with the linguistic and religious differences and lastly, the rapid rate of population growth and slow rate of economic development in general. This great task can be achieved in educational institutions with the help of the youth of today who are architects of the destiny of the future.

Education as an Agent of Empowerment of Society

Education has an ennobling and humanizing effect on man. It has a great unifying effect for promoting national integration. It is an important discipline contributing to individual evolution and national progress. In a great democracy, which aspires for stability and vigour, education is as much a DIRE NECESSITY, AS IT IS A MORAL RESPONSIBILITY. Whatever the constitutional safeguards, worthy administrative changes, removal of social and economic disparities, cultivation of common values and propaganda to create a sense of emotional integration, the pivotal and contributory role of education cannot be denied. The temper of a nation is nowhere more clearly expressed than in its educational system. It has to train the young so as to enable them not only to reap full advantage of potentialities but also to make them a contributory factors for social welfare. The India of tomorrow has to be built by the younger generation. Education is the major social instrument to foster the all round development of the student with integrity, moral and human values. It must stem from the roots and culture of the society, its moorings, living conditions, problems, goals and aspirations. Only then can education become relevant to life and contribute to the development of the individual and his society. This is achieved by the four pillars of education as published by Delors Commission Report – UNESCO:

(I) Learning to know: by having a broad overview of things and the skills to work in depth on selected fields, learning to learn and thereby benefit from the opportunities to learning throughout life.

(II) Learning to do : by acquiring vocational skills and competencies to work in different situations and to work in teams.

(III) Learning to live together and appreciating other cultures and people, respecting pluralism, peace and managing conflict.

(IV) Learning to be : so as to develop one's own personality, acting with autonomy, judgment and personal responsibility.

Gandhiji wanted education to be closely related to the social life situation in a concrete manner. It was to aim at the development of social efficiency and responsibility. Education should be geared to be in tune with social demands, cultural imperatives and national requirements.

To Gandhiji, every individual human being was significant and had the capacity to contribute immensely to the society and humanity. To him, real education did not consist in packing the brain with information, facts and figures, or in passing examinations by reading prescribed number of books, but in developing the right character in young minds. Addressing the college students once he said, "Your education, if it is vital thing, must shed its fragrance in your surroundings. You must devote a certain portion of your time daily to serving the people around in a practical manner. You must, therefore, be prepared to take the spade, the broomstick and the basket. You must become voluntary scavengers of this holy place. This would be the richest part of your education and not learning by heart literary theses."

College and Society Linkage

An integration between an educational institution and society has to be there because the ultimate objective of the educational institution is to produce socially efficient members of the society. This is possible only if there is a relationship between the educational institution and society. Whether the two work together or not, whether they work together consciously or unconsciously, positively or negatively, they affect each other. When the educational institution works towards the appreciation and understanding of racial minorities and the community discriminates against certain groups, youth are forced to choose between conflicting values, But when the youth see the same values in operation in the community, in them will grow a consistent appreciation of the real values. This is how the community affects the work of educational institutions. The privileges of having higher education is the gift of the society, the contribution of a common man who himself do not have privilege of higher education. It is through his contribution, the result of his labor by his sweat and toil that educational institutions are established and maintained; instructions imparted. He believes that educational institutions and the products coming out of them will do goods to them and to the society of which he is a part. Wherever we are, whatever we do, we have an obligation to common man. The common man in society has realized that the professional skills and knowledge gained through educational institutions provide means for possible upward economic and social mobility. We now have a situation, wherein the actions and performances of educational institutions are being closely scrutinized both by the government and the people at large.

Extension

The UGC in the document 'Development of Higher Education in India' 'A Policy Frame on Higher Equation' recognized "Extension" as the third dimension of the higher education system in addition to teaching and research. The UGC (1978) declared: "If the university system has to discharge adequately its responsibilities to the entire education system and to the society as a whole it must assume extension as the third important responsibility and give it the same status as research and training. This is a new and extremely significant area which should be developed on the basis of high priority." So extension has been introduced by a number of universities and colleges to serve the society. These extension programs need the whole hearted involvement of administrators, principals, staff and students of the educational institutions. They need to spell out and implement these extension services as part of their MORAL COMMITMENT for the well being of the community in their neighborhood and the nation. Only such understanding, commitment and dedication can create a conviction for continued, meaningful association with extension services.

The Department of Extension and Communication, Faculty of Family and Community Sciences, The Maharaja Sayajirao University of Baroda is carrying out extension activities in the urban and rural communities of Baroda Districts. The thrust areas of project undertaken are environment education, women empowerment, entrepreneurship Education, reproductive Health, Income generation, moral education, recreational activities and many more.

The Adult and Non Formal education is one of main features of our Department. This time our department got the chance to carry out Functional Literacy project with coolies of Vadodara Railway Division

Definition of Functional Literacy

The 1962 World Conference on Literacy and Society held in Rome took literacy to mean the fluent reading of ordinary newspapers of the equivalent of five years' ordinary schooling. From the Philippines comes the following definition of literacy for good citizenship: "A good citizen should be able to read with understanding newspapers, bulletins advertisements, tax notices and letters, and to write an ordinary letter."

Objectives of Functional Literacy

A meeting of Experts on Literacy held by UNESCO in 1962 recommended unanimously that the objective of functional literacy should be defined as follows:

"A person is literate when he has acquired the essential knowledge and skills which enable him to engage in all those activities in which literacy is required for effective functioning in his group and community, and whose attainments in reading, writing and arithmetic make it possible for him to continue to use these skills towards his own and the community's development."

"In quantitative terms the standard of attainment in functional literacy may be equated to the skills of reading, writing and arithmetic achieved after a set number of years of primary or elementary schooling."This is the type of goal which is aimed at the most national literacy programmes, although it would be undesirable to give too much publicity to the objective of the citizen's ability to read tax notices.

Title of the project: To promote Functional literacy among the Class IV employees of Western Railway Division.

Objective: To promote functional literacy amongst the Class IV employees of Western Railway Division.

Colloborating Agencies

The functional literacy project was a joint collaboration Western Railway Division , YMCA and Faculty of social work.

The whole project was financed by Damodardas Jewellers. We were invited as resource faculty to impart functional literacy amongst the Class IV employees of Western Railway Division.

Beneficiaries

The selection of beneficiaries was done by employees of Western Railway Division. It included coolies, gangman/ Trackman and class IV employees of Railway. Both male and female employee of Railway participated in this project.

Teaching Aids

Different teaching aids like charts, flipcharts, puppets, specimen were used for conducting the functional literacy classes in the training centre of Vadodara Railway Division.

Teachnig Methods

Several innovative methods were planned and used for teaching the functional literacy content. The important once were Exhibition, Educational games, Lecture, Role play, Drama, and Street play.

Content of The Functional Literacy

The content focused and stressed an the following sub content.

(a) Alphabet in Hindi
(b) Simple word in Hindi
(c) Sentence formation in Hindi
(d) Paragraph formation in Hindi
(e) Alphabets in Gujarati
(f) Simple word in Gujarati
(g) Sentence formation in Gujarati
(h) Paragraph formation in Gujarati

Approaches Used

The individual approach was used to solve their learning problem and to cope up with the content The group approach was used to teach. The educational games were used to evaluate the progress of learning and to retain the interest in learning, different types of performances like drama, street play and puppet show were developed on recent social issues like de-addiction, importance of education, and balance diet.

METHODOLOGY

The complete functional literacy project was conducted from 14th Dec 2009- 6th Jan 2010 . The final year students of Department under the supervision of teaches Incharge executed the whole programme.The duration of inputs was 2 hour/ daily The period was divided into three parts i.e. Lectures on functional literacy topic, educational game was used to evaluate the learning and followed by group performance on social issues.

The functional literacy project was divided into four phases.

(a) Rapport building Stage
(b) Planning and Organizing Stage
(c) Implementation Stage
(d) Evaluation stage

(a) Rapport Building Stage

The functional literacy project was inaugurated by DRM, ADRM, President of VMCA, Dean, Faculty Of Social Work, and Sponsor i.e. Damodardas Jewellers The function was graced by the beneficiaries i.e coolies, gangman, and class IV employee of the Vadodara Western Railway Division. All the third year students of Department visited the training Centre of Vadodara Railway and had organized exhibition. The exhibition focused on outreach activities of department, teaching methods and materials used, thrust areas of non-formal and adult education program. The students explained the beneficiaries regarding the different outreach activities and project undertaken by the departments. The students interacted with the beneficiaries to evaluate their level of knowledge, and their understanding in Hindi and Gujarati so that they could plan their further inputs keeping in mind the progress of the beneficiaries.

(b) Planning and Organising Stage

The programme of functional literacy was divided among 42 third year students. Every day two groups were responsible for organizing the content, developing educational game and script for the group performance. The project inputs were constantly guided and supervised by the lectures of the department. Every day content focused on three strategy i.e lecture methods, educational game and group performance. The alphabet chart of Hindi and Gujarati language were used for teaching and for creating an effective educational environment. The main emphasis was on learning through play way methods. The educational games were developed like Match A with B, Identification of object, Identification of alphabets and passing the parcel. The total concentration of the student was teach using innovative methods so that learning becomes easy and long lasting.

(c) Implementation

After the planning and organizing stage, implementation of the programme was done as per the planning of the coordinator. The content followed theory of simple to complex i.e teaching alphabet then simple words, simple sentences and paragraph formation. The beneficiaries were encouraged to actively participated in each and every activities of the programme so that they could develop their self confidence. They were also invited in the front to give brief self Introduction and their views regarding training programme.

(d) Evaluation

At the end of project valedictory programme was organized on 6th January 2010. The interesting feature of the programme was to evaluate how much beneficiaries have learnt during the programme. To evaluate blackboard was displayed in front of beneficiaries and each one of them had to write on the blackboard and had to express their views regarding training programme.

At the end certificates were distributed to the beneficiaries. At the end Railway official appreciated the efforts of the Department of Extension and Communication. A questionnaire was developed to gather background information and to check the effectiveness of the functional literacy project. The questionnaire was given to the respondent and students assisted then to fill up the questionnaire. The data was collected and analysis was done using quantitative method. The results were as follows

Table 1 Percentage Distribution of The Respondents According To Their Age.

N=15

Sr.No.	*Age (Years)*	*Frequency (f)*	*Percentage (%)*
1	25-50	6	40
2	51-70	8	53.33
3	Above 70	1	6.66

The table 1 shows that the majority (53.33%) of the respondents age were ranging from 51-70 years. Forty (40%) of the respondents age were ranging from 25-50 years. Very few (6.66%) of the respondents age was above 70 years

Table 2 Percentage Distribution of The Respondents According To Their Sex

N=15

Sr.No.	*Sex*	*Frequency (f)*	*Percentage (%)*
1	Male	10	66.66
2	Female	5	33.33

The table 2 shows that the majority (66.66%) of the respondents were male. 33.3% of the respondents were female.

Table 3 Percentage Distribution of The Respondents According to the Number of Family Members In The Family

N=15

Sr.No.	*Number of family members*	*Frequency (f)*	*Percentage (%)*
1	1-3	3	20
2	4-6	9	60
3	Above 6	3	20

The table 3 shows that the majority(60%) of the respondents have four to six members in the family whereas equal (20%) percentage of the respondents have one to three family member in the family.

Table 4 Percentage Distribution of the Respondents According to their Occupation

N=15

Sr.No.	*Type of Occupation*	*Frequency (f)*	*Percentage (%)*
1	Clearner	5	33.33
2	Gangman/track man	5	33.33
3	Coolie	5	33.33

The table 4 shows that equal (33.33%) of the respondents were occupied as clearner, trackman and coolie.

Table 5 Percentage Distribution of the Respondents According to their Monthly Income

N-15

Sr.No.	*Monthly Income (Rs)*	*Frequency (f)*	*Percentage (%)*
1	Below Rs 5,000	5	33.33
2	Rs. 5,000-Rs 15,000	10	66.66

The table 5 shows that majority (66.66%) of the respondents had their monthly Income between Rs 5,000-Rs 15,000, whereas nearly thirty five percent of the respondents had their monthly income below Rs 5,000.

Table 6 Percentage Distribution of The Respondents According to their Opinion Regarding the Effectiveness of the Training Program

N=15

Sr.No.	*Effectiveness of the programme*	*Frequency (f)*	*Percentage (%)*
1	Excellent	2	13.33
2	Very Good	11	73.33
3	Good	2	13.33

The table 5 shows that high majority (73.33%) of the respondents opined that the training programme was very good whereas equal(13.33%) percentage of the respondents opined that the programme was rated as excellent and good.

The verbatim of the participants are as follows:

1. Programme Bahot Accha tha! Signature Karna Sikhne Ko Mila.
2. Padhne Ko mila.
3. Jethalala Aur cirgratte wala Natak Bahot Accha Laga.
4. Padhai Karna Sabse Accha Laga.
5. Sabhi Sishko Ne Bahot Accha Padhaya.
6. Jo padhate the wo samaja Aata.

Conclusion

Overall, it was a very challenging project to promote functional literacy among the employee of Western Railway Vadodara division. It was challenging yet interesting project. The Railway officials also appreciated this efforts and contribution in teaching their employee. If all of us contribute bit by bit then day is not far when each one of us will enjoy the environment of total literacy. Let us join hands and complete the literacy chain.

References

- **Chandra. S** (2003) "Adult Education and Non_Formal Education, Surjeet pulications, Delhi pp. 85-86.
- **Rajammal P. Devdas,** "Community and Social services as curricular component in higher education" p. 5 to 8
- Proceedings of the First national Convention of Accredited Institutions , 19th and 20th October 2001, pp. 197-199.
- **Sekhar.B** (2006), "University Extension Services" University News Nov 2007, p. 6.
- **Ram Takwale** (1997) "emerging perspective and paradigms in higher education", University News May 19,1997 p 17.

6

Environmental Education to Environmental Ethics Education: Need of a Paradigm Shift For Sustainable Development

Dr. V.K. Rai
Dr. R.P. Rai

Nature is a wonderful book authored by God and it does not belong to man rather man belong to it. The Sun, the Moon, the rivers, the forests, the land the animals themselves are gifts of nature. They need to be cultivated, not desecrated, they need to be preserved, not polluted, they need to be conserved, not wasted, these are central teachings of our religions. Unfortunately, we have forgotten the conservation ethic in the recent past and we have been disrespectful to mother earth. Perhaps the fist statesman to appreciate the importance of nature in the recorded history of Koutilya who in his celebrated book Arthasastra ordained that kings have the primary responsibility for protecting forests and wild life. Environmental Issues emerged only after the impact of industrialization, modern economic development and population pressure on natural resources began to be felt. John Ruskin in his book "unto the last" flayed the disasters created by industrial revolution and insisted on giving priority to the need of human beings to live surrounded by beauty, W.S. Jevons, known as the father of neo classical economics, raised the problem of what is now termed as sustainable development when he posed the question of what would happen to the British ship building industry and also for expanding the railway network in India. It is a fact that environmental problems were not felt very acutely during the 19th century. It was during 20th century that the environmental crisis emerged in acute form since it has seen an unprecedented technological progress in several areas such as agriculture, industry, information technologies, space, bio technology, energy and at the same time population explosion, rapid industrialization and high levels of pollution, commercialization of agriculture and quantum jump in economic activity have diluted the pleasure of advancement and development. We have now realized that such progress is not ecologically, economically and socially sustainable. Our fast economic growth may give a television in every tenth home, perhaps a car in every hundredth home but it will leave the capital resource of the earth inexorably depleted, our forests denuded our rivers polluted, our lands salineated and the cost of such unsustainable growth would be so high that we would be forced to regret that why we did not pay timely attention to the demands of the sustainable growth. Moreover, it is an unadulterated truth that we are not using our resources, we are abusing them and overlooking the dire need of conservation of resources and environmental protection. We indeed seem to be mindlessly and selfishly mortgaging our future to have good time today. Hence the need of the hour is thus adopting sustainable strategies for an environmentally benign and socially forward looking development process.

It would be in perfect order to clarify the concepts mentioned in this paper.

Environmental Education

Environmental education is a kind of education which seeks to make people fully aware of the problems connected with their environment and motivates them to tackle these problems with a sense of responsibility and with technical skills which will enable them to contribute to their solution along with other member of their community. It includes in its ambit not only conservation but also everything that relates to man and his environment.

Sustainable Development

Sustainability the implies meeting current human needs while preserving the environment and natural resources needed by future generation Renowned Gandhian Economist Prof. J. C. Kumarappa has opined that we are obsessed with the money economy. Monkey eats less but destroys more in contrast to the bird economy where the wastage is comparatively less than that of the monkey economy. In the third type of economy called the mother economy in which the child sucks milk from her mother's breast but does not harm and the mother's loss of milk can the supplemented by other means. Then there is the real economy aimed at sustainable development which keeps in view the requirement of the future generation apart from the present generation and puts premium on fulfilling the needs rather them greed which the nature is incapable of affording us.

Environmental Ethics

The field of environmental ethics concerns human beings ethical relationship with the natural environment. Ethics is related to the moral principles that govern a person's behavior. While numerous philosophers have written on the topic, environmental ethics only developed into a specific philosophical discipline in the 1970's. This emergence was no doubt due to the increasing awareness in the 1960's of the effects that technology industry, economic expansion and population growth were having on environment. The development of such awareness was aided by the publication of two important books at this time. Rachel Carson's Silent Spring First published in 1962 alerted readers to how the widespread use of chemical pesticides was posting a serious threat to public health and leading to the destruction of wildlife. Of similar significance was Paul Ehrlich's 1968 book, "The Population Bomb" which warned of the devastating effects the spiraling human population has on the planet's resources. The job of environmental ethics is to outline our moral obligation in the face of such concerns. In a nutshell, the two fundamental questions that environmental ethics must address are: what duties do humans have with respect to the environment and why ? If we think that we, as human beings will perish, if we do not constrain our actions forwards nature, then the ethics is considered to be anthropocentric. Anthropocentrism literally means human centeredness and in one sense all ethics must be considered anthropocentric since human beings can reason about and reflect upon ethnical matters. However, some thinkers have claimed that ethics must be extended beyond humanity and that moral standing should be accorded to the non-human natural world. Some have claimed that this extension should run to sentient animals, others to individual living organisms and still others to holistic entities such as rivers, species and ecosystem. Under these ethics, we have obligation in respect of the environment because we actually owe things to the creatures or entities within the environment themselves. Determining whether our environmental obligations are founded on anthropometric or non anthropocentric reasoning will lead to different accounts of what these obligations should be.

It has been rightly observed that man is his own enemy. All inventions and discoveries have improved his lot but at the same time they threaten to his very existence. Animals adapt themselves to their environmental but man besides such adaptation alters the nature of his environment to suit his immediate needs which spells disasters.

Moreover, for living a health and happy life, human beings need to maintain a three fold harmony-harmony with themselves harmony with society and also with nature itself. It is unfortunate that the emphasis has been only on the first two on account of the gross materialistic philosophy developed in the west. It is also true that nature instead of satisfying human needs has become an object of satisfying their greed. Mahatma Gandhi also warned mankind against this catastrophe, saying that nature can satisfy human needs and not their greed. The future of the whole would is at stake due to environment related problems and both developed and developing countries are afflicted with this conundrum and it is rightly and that do not breath in the developed countries and do not drink water in the under developed countries. In order to tackle this menace there has been paradigm shift from economic centric approach to social centric recently. Here are some suggestions to stem the rot that has set in on environment related scenario today.

(I) Respect nature and living resources and revive past beliefs and traditions regarding the conservation of plants and animals. In the ancient Indian, Greek Chinese and Egyptian literature and natural forces and the associated phenomena like the Sun, Moon, mountains, rivers and trees etc. have all been depicted and regarded as objects of warship. The great physician Charka mentions in his 'Samhita' that medicinal plants and herbs should be taken after worshipping them and obtaining their permission. The stand of our forefathers in respect of paying reverence to natural forces was vindicated when the club of Rome Published its fist report concerning the limits of growth.

(II) Change consumption patterns, avoid consumerism and boycott environmentally detrimental commodities.

(III) Love the native land and oppose any activity which destroys nature and environment.

(IV) Sensitize people for adopting small families.

(V) Take the support of non governmental organizations for protecting an environment.

(VI) Organize the plantation function, cleanliness drives which help to protect plants and get optimum satisfaction out of it.

(VII) Initiate and organize group discussion seminars and workshops regarding man, environment, pollution, conservation, global warming and ozone depletions etc.

(VIII) More prominence should be given to organize poster competition, essay writings, and dramatization which easily help to understand the importance environment for better life.

(IX) Create social awareness by publishing books on environmental problems.

(X) There should be ceiling on our desires which have the following fore pillars:-

(I) Do not waste food

(II) Do not waste money

(III) Do not waste time

(IV) Do not waste energy

(XI) Provide help in the awakening of environmental protection phenomenon which can include personality, family, village and community, urban, national and global awakening.

(XII) Use clean and safe water.

(XIII) Keep school, home, and surrounding clean.

(XIV) Take appropriate steps to make provisions for the depositing waste food, garbage and animal waste in composite pits.

(XV) Use modern and scientific method and techniques of preventing water air and soil pollution.

(XVI) Avoid the hunting of animals and birds.

(XVII) Provide essential information regarding family planning and over population.

(XVIII) Integrate the view points of at least three disciplines i.e. economics, sociology and ecology. The economist seeks to maximize human welfare within the constraints of existing capital stock and technology, the sociologist lays emphasis that the key actors are human beings whose pattern of social organization is crucial for devising viable solution to achieving sustainable development and ecologist who stresses the integrity of ecological sub-systems for ensuring over all stability of the global ecosystem.

All said and done efforts should be made to simultaneously address developmental and environmental imperatives for realizing the concept of sustainable development as coined by Brundtland commission of 1987.

References

- **Attfield, Robin,** (1983) The Ethics of Environmental Concern, Oxford: Basil Blackwell.
- **Benson, John,** (2001) Environmental Ethics: An Introduction with Readings, Landon: Routledge.
- **Bookchin, Murray and Foreman, Dave,** (1991) Defending the Earth, New York: Black Rose Books.
- **Callicott, James Baird,** (1980) Animal Libration: A Triangular Affaire, Environmental Ethics 2: 311-328.
- **Ehrlich, Paul,** (1968) The Population Bomb, New York: Ballantine Books.
- **Golding, Mark,** (1972) Obligations to Future Generations, Monist, 56 (85-99).
- **Mies, Maria and Shiva, Vandana,** (1993) Eco feminism, Landon, Zed Books.

- **Parfit, Reasons and Persons,** (1984) Oxford: Clarendon Press.
- **Passmore, John,** (1974) Man's Responsibility for Nature, New York: Scribner's.

7

Enhancing Elementary Education Through Teaching Learning Materials (TLM)

Ms. Varsha Parikh
Ms. Sheetal Onkar

Primary education is the first years of structured education that occurs during childhood. The major goals of primary education are achieving basic literacy and innumeracy amongst all the students as well as establishing foundations in science, geography, history and other subjects. After post independence period in India, the quantitative achievements are impressive but there is a lot to desire on the qualitative front. Enrolment at primary stage jumped almost five fold from 20 million in 1950-51 to 102 million in 1991-92, the increase in the upper primary stage is far higher from 3 million to 35 million. But on qualitative side, the system lacks flexibility and inhibits initiative and innovation.

Talking about quality of education to a large section of society, it is the responsibility of education to promote the emergence of an egalitarian and integrated society, but education itself is tending to increase social segregation and to perpetuate and widen class distinctions. Government schools are becoming poorer and private schools are expanding with vested interest on their economic grounds. General observations and studies have shown that enough care is taken by private schools to encourage creative expression through visual aids, arts, crafts, music, etc. A wide variety of expressive materials is made readily available and a warm friendly atmosphere is provided in the private schools so, that learning can be achieved at its best. But when we look at the government schools, it has been found that systems are collapsing. It is more painful and harmful that the mass is losing its faith in these systems. This is a serious concern to think over and hence, alternative measures need to be taken to provide quality education to the masses to minimize the gulf between the classes and masses. If we can't restrict alternative channels of education on economic grounds, we can't expect social harmony and social service from the deprived group. Strengthening of existing common government school systems may serve the purpose.

In the schools teaching provides the teacher an opportunity for doing something creative i.e. for moulding personality and minds. Since the goal of teaching is desirable learning, the quality of teaching can be tested only in terms of the quality of learning to which it leads. We can expect some return positively when teaching and learning are satisfactory.

On the other hand, it is not uncommon for students completing six years of primary schooling in government public schools to lack even rudimentary reading and writing skills. Not only that even the high drop out rates at the primary / elementary stage indicate that the system is too weak to retain the children in schools, even at the initial stages of learning. So, quality of education can be improved by redesigning the system in terms of content and teaching methods.

If quality education is to be improve a two-pronged efforts will have to be made.

(1) to re-design the system in terms of content and teaching methods

(2) provide amenities to the school.

As Gandhiji suggested we need education of 3-H, i.e. Head, Heart and Hand. Training that teachers receive prepares them for the (teaching) role that have to play, how to deal with interface between schooling and society and many more. With the realisation of significance of the role of the teacher in education, it is natural that more attention needs to be given to teacher-education it-self.

Need for capacity building of NPSS School Teachers

The school is responsible for the social and emotional development of children as well as for sound academic instruction. In school, the only way to raise standards in education is to improve the quality of the teaching. The only way to remedy deficiencies in any school is to obtain more and better instruction. Quality teaching results in improved learning and improvement in the all-important attitude towards the learning on the part of the student. A key to excellence in teaching is an acceptance and understanding of all children and their individual differences. The essence of best teaching is that the subject matter has to be communicated effectively to the students to make them understand the basic ideas. Effective communication can no longer be possible with words alone. Our traditional "chalk and talk" method finds it difficult to motivate learners. The teacher often understands the difficulty of conveying ideas and information without using resources beyond words.

Teachers play very important role in raising standard of education. Informed teachers know there is rich mine of inexpensive materials like pamphlets, pictures, charts, posters, from discarded school books and exhibits of various types. To enable learners to keep pace with this widening frontiers of knowledge our teaching has to be geared up.

Looking to the present scenario, there is vast difference in the teaching performance of private and government schools.

Talking about elementary / primary schools of Nagar Prathmik Shikshan Samiti (NPSS), situation is quite different. Here, teacher can't ignore the fact that children coming in these classrooms are socially and economically deprived. These children display hostility, differences or withdrawals. The fact that children differ in abilities both physical and mental is recognised. Even the uniqueness of children in the number, kind and degree of intensity of their interest is also recognised. Here, teacher is all the more taxed in finding out new ways of presenting the same information, because these students need to get more interested and more able to work with concrete, perceptual experiences. Not only that but also to meet individual differences of students, TLM can play significant role.

As there are varieties in TLMs, it is necessary that the teacher should have a clear enunciation and the trick of putting thoughts properly. Hence, teacher especially of primary classes must have knowledge of adopting TLMs as per the purpose, content, pupils status and her own ability, to permit and encourage use of variety of TLM. Wrong preparation or misuse of TLM is likely to spoil the lesson in hand. Hence, TLM should be prepared and used with care and caution and not merely regarded as a means of making lesson attractive. This can be obtained by undergoing proper training in preparing and using TLM.

Another reason, we are aware that national government is trying to bring education system in the main stream through the efforts of operationalising the national policy on education, which proposes various sub schemes. A sub scheme of developing teaching learning material (TLM) was introduced in the year 2002, under Serva Shiksha Abhiyan (SSA). In the line of national programmes, under Serva Shikshan Abhiyan, on one hand huge flow of money and strenuous efforts on the part of state government are there. Massive budget under TLM grant i.e. of Rupees 500 / - to each of the upper and lower primary school teacher of the government schools are provided every year, but no training, guidance or encouragement from the system or top authorities are provided to the teachers in this area, which lead teachers to become inefficient and ineffective for their assigned task. Because, majority of the teachers are unaware about effective utilisation of the TLM grant, as they lack the ability to design and develop different types of TLM. So, existing situation calls for recasting strategies and priorities by fostering growth of teachers who try to teach on the growing edges of children's lives. Hence, there is an urgent need to plan interventions that has to be specifically designed to build capacity of NPSS schoolteachers in developing TLM and also to enable them to make proper utilization of big chunk of the money.

The NPSS school teachers who are rarely exposed to in – service training programme and who always do everything else first and teaching at the last, need to be trained in proper preparation and use of TLM tricks of trade. This will make teaching learning quicker and interesting and also improve quality of education in NPSS School. Thus, a project to start resource cell of TLM was conceptualised in the Department of Home Science Extension and Communication at the M.S.University of Baroda, Gujarat.

Conceptualising the Project

The Department of Home Science Extension and Communication (HSEC) undertakes various programs of education, development and welfare. The course content and practical exposure of student in the Department of HSEC are mainly in the social and developmental areas. The department is training the students for disseminating knowledge to urban and rural of formal / non-formal group through the use of various methods with effective use of TLM like chart, poster, flash card, puppet, mobile etc.

It has been found that these TLM (Chart, poster, flashcard, model, mobile, puppets) are popularly known and most suited means to supplement information in formal and non-formal environment. TLM if prepared and used effectively in teaching especially at primary level it helps to clarify, establish and correlate accuracy, concepts, interpretations and appreciations; increase knowledge; arouse interest and even evokes worthy emotions and enriches the imagination of the children. Though government has started providing grants to improve teaching pattern in the government schools, but it is not enough as teachers have lack of expertise in making and using the teaching learning materials. Not only that TLMs which are available in the market are neither up to the mark nor according the requirement or level of the students. And they are very costly also so, within small grant of money teacher can't afford to buy for all the subjects. The universities, which are considered as institutions of higher learning, have a major role to play to bridge this gap. So, it was observed that this kind of project is really in demand to use government grant in a right manner with the right purpose. However, looking tochanging world concept as well as shrinking of resources and collapsing government system these kind of collaboration of government and academic institutions are need of an hour. The present project is a model example for the same.

Importance of TLM in teaching and learning

Teaching Learning Material deals with a subject that is in fact, as old as history itself. These teaching learning materials are visual materials, visual means of expression and communication employed by men and women everywhere from the dawn of history. TLM is any device that assists an instructor / teacher to transmit to a learner facts, skills, attitudes, knowledge, understanding and appreciation.

According to Kochhar (1997), In order to achieve the purpose of good teaching the teacher like other craftsman has to use certain skills- commonly styled as "Teaching Learning Materials". These TLM are the external modes or forms which teaching may take from time to time. Teachers often use representative teaching learning material (TLM) to illustrate new words as well as abstract relationships and concepts. (TLM define in TLM Grant Module, 2002).

As we know, learning takes place at three levels – direct experiences, vicarious experiences and symbolic experiences. Thus, teaching – learning materials (TLM) are quite helpful in instruction. They supply a concrete basis for conceptual thinking; they give rise to meaningful associations. Researchers have also recommended that in education we should appeal to the mind of the subject chiefly through the visual and auditory sense organs, since it is experienced that 85 percent of our learning is absorbed through these sense organs.

In teaching learning process teacher is a mediator between the students and unknown knowledge. She explains the subject well in a clear manner. The students learn to understand in the same way the teacher understands. However, sometimes due to difference in language, type of course, learning styles, complexity of course content, teacher's abilities and other differences, communication may not take place in the desired direction. Such a time, the teacher needs to supplement her teaching with variety of teaching learning materials. This will help to establish commonality of thought and understanding between herself and the students. In such a situation, in order to build a common platform of understanding and to have correct and similar concept development among students with varying speed of learning, a teacher must use TLM with her verbal explanations. Teaching Learning Material when used intelligently can promote the most effective kind of learning among children in the schools. Educators have found that many teaching problems can be solved partly or wholly, by the proper use of the rich experience that can be gained through Teaching Learning Material (TLM).

For good teaching, TLM should be adopted according to purpose, content, pupil's status and teacher's ability. Various types of teaching learning materials can be used for teaching in formal situation at various levels. The main concern of a good teacher is to get her student learn.

According to John Mander, there are five main reasons, which might justify the use of these teaching expedients. They are:

- To teach something more thoroughly so that the children may retain the subject matter taught;
- To teach something more quickly. This will result in "covering more ground" in a given time, and thus give a better chance of "getting through the syllabus,"
- As a means of creating or sustaining interest ;
- As a means of integrating a number of separate pieces, of work already learned by other means, and
- As a means of bringing with the experience and understanding of children something which is new to them.

Thus, a proper use of these tricks of trade makes learning quicker and interesting.

Objectives of the Project

Major Objective

To start a resource cell of Teaching Learning Material (TLM) in the selected primary schools of Nagar Prathmik Shikshan Samiti of Baroda.

Specific Objectives

- To impart training in developing teaching learning materials among the primary school teachers of Nagar Prathmik Shikshan Samiti of Baroda.
- To develop abilities in designing and developing TLM among the primary teachers of Nagar Prathmik Shikshan Samiti of Baroda.
- To study the reactions of the primary school teachers towards the project activities.
- To evaluate understanding and ability of primary school teachers in the preparation and use of TLM.

METHODOLOGY

In Baroda City, under Nagar Prathmik Shikshan Samiti, there are 16 CRC centers, with 122 elementary schools. After making informal visits to different CRCs, CRC–2, near Gorwa area of Baroda was selected keeping in mind the criteria viz; Good strength of the students, Demand from CRC teachers to NPSS office for training in TLM, Interest of the teachers, Availability of Nagar Prathamik Shikshan Samiti Schools within city area. Besides these reasons when government is emphasizing on the girls' education, in CRC-2 enrolment of girls students are more compared to other CRCs. Hence, CRC –2 which consists of in total 7 different schools viz. School number 8, 9, 10, 17, 22, 37, and 46 having in all 33 teachers in lower primary schools (std.1 to 4) were selected for the project.

The project proposal mainly emphasizing on different types of TLMs covered under project, duration of project work and budget were prepared and permission from administrative officer of Nagar Prathmik Shikshan Samiti, Baroda was taken for the same.

For the project finance, as well as permission was taken from the administrative officer of NPSS. He approved the project and allowed to utilize TLM grant of lower primary school teachers of CRC –2, to carry out TLM project activities. In all, 33 teachers of lower primary schools of NPSS of Baroda, each with TLM grant of Rs. 500 /- were involved in the project activities.

Since TLM scheme was introduced under SSA in 2002, by the government of India it's essential to know about efforts done to achieve objective of the scheme, by NPSS in Baroda. Hence, a pilot study aiming to find out whether primary school teachers of NPSS had any previous training or knowledge about preparation and use of TLMs and whether they use TLM in their teaching programs was conducted. A checklist was prepared to collect background information of all the 33 teachers.

The major findings of the pilot study were as follows;

- All (100 percent) the teachers were using TLM in teaching as per the subject requirement.
- All (100 percent) the teachers reported that they had no knowledge about preparation of TLM, except chart. In the case of chart, 51 percent of the teachers reported that they can make it, according to their imagination.
- High majority (87.8 percent) of the teachers buy the TLM, available in the market from their TLM grant, every year.
- All (100 percent) the teachers expressed their desire to undergo training in TLM under the project.
- All (100 percent) of them had shown their desire to learn charts, posters, flash cards, puppets, model and mobile, under the project.
- Very few teachers (39.3 percent) expressed strong desire to learn model followed by (18.18 percent) diagram and (12.12 percent) map as TLM under the project.

Results of the Pilot study played important role in the selection of teaching learning materials under the project. Other criteria viz; Provision of budget to prepare teaching learning material, Nature of the subject to teach, Maturity level of the learners, Duration of the project, Availability of the TLM with the teachers and Interest shown by teachers in TLM were also kept in mind during selection of teaching learning materials for the development.

Three different types of TLMs were selected under the project viz. charts / poster, flash card and puppet. Since, few teachers also showed strong desire to learn model and mobile as TLM, it was also covered under the training programme content. The content of the training programme was decided with the help of experts in such a way that teachers can prepare and use each selected type of TLM effectively in their classroom teaching. The booklet on preparation and use of TLM was prepared and distributed to the teachers mainly for the purpose of further reference.

Execution of the project

Steps for the execution of the project

(i) Conducting training cum workshop

(ii) Preparation and use of TLM

(iii) Starting a resource cell

(i) **Training cum workshop programme.** Under this, Technical sessions of the experts were organised which was followed by Workshop. The venue of the training program was decided as school number 8, as all the co-ordination and management of CRC- 2 activities were carried out from the school No.8 of Gorwa. In all, 15 days training cum workshop was conducted with the teachers. The Content and Methods used in training cum workshop programme on TLM was as follows:

(ii) **Preparation and use of TLM.** For the final preparation of TLM, adequate practices were given to the teachers, which helped them to develop their skills in making effective TLM. Looking to the nature and purpose of the content suitable TLMs viz, chart or poster, flash card and puppet (glove / rod / finger / human) were decided. A unit plan was prepared and executed for the final preparation of TLM by approaching each of the 33 teachers using source book published by NPSS for primary section. During preparatory stage teachers were guided to prepare layout for charts, posters, and flash cards according to the content.

Each lay out was checked in terms of visuals, lettering, colouring scheme and other necessary aspects of visual aids, before teachers prepare final visual aids. In the first round, all the teachers were guided to prepare chart or poster whereas in the second round they were directed to prepare their flash card

Content and Methods used in training cum workshop programme on TLM.

Sr.No	*Content*	*Methods used*
1.	• Layout in TLM • Lettering in TLM	Lecture cum Demonstration
2.	• Inauguration of training programme • Importance and types of TLM • Concept, Types and Purpose of using Charts in Classroom • Concept, Characteristics and Purpose of using Poster	Discussion cum Demonstration
3.	• Concept, Characteristic, Advantages, Size, number and use of flash cards	Lecture cum Demonstration
4.	• *Concept, Purpose and use of simplified model in the classroom*	Lecture cum Demonstration
5.	• Concept and Purpose of using Mobile	Discussion cum Demonstration
6.	• Types, Purpose, use, Advantages and Limitations of puppet (glove, rod and finger)	Discussion cum Demonstration
7.	• Preparation of lay out of charts, poster and flash card. • Actual preparation of chart/ poster, flash card, glove puppet.	Discussion cum workshop
8.	• Concept, preparation and use of live puppet • Storage of teaching learning material	Discussion cum Demonstration
9.	• Actual preparation of live puppet	Discussion cum workshop

set. In the third round, they were guided to prepare puppets (glove/rod/finger/human) also discussed the materials and drafts for different parts of glove/ human puppet were discussed (according to characters) with the teachers. And in the last round preparation of model and mobile were covered. Each round was lasted for 15 days.

- Total twelve Charts covering various topics like formulas of multiplication, basics of calendar, difficult words in Gujarati and others were prepared.
- Total twenty-one Posters covering various topics like Air pollution, cleanliness, and water pollution and others were made.
- Sets of fourteen Flash cards covering various topics like stories, houses, English alphabets and others were prepared.
- Total six Models covering various topics like, types of fruits and vegetables.
- Total five Mobiles covering different topics like digit of moon and others were made.
- In all, the teachers prepared 68 different types of puppets including Glove, Rod, Finger and Human.

After the preparation of TLM it was used by respective teacher in his /her classroom teaching as per the requirement of the topics under the different subjects. A supervision schedule was planned and executed to check the effectiveness of TLM during classroom use. Project worker supervised each type of the TLM prepared under the project during its use in the classroom. It was found that use of chart, poster, and model was very efficiently done by the participants, whereas in flashcard and puppet some of the participants were found deficient in using appropriate skills like effective manipulation, voice modulation etc in the beginning.

At the end of the supervision, necessary inputs were given by the project worker to the teachers wherever required like voice modulation during puppet show, effective manipulation of puppets, involvement of children while using flash cards etc., which helped teachers to enhance their ability and confidence.

In their verbal feedback, teachers reported that, use of TLM has indeed changed the classroom atmosphere. According to them students have started becoming more interested and attentive, were able to memorize facts and information as well as colors and could properly relate with teaching materials used in the classroom for the same.Informal feedback was collected from the students of various standards, where in they reported that they like to learn through TLM, as they found teaching more interesting, could remember information for long time, with clear concept, picture, color.

(iii) **Starting a Resource cell** To start resource cell, development of TLM alone is not enough, but its storage is equally essential. Hence, a local resource was mobilized where corporator of Gorwa area, Baroda of CRC-2 zone was approached and convinced to for storage facility. He gave two steel cupboards for the storage of TLM from the corporation fund.

To make systematic and effective use of resource cell, a set of rules and regulations was prepared by with the help of CRC coordinator. In the CRC meeting, with the general consent of the teachers, along with CRC in-charge, two teachers were selected as resource cell in-charge for the coming year of 2005-2006. They were made responsible for issuing-borrowing of the TLMs, maintenance of registers as well as TLMs, Teachers of all the seven schools were explained rules and regulations to strictly follow for the better use of this resource cell.

Results and Discussion

A reaction scale was developed by the project worker for the purpose of knowing reactions of the teachers towards various aspects and content of the training programme, focusing on preparation and use of TLM.

Rating scale on graphic aids and puppets prepared by Shah and Joshi (1992), were used for evaluation of teachers' performance on preparation and use of TLM, during supervision.

Reactions of the teachers towards the training programme

The teachers reported that:

- All (100.00 percent) had attended training programme on TLM conducted by the project worker and also attended exhibition prior to the training.
- All liked the training programme very much.
- All found that physical facility, time and language during training suitable.
- High majority (78.78 percent) of the teachers had not attended any training programme related to TLM previously.
- All were using TLM to reinforce concept in the subject.
- High majority (75.75 percent) of the teachers were using TLM for all the subjects.
- Majority (63.63 percent) of the teachers felt the need of TLM for Maths subject, followed by (48.48 percent) for Science and Gujarati.
- High majority of (87.87 percent) the teachers were using charts followed by more than fifty percent (57.57 percent) using model generally readily available from the market in teaching before this training program.
- High majority (96.96 percent) of the teachers reported that this training helped them to learn about different types of TLM.
- High majority (90.90 percent) of the teachers reported that this training has enabled them to prepare different types of TLM independently.
- Majority (69.69 percent) of the teachers reported that they learnt puppet quite satisfactorily followed by learning of chart (66.66 percent) followed by (60.60 percent) learning mobile and flashcards.

In the use of TLM by the teachers during supervision following findings were revealed ;

- Majority (57.57 percent) of the teachers obtained average scores in the range of 26-50, in the preparation of TLM (chart, poster, flashcard, model and mobile) followed by few participants (27.27 percent) obtaining high score in the range of 51-75, which indicates that to obtain best results still teachers require more practice.
- High majority (90.90 percent) of the teachers obtained high scores in the range of 7-12 as far as using TLM in classroom for teaching purpose was concerned, which indicates that teachers were able to use TLM in a correct and effective manner.
- All (100.00 percent) the teachers obtained high scores in the range of 7-12 in the use of flash cards.
- Little more that fifty percent (57.14 percent) of the teachers obtained high scores in the range of 19-27 in the preparation of glove puppet, they found making of glove puppet little tough.
- All (100.00 percent) the participants obtained high scores in the range of 33-48 in the use of the puppet.

Conclusion With Suggestions For Future

- From the results of the supervision, it is known that TLMs were effective in changing classroom environment as well as to reinforce the skills in reading, writing, in numeracy, to make the concept clear. The reactions of the students, the enthusiasm of the teachers and CRC coordinators and members of government organization supporting the program in one of the CRC zone towards starting a resource cell was favourable. These results and observations signify the need for developing and using TLM to hold the attention, develop interest and motivate students in teaching program.
- Planning such kind of interventions, which lead to develop great satisfaction and also found worth of using grant

money, could solve a major complaint of teachers towards readymade TLM available in the market.

- Effectiveness of proper preparation and use of TLM was visible through this project. It could be seen that teachers were found with better confidence and great enthusiasm. Even positive effective of use of TLM was seen on quality of teaching too as they enjoy learning and vice a versa.
- During the project activities, keen interest and desire was shown by other CRC coordinators and primary school teachers to replicate same project in other schools. Even upper primary school teachers also expressed their strong desire to under-go the same kind of TLM training programme.

It can therefore, be concluded that this type of project which direct the national investment to its correct path and also boost backbone of the education system i.e. teachers by strengthening their capacity in the work are really in demand and there is an urgent need to take up such kind of work. However, NPSS can link it up with such academic institutions and strengthen national programme of education in a real sense, by proposing this project work as a model example.

Recommendations for the Further Studies

(1) A similar action project with rest of the CRC's lower and upper primary school teachers of NPSS of Baroda can be carried out

(2) An action project using other visual aids like bulletin board, flannel board can also be carried with NPSS schoolteachers.

(3) A research study to under check effectiveness of use of TLM on primary / elementary school children can be conducted.

References

- **Chand P. G., Vijaya S. and Shukla S. R.,** (1998) Teachers as Transformers, learning from outstanding primary school teachers, UNICEF, Gandhinagar.

- **Chand Tara and Pahuja N.P.**, (2004) Essentials of Instructional Technology, New Delhi. Anmol Publications Pvt. Ltd.
- **Chandra A. and Shah A.**, (1989) Fundamentals of Teaching Home science, New Delhi, Sterling Publishers Pvt. Ltd.
- **Dhama, O. P. and Bhatnagar, O. P.** (1991) Education and Communication for Development, New Delhi, Oxford and 1BH publishing Co. Pvt. Ltd.
- **Ghar Parikshit and Zala Shwetambari,** (1991) Khushgul, Shishumilap Baroda.
- **Lahkar Indrani**, (1998) An action project to promote literacy in the primary schools of Baroda through the use of Games.
- **Mehta N. and Maniar A.**, Designing Graphic Aids, August 2000.
- **Mehta. N**, (1998) Effectiveness of instructional package in promoting environment concern among V standard students of English medium schools in, Baroda.
- The effective Use of Type, Colour and Graphics, New Delhi, Viva books Private Limited.
- **Rao Usha**, Educational Technology, New Delhi. Himalaya publishing House.

8

Leadership Training

Dr. O.P Mishra
Prof. A.K. Singh

Leadership is and has been described as the "process of social influence in which one person can enlist the aid and support of others in the accomplishment of a common task".[4] A definition more inclusive of followers comes from Alan Keith of Genentech who said "Leadership is ultimately about creating a way for people to contribute to making something extraordinary happen."[13] According to the late Jules Masserman, American psychoanalyst and former member of the faculty of Northwestern University medical school, leaders must fulfill three functions: the leader must provide for the well-being of the led, provide a social organization in which people feel relatively secure, and provide a set of beliefs.[11] In the words of Hoyle (1995) "A leader is a person who influences a group of people towards a specific result. It is not dependent on title or formal authority. Leaders are recognized by their capacity for caring for others, clear communication, and a commitment to persist."[10]

An individual who is appointed to a managerial position has the right to command and enforce obedience by virtue of the authority of his position. However, he must possess adequate personal attributes to match his authority, because authority is only potentially available to him. In the absence of sufficient personal competence, a manager may be confronted by an emergent leader who can challenge his role in the organization and reduce it to that of a figurehead. However, only authority of position has the backing of formal sanctions. It follows that whoever wields personal influence and power can legitimize this only by gaining a formal position in the hierarchy, with commensurate authority.[8] Leadership can be defined as one's ability to get others to willingly follow. Every organization needs leaders at every level.

Literature available in the field of Extension Education have defined the term **Leader** as a person who has been spontaneously considered, or chosen, as being influential in a specific situation or situations. In simple words **Leader** is a person who effectively influences a group to co-operate in setting and achieving goals. **Leadership** has been defined as the process of influencing the behavior of the individual in a given situation or situations.[5] **Rogers and Olmsted** defines **Leadership** as "an activity in which effort is made to influence people to cooperate in achieving a goal viewed by the group as desirable."[18&19]

Types of Leaders (Classification of Leadership)

There are several classifications of leaders or leadership available in the literature on leadership.[5,6,12,14,18&22] However, some of the important classifications have been presented below.

Whyte has classified leaders into four categories:

(1) **Operational Leaders**: Those persons who actually initiate action within the group, regardless of whether or not they hold an elected office.

(2) **Popularity Leadership**: It means the popular person is elected to a position of leadership because he is well liked by the members. Such an individual may or may not be the actual leader of the group. If such persons who hold elective positions do very little about initiating action for the group, and are mere **figure headed** or **ornamental leaders** are called **nominal leaders**.

(3) **Assumed representative type:** It refers to a person selected to work with a committee or other leaders because the later have assumed that he represents another group they desire to work with, he may or may not be a leader of the group.

(4) **Prominent talent:** It refers to artists, musicians and other prominent talent who have exhibited an outstanding abilities and accomplishment in their respective fields. It may include the experts and intellectual leaders.[18]

Another Classification divided leader into

(1) **Professional Leaders:** The professional leader is one who has received specialized training in the field in which he works full time as an occupation, and is paid for his work. Extension Officer, Gram Sevak, etc. may be cited as professional leader in the field of extension work.

(2) **Lay Leaders:** The lay leaders may or may not have received special training, are not paid for their work, and generally work part-time with local group organizations, eg., Gram Sahayak , Gaon Sathi, Youth club president etc. Lay leaders are also called Volunteer Leaders, or Local Leaders or Natural Leaders. These local leaders may be either Formal Leader or In-formal leaders, depending on whether they are regular office-bearers of organized group or not.

Perhaps the **most significant classification** from the view point of modern research as well as practical application of the results of research, is the one designating leaders into the following three types.

1. **Autocratic Leader**: This type of leaders operates as if they cannot trust people. They think their subordinates are never doing what they should do; that the employee is paid to work and, therefore, must work. Such leaders determine all policies, activities, and goals of organization. They take no part in work except when conducting meetings, telling others what to do or demonstrating. Members are uncertain about what to do and usually take actions they are told to take. Leader is personal in both praise and criticism of the work.

(2) **Democratic Leader**: This type of leaders shares with the group members decision-making and the planning of activities. The participation of all is encouraged. They work to develop a feeling of responsibility on the part of every member of the group. They attempt to understand the position and feelings of the employee. If they criticize, they do so in terms of results expected, rather than on the basis of personalities.

(3) **Laissez-fair Leader:** This type of leaders believes that if they leave workers alone the work will be done. They seem to have no confidence in themselves. If at all possible they put off decision making. They tend to withdraw from the work group. They give minimum guidance. They remain in the background and seldom express an opinion or work with organization. Members have almost complete freedom and operate with a minimum of rules. Members often act as leader in making decision that guide the organization.[18]

Classification on the basis of number of task to be performed

1. **Monomorphic Leader:** It refers to one leader for one aspect. Such types of leaders are found in modern and urbanized societies.
2. **Polymorphic Leader:** It refers to one leader for several aspects. Such types of leaders are found in traditional and rural societies.

Pattern of Farm Leadership

Dahama and Bhatnagar (1990) in their book titled Education and Communication for Development have discussed following pattern of farm leadership identified by various Indian scholars.[5]

M.S.K. Reddy (1960) and **J. Rao** (1966) have classified leaders into following categories.

(1) Traditional Leader

(2) Caste Leader

(3) Political Leader

(4) Functional Leader

B.N.Sahay (1966) has classified leaders into following categories.

(1) Traditional leader

(2) Emergent Leader: Those who are traditional leaders keeping themselves up-to-date with the current conditions and social institutions.

Deshmukh (1966) has classified leaders into following categories.

(1) Formal Leader

(2) Informal Leader

(3) Composite leaders: Those who hold position in the village organizations and at the same time are recognized by villagers as their leaders.

S.V. Reddy (1972) has classified leaders into following categories.

(1) Agricultural Leader

(2) Social Leader

(3) Agro-Social leader

J.P. Yadav, *et al.* (1972) have classified leaders into following categories.

(1) Agricultural Leaders

(2) Traditional Leaders

(3) Political Leaders

(4) Opinion-making Leaders

(5) Decision-making Leaders

(6) Caste Leaders

Pattern of Leadership in Rural India

Rural India has seen various pattern of leadership before and after independence. However, some of the prominent patterns of leadership have been discussed below.

1. **Leadership based on heredity and caste structure**:
   - (i) Landlords/ Zamindar
   - (ii) Village Headman
   - (iii) Patel/ Lambardar
   - (iv) Village priest
2. **Leadership based on occupational patterns and functional groups:**
   - (i) Governed by the caste structure
   - (ii) Influence is not wide spread
   - (iii) Restricted to a particular group of people
3. **Personal Leadership**
   - (i) People are respected for their knowledge
   - (ii) Wide experience
   - (iii) Authority, mastery of knowledge and skill in a particular field
   - (iv) Truly lead the group
   - (v) Educated youth who return to their villages and fallow a vocation
   - (vi) Ex-Service men who settle down in their home village after retirement
   - (vii) Others who maintain close contact with their home village
   - (viii) Resident school teacher
4. **Political and Social type of Leadership**
   - (i) Emerged during Independence movement of India.
   - (ii) Large number of political and social workers who have chosen the village as their venue of work.

After Independence and launching of Panchayati raj, Cooperatives, Extension progremmes etc. a new type of leadership has evolved in rural India.

(i) Democratic leader, educated leader, and elected leader

(ii) Traditional leader also exercise influence e.g. Sarpanch of panchayat, Director of the cooperative society etc.

On the whole it can be said that the best leader is one who develops leadership in others.

Role and Functions of a leader

The functions of local leaders are varied, and depend upon specific group situations and the personal abilities they possess. In rural extension programme the function of local leader vary from place to place and in accordance with the nature and scope of the job to be performed. However, the major function of local leaders is to set an example for others to follow. Their role and function are highly related to each other and are sometimes mixed so much together that it becomes difficult to differentiate between the two. The overall function of local leader is to lead the community in different ways under a variety of situations. Local leaders show special interest and initiative in a local programme. They catch new ideas first. They serve the community without profit motive. Their reward and incentive is the satisfaction they derive from their own action.[22]

One of the important roles which a local leader has to play in the community is that of the initiator.[9] If he waits for others to initiate action, then he is a leader in a nominal sense only. Leader helps group in two ways: (i) helps in making progress towards their working goals, and (ii) helps in keeping the group in a healthy working condition. Some of the roles expected from him are:

- Assist the group in identifying its needs.
- Aid to the group by setting some examples before them.
- Move the group towards the goal.
- Encourage and improve interaction among group members.

- Keep the group together.
- Make resources available to the group.

According to **Hall (1950)** a leader is expected to perform the roles of Initiator, Orientator, Facilitator, Encourager, Harmoniser, Summariser, Fact-Seeker, Fact-Giver, Compromiser, Expediter, Spokesman, Status Role, Recorder, Evaluator, and Analyzer.[7]

Sanderson (1940) has suggested following six roles for a leader:

1. **Spokesman:** He has to speak for the people he is representing.
2. **Harmonizer:** He has to deal in tactful way with persons who create conflicts in the group and bring them together in working toward group goals. He has to show his superiority by showing some useful ideas to the members of the group.
3. **Planner:** He has to realize the need of the group in advance and must have plans to fulfill them. He has to interpret the purposes of the group into practical goals. He opens the potentialities of available resources.
4. **Executive:** He helps the group in carrying out the plans and policies. He gets things done. He stimulates others and promotes solidarity.
5. **Symbol:** He has to be loyal to the ideals of the group in words and action. He must not be self-interested. He represents the group only when his direction is that of the group.[20]

Bass (1960) has identified the following important roles of a leader: [2]

1. Figurehead: Ceremonial, Status role
2. Mobilizer: Integrator, linking pin, supporter, binder, catalyst.
3. Liaison man: He acts as an ambassador. He develops a net-work of high status contacts.

4. Negotiator: He resolves the problems, he negotiates.
5. Monitor: He commands, controls and evaluates.
6. Disseminator: He informs and acts as a spokesperson.
7. Resource allocator: He distributes scarce resources aimed at maximum output with minimum input.
8. Entrepreneur: He innovates.
9. Goal setter: He guides.
10. Motivating activator: Prime mover. He inspires.
11. Visionary: Hero.
12. Developer of men: Man maker.

The function of leader is to stimulate interaction, sentiment and action.

Identification/ Selection of Local Leaders

Locating local leaders is not an easy task. But the following methods have been tried and proved to be workable in this respect. [22, 14 & 6]

1. **The Discussion Method:** Through discussion (on any subject) the person with sound knowledge and ability is soon recognized and a mere talker easily spotted. Discussion gives encouragement and assurance to the potential leader to express him and over a period of time may make him more confident in accepting some position of leadership, and emerge as a valuable leader.
2. **The Workshop Method:** In this method, a large group is broken into smaller groups, where people discuss and make decisions and present their decisions. The development workers act like a consultant and observe the deliberations. This will give him a chance of locating the leaders.
3. **The 'Group Observer':** The extension worker/ development worker should watch a community or group in action and then he will be able to spot potential leaders. He may observe the community in any type of situation. For obtaining the best results, the group should not be aware of this.

4. **The Questionnaire or Socio-metric Method:** This requires interviews of the villagers, or the community members according to a prepared questionnaire. This may have questions like: whom they ordinarily consult for advice on farming, advice on home affairs, and advice for the village problems, who make decisions about community affairs in the village and so on.[16] (J.L.Moreno, 1953)
5. **Election Method:** Another method of identifying a local leader is that of election. In helping groups elect the right people for the right job, state clearly to the group the position required as well as the kind of job each person must be qualified to do. With an understanding of the kinds of the work each leader or officer is to do or should do, the group can vote more wisely.
6. **Seniority and Past Experience:** In some communities the oldest person is supposed to have the most knowledge and experience and normally can add stability to the group. But this may not be a proper way of locating a leader. "The best type of leader is one who develops leadership in others."
7. **Key Informants:** In a community people may be asked to indicate opinion leaders in that area. This is cost saving and time saving when compared to sociometric method.
8. **The Self Designating Techniques**: Consists of asking a respondent a series of questions to determine the degree to which he perceives him self to be an opinion leader.
9. **The reputational method**: In this method extension workers ask 3-4 persons like school teacher, banker, etc. to name who they consider to be the most interested in the general welfare of the community. Then the names obtained are sorted by frequency mentioned, and those of high frequency are accepted as possible leaders.
10. **The decision making or tracer method**: First extension worker select certain actions to analyze, then

he trace down what happened or who did what in order to identify the persons who made or led in making the main decisions related to the events or action selected.

11. **The formal position incumbent method**: Local people holding certain position in selected organizations and public offices are selected as leaders.
12. **The social participation method**: The most active people in the community in terms of participation in existing organizations are identified to be the local leaders.

Training of Local Leaders

The objective of training local leaders is to make them good teacher, capable of passing on many ideas and thrust with a perfect understanding of the people with whom they are working. The training of local leaders brings about changes in their attitude and alters their knowledge, skills and sensitiveness towards themselves and others. This in turn leads to changes in the actual performance of the leaders in carrying out their role.[22]

In a training programme, it is necessary for local leaders to have a clear cut concept of *what they are to do and why.* It assumed that leadership is something that can be taught and learned. If one assumed that certain person are born leader, then there is little to be offered in the line of training. *A programme of developing leaders must assume that the person to receive the training have average or normal ability to learn.* Taba (1953) has given following objectives of leadership training.[23]

1. Mastering fundamental concepts that would serve as a framework for understanding and interprating group behavior, social learning and cultural differences.
2. Method of identifying and analyzing problems. The ability to see problems in perspective.
3. Develop competence in group processes: cooperative thinking, exchange and analysis of ideas, facts and teaching; processes of converting discussion into

consensus; ability and disposition to conceive group goal; respect for and understanding of others.

4. Acquire technical skills necessary to carry out a job. Diagnose solution, learn how to approach problems, plan appropriate educational procedures, learn skills in handling appropriate diagnostic techniques, conduct open discussion, learn team work with other leaders, etc.

Leadership Skills

It is important to note the behavior of the person with leadership traits. The different areas of behavior can be clustered into at least three behavioral categories such as intellectual, personal and interpersonal and group behaviours.[21]

Intellectual / Cognitive Skills of a Leader

1. The leader is responsible for figuring out what is wrong and showing others how to solve problems whenever necessary.
2. Effectively handles imaginary and abstract areas and sees a wide perspective, sees the complete picture while others may focus on parts.
3. Plans minutely and goes through it.
4. Visualises the future and sees the consequences of decisions.

Personal Skills of a Leader

1. Judges the efficiency of own decision, directions or suggestions; gauges appropriateness of own timing in these same areas.
2. Tendency to cope with unpleasantness.
3. Ability to absorb interpersonal stress.
4. Ability to tolerate ambiguity, delay or frustration.

Interpersonal Skills of Leader

1. Ability to listen, observe and recognize the skills and abilities of others.

2. Has the ability to inspire confidence in others and interact with others easily.
3. Perceives and articulates undated feelings, recognizes and states goals, problems, ideas and interests of groups.
4. Having the capacity to structure social interaction systems for specific purposes.
5. Follows well.
6. Ability to support members of the group; accepts responsibility, is able to determine appropriate behaviours and courses of action.
7. Ability to direct activity, organize others, delegate responsibility and establishes the mood of the group.

Is it Possible to teach Leadership?

There is evidence throughout the literature that leadership can be taught or developed. It does not appear that any one type of person holds a monopoly on knowing it all. Rather, leadership is an evolution and a combination of skills, experience, knowledge and intuitive understandings. Certain situations seem to bring about leadership - like personality traits or innate abilities, allowing an individual to solve problems for others as an outgrowth of a given time or place. Stressing the need of leadership development programmes is a must if human resources development strategies a·e to reach into the uppermost ranks of organizational life.[21]

Criteria for Leadership Training

Leadership training should have education and behavioural foundation for bringing desired impact. **Sinetar (1995), and Kumar and Hansra (2000)** have suggested following leadership training criteria. [21&14]

- Training should provide a climate in which participants feel free to discuss and express themselves.
- It should develop an atmosphere of mutual interests, problem-solving and mutual respect among members.

- It should start with need assessment in order to develop the programs to meet the requirement and interests of all the members of the particular group.
- It should continually clarify developmental goal through mutual discussions, practices and surveys.
- It should utilize role playing to allow for as much open discussion as appropriate and to maintain an arena in which human feelings and attitudes are regenerated.
- Utilize one-on-one counseling methods to augment the developmental programs, thus developing a sense of "self" within each individual.
- The training should help in acquiring and reinforcing values like justice, equality, honesty, solidarity through day-to-day working.
- The training venue and set-up should be realistic, closer to the village life so that they can relate with their own situation.
- Training should involve the participants at all the stages of training programme like planning, organizing and evaluation of leadership development programme.
- Participatory method of training (e.g. Workshop, role play, field visit, group discussion etc.) should be used instead of trainer dominated method like lecture method.
- Modern training aids like computer, internet, LCD Projector should be used for imparting training.
- The period of training programme may vary from a day to a few weeks depending upon objective of the training programme and interest of the participants.
- Training for leadership development should be a continuous programme.

Methods of Leadership Training

Methods of leadership training may be categorized into two groups: (i) Formal methods, and (ii) Informal methods. *Formal methods* of leadership training are those which are structured to achieve specific goal and are usually setup by someone seeking to train and develop leadership in others. *Informal methods* are not structured, but are those which the individual utilizes in personal leadership.

Informal Methods

In training of leaders one of the requirements is that the leaders learn to understand and deal with people. This may be achieved through personal observation and supply of reading materials that relate to human behavior. Some methods used are:

1. ***Observation.*** Noticing how others have performed.
2. ***Reading***. Studying printing material often found in the form of leader handbook, news letters, circulars, bulletins, etc.
3. ***Talking.*** Speaking with other leaders in the same or related field of interest and also with members to determine consensus.[22]

Formal Methods

There are several formal methods of leadership training. The local leader may take advantage of formal training programmes in the quest of becoming a better leader. Formal methods are either used individually or in combinations. Some of the important formal methods of leadership training available in the extension education literature have been discussed below.[20,22,15&6]

1. ***Lecture:*** This is probably the most common method. Through this method local leaders under training are given enough material for thought, but little opportunity for self expression. The lecture method is effective in certain situations, but should usually be supplemented by other methods, depending on the objectives to be attained. *This method is good for presenting new information.* This is used to pass more information in less time.

2. ***Discussion and Workshop:*** Discussion is considered to be a group cooperative effort where members of a class or a group meet together to try to understand and to solve some particular problems common to them. *Discussion is organized conversation*. The underlying theory is that no one knows all the answers. Its merit lies in exchange of views or insights and adds to the understanding of a subject.

   Workshop is a gathering for providing hands on experience. Widely used, the method provides flexibility and emphasizes individual proficiency. It has a mix of theory and practice. The end result may be tangible like preparation of an audio-visual aid.

3. ***Forum, Panel and Symposium:*** In a forum or a panel, three or four individuals explain certain phases of a particular subject. In a symposium, two or more speakers with different point of view or areas of interest discuss the issue.
4. ***Audio – Visuals:*** Role playing, socio-drama and demonstration.
5. ***Field trips:*** Local leaders or potential leaders visit other groups and observe the actions and behavior of a successful organization. Field trips help the potential leaders to observe and have conversation with those already having leadership positions. Experiences gained through field work supplements the learning in the class room.
6. ***Apprenticeship:*** The local leaders or potential leaders see someone operating with a view to learn some of the activities and ways to handle problems in the field of leadership. This serves as an instrument for the local leaders to acquire a better understanding of the job.
7. ***Training group:*** This brings several local leaders to the training sessions at the same time. These people reinforce each other since each of them has experiences of his own.
8. ***Direct assistance from experts:*** This may come in the form of advice.

9. ***Buzz group:*** In this method the groups are subdivided into small groups and each selects a chairperson. The proceedings of each group are recorded. This gives several persons an opportunity to lead the discussion and practice leadership role. This technique is a very useful method of training.
10. ***Leadership Training Camps:*** Periodical organization of training camps gives the local leaders opportunity to get both practical as well as theoretical experience about their work.
11. ***Giving responsibility to local leaders:*** Giving everyone a job through which self confidence may be attained by achievement in the activities useful to the group is an essential for development of leadership.

Trained local leaders are very much useful in extension work. They can reach large number of people in the villages. They have high degree of credibility in the minds of local people. Therefore, extension worker should frequently contact them in person as well as by correspondence or mobile phone which is very much common these days. Leader should adopt new practices as well as influence others to adopt. Local leader's cooperation should be ensured in rural and agricultural development programmes and extension work. Due recognition should be given to local leaders' activities. Local leaders' contribution should be evaluated in order to make it more effective. If local leaders are used properly, volume of coverage will increase. Cost will be reduced as they are not paid. Local leaders themselves become better taught by their own experience. People readily accept the idea of local leaders.

References

- **Adair, J,** (1984) *Skills of Leadership.* Gower, London.
- **Bass, B.M,** (1960) *Leadership , Psychology and Organizational Behaviour*. Harper, New York.
- **Bhatia, S.K. Athreya, M.B,** (2007) *Team Leadership: Concepts, Roles, Strategies and Attributes.* Deep and Deep Publications Pvt. Ltd., New Delhi.

- **Chemers, M. M,** (2002) Cognitive, social, and emotional intelligence of transformational leadership: Efficacy and Effectiveness. In R.E. Riggio, S.E. Murphy, F.J. Pirozzolo (Eds.), Multiple Intelligences and Leadership.
- **Dahama, O.P, Bhatnagar, O.P,** (1990). Education and communication for development. Oxford and IBH Publishing Co. Pvt. Ltd., New Delhi.
- **Dubey,V.K. and Bishnoi, I.**,(2008). Extension Education and Communication. New Age International (P) Limited Publishers, New Delhi.
- **Hall, D.M,** (1950). The Dynamics of Discussion. Inter-state Printers and Publishers, Danville, Illinois.
- **Henry P. Knowles; Borje O. Saxberg,** (1971). Personality and Leadership Behaviour. Reading, Mass.: Addison-Wesley.
- **Hepple, L.M,** (1956). Group Organisation and Leadership in Rural Life. Lucas Brothers Publishers, Columbia, Missouri.
- **Hoyle, John R,** (1995). Leadership and Futuring: Making Visions Happen. Thousand Oaks, CA: Corwin Press, Inc.
- http://en.wikipedia.org/wiki/Leader
- **Kamath, M.G,** (1961). Extension Education in Community Development (pp. 334-361). Directorate of Extension, Ministry of Food and Agriculture, Government of India, New Delhi.
- **Kouzes, J., and Posner, B**, (2007). The Leadership Challenge. CA: Jossey Bass.
- **Kumar, B. and Hansra, B.S**. (2000). Extension Education for Human Resource Development. Concept Publishing Company, New Delhi.
- **Mishra, D.C,** (1990). New Directions in Extension Training. Directorate of Extension, Ministry of Agriculture, New Delhi.
- **Moreno, J.L**, (1953). Who Shall Survive? Foundation of Sociometry. Beacon house, New York.
- **Pilania, G.P,** (1991). Leadership. RBSA Publishers, Jaipur.
- **Reddy, A.A**, (1993). Extension Education. Sree Lakshmi Press, Bhopal.
- **Rogers, F.E. and Olmsted, A.G,** (1957).(eds) Supervision in the Co-operative Extension Service. National Agricultural Extension Centre for Advanced Study. Madison Wisconsin.

- **Sanderson, D,** (1940). Leadership for Rural Life. Associate Press, New York.
- **Sinetar,M.,**(1995). Developing Leadership Potential. In Watson, C.M. Edited Dynamics of Leadership. Jaico Publishing House, Bombay.
- **Singh, S.N,** (1961). Leadership and Group Methods of Education. In M.G.Kamath (Ed.), Extension Education in Community Development(pp.334-361). Directorate of Extension, Ministry of Food and Agriculture, Government of India, New Delhi.
- **Taba, H,** (1953). Leadership training in intergroup education. American Council of Education.
- **Watson, C.M,** (1995). Dynamics of Leadership. Jaico Publishing House, Bombay.

9

Transparency in Leadership Communication: The Need of the Hour

Prof. Aparna Rao

"It takes 20 years to build a reputation and five minutes to ruin it. If you think about that you'll do things differently."-
Warren Buffet

This chapter 'Driving Growth with Transparent Leadership Communication' is an attempt to highlight the crucial role of transparency in leaders' communication approaches. Organizations like Transparency International, Acts like RTI, Freedom of Information, the Sarbanes-Oxley and more in nations across the globe indicate the efforts of organizations for transparent communication and good governance. The chief purpose of these efforts is to ensure good governance, thereby enabling the Governments and the private sector to 'operate efficiently, effectively, and transparently with greater accountability. It would be observed from these trends that the demand and need for transparency in public and private organizations is only growing. A study of organizational communication patterns would reveal an interesting connection between organizational success and transparent leadership communication. Success here is defined as achievement of the goal of the organization in the context of the situations described in the cases.

Data is represented in the form of examples and cases about leaders who have succeeded in overcoming challenges chiefly due to their communication styles. The findings show a correlation in transparent communication by leaders and organizational success. There is also an interesting case of a company turnaround after the introduction of transparency in organizational systems. The transparency actually enabled streamlining of the various processes, leading to improved profits and company credibility.

METHODOLOGY

The chapter is based on secondary literature. This is represented in the form of cases. Each case is described in the format of Situation, Communication Approach, and Outcome. There are four case examples showing how transparent leadership ensured growth. Cases V & VI show the results of lack of transparent leadership and communication. The case examples range from known to unknown companies from across sectors.

Findings from interviews of employees in five private organizations selected at random in Mumbai are also given. The organizations are from the sectors of education, retail and telecom. The common features in the cases indicate the correlation between leadership communication techniques and employee performance. These are discussed in the conclusions. The source of information for each case is mentioned at the end of each case, as well as in the section, References. Details of books and Internet sources referred to are listed in the References section.

Case I – Marbury Engineering

Situation

This civil engineering firm in Albany, Georgia, USA was reeling under pressure of closure if something drastic did not happen in twelve months. The onslaught of severely depleted financial sources, high debts and the line of credit from banks being cut off presented bleak prospects. To top it all another firm made a job offer with a pay hike to all 12 employees. Ritchey the owner realized the trust his employees had in him when they rejected the offer. He knew he had to do something radical.

Communication Approach

He focused his attention on the staff. He called for a meeting, informed them clearly that the firm was in serious financial trouble, and that each of them would have to take 'an immediate salary adjustment' to take them through. He then passed around envelopes containing a substantial salary increase for each employee. When they opened their envelopes, they couldn't believe it. "We thought you said we were in serious financial trouble!" they said. "We are," Ritchey replied. "But I'm counting on each of you to do much more than before. So I'm paying you up front for what I expect you to do. If we do what the business needs, you will earn this increase."

Ritchey realized that he had to acknowledge his employees for their trust in the company, and adopted this unique approach. Together they developed Vision and Mission statements defining win-win outcomes for all stakeholders.

Ritchey then approached the bank for reducing the existing monthly loan payment, based on a level of payment that he could sustain, without defaulting on installments. Due to their record, this was granted.

Results

The Company saw a turn around in twelve months -

- The employees worked at streamlining processes, reducing the number of steps for completing projects, and met deadlines earlier. Projects that earlier took up to seven days to complete were now done in one or two.

- Quality increased and costs were reduced, even though the owner was less involved in each project.
- The result of this was that revenues increased by about 30%, ME met every payroll and bank payment on time.
- In the longer-term revenues nearly tripled, with an almost equal increase in salaries of employees. The company evolved and grew into a network organization - Marbury Associates, Inc. (MA, Inc.).

Case II: Project SLV – 3, ISRO

Situation

In 1973, Dr. APJ Abdul Kalam became the Project Director of the Satellite Launch Vehicle Program, SLV-3. The goal was to put India's satellite 'Rohini' into orbit by 1980. The team contained thousands of scientific and technical staff. They were ready by August 1979. As Project Director, he went to the control centre for the launch. The computer went through the checklist with four minutes to the launch. The program put the launch on hold, and the display showed that some control components were not in order.

Four experts in Dr. Kalam's team said it was all under control and that they had enough reserve fuel. So he decided to bypass the computer and switch to manual mode. In the first stage everything went off well, but in the second stage a snag developed. The entire rocket system fell into the Bay of Bengal. It was a big failure. Prof. Satish Dhawan, Head of ISRO, had called for a press conference the evening of the launch. Journalists from all over the world were present. Prof Dhawan personally conducted the conference. As leader of the organization, he owned the entire responsibility for the failure. Actually, Dr. Kalam, as Project Director, felt it was his failure.

In 1980, they successfully launched the satellite. This time, Prof. Dhawan invited Dr. Kalam to handle the press conference.

Communication Approach

As leader of the organization, Prof. Dhawan communicated that 'when failure occurred, the leader of the organization owned that failure. When success came, he gave it to his team. The best management lesson I have learned did not come to me from reading a book; it came from that experience.' Prof Dhawan showed his entire team that a leader has to lead by precept. He didn't just convey this through lip service; he demonstrated it through his actions.

Results

- The SLV-3 team worked overtime to ensure a successful launch
- They met the 1980 deadline, and were successful in the second attempt

Case III: Wal-Mart and Procter and Gamble Contract Situation

In the late 1980s, Sam Walton, Chairman, Wal-Mart and John Smale, CEO, P&G tried an experiment in business relationships. They were to align their business systems with each other with the aim to improve the bottom line for both organizations. It began with P&G managers from functions like advertising, information services, logistics, sales, manufacturing, distribution and finance moved their families from the P&G headquarters, i.e. Cincinnati, Ohio to Wal-mart's headquarters at Bentonville, Arkansas. They formed a task force with Wal-Mart counterparts to study how each did business and develop totally aligned systems to better serve the consumers who bought P&G products in Wal-Mart stores. The challenge was to eliminate the competition between P&G and Wal-Mart in this project. So far, there had been competition between them for profit margins.

Communication Approach

On the first day of work of the new team, Mr. Sam Walton entered, 'unannounced and unexpected.' He asked for the P&G

folks and was informed by the receptionist that they were all at the bank, caught in the red tape for their home mortgages. The local bank seemed hesitant to approve mortgage loans for so many out of town people together. Sam immediately called up the bank and said that he was willing to do whatever was required to expedite the loans for the P&G partners.

Results

- Needless to say, the loans were quickly approved.
- With his phone call, Sam communicated that he took the partnership seriously, and acknowledged that the onus of successful execution of the contract lay on him.
- The managers from both companies got the message that they were a team, and not competitors.
- They worked together for the same end.
- The changes that were introduced fulfilled consumers' needs better, faster and cheaper.
- Sales volume and profits of both P&G and Wal-Mart showed a dramatic improvement.

Case IV: Stu Reed, Motorola – IABC 2007 EXCEL Award Winner

Situation

Before he became President, Motorola's Mobile Devices Business, Stu Reed was Executive Vice President, Motorola's Integrated Supply Chain, which includes all customer fulfillment centers, logistics providers, manufacturing facilities and procurement. When Reed joined Motorola from IBM in 2005, he took up the challenge of helping to improve Motorola's growth and profitability through its supply chain function.

His charter: transform the four decentralized business-unit-specific supply chains into a single integrated organization that would seamlessly support the entire company. Specifically, he sought to engage and mobilize 36,000 employees and contractors—more than one-third of Motorola's global workforce.

Communication Approach

Reed recognizes communication as a vital ingredient to success. Supply Chain is not an area traditionally known for excellence in communication leadership; Reed however, 'recognized that a solid communication plan was an essential component of lasting transformational change'.

He is known to be 'an authentic, straight talker who interacts regularly with all levels of his workforce, both face-to-face and through communication vehicles that enable him to share supply chain strategy, expectations and successes.'

'Communication in the Integrated Supply Chain function is planned, strategic and evaluated. Reed has worked closely with his communication director to execute a comprehensive communication plan that addresses the needs of both internal and external stakeholders.'

'Reed was actively involved in developing a set of consistent messages aligned with Motorola's business strategy. He also made it easy to put these messages together in an engaging and compelling format. By using a collaborative approach in developing meaningful and consistent messages, and continuously reinforcing them through leadership actions and organizational initiatives, Reed was able to engage employees to help achieve business success.'

'The Award Committee found that Reed communicates with clarity of purpose, ensures effective stakeholder communication, supports effective information sharing, is consistent in his communication behavior and expects the same of his team. These are the ingredients for communication competence in business as identified in research sponsored by IABC's Research Foundation.'

'Reed has a great deal of experience and an acknowledged position in supply chain management. He manages a cross-cultural workforce that includes operations in countries such as China and India'.

Results

- In 2005 when Stu Reed joined Motorola was not included in AMR Research's Top 25 Supply Chain List. Seven months later, Motorola was ranked #15.
- Eighteen months later, Motorola moved up three spots to #12 on AMR's 2007 list.
- Motorola's supply chain and realizing efficiency and productivity gains for the organization are transformed.
- The supply chain is now a distinct competitive advantage for the company.

Case V: Enron – A Case in Miscommunication and Lack of Transparency

The incredible rise and fall of this energy giant in a span of 15 years, is a lesson in itself. The fundamental means and methods of communication were based on vagueness and miscommunication.

The unhealthy accounting practices were brought to the notice of Kenneth Lay, the Enron CEO in 2000, and to another acquaintance who worked with Enron's accountants – Arthur Anderson in confidence, by Sherron Watkins who was then Vice President, Corporate Development. The practice of projecting manipulated figures reflected in the overall communication of the company – internal as well as external. The meteoric rise in the revenues of the company appeared too good to be true. Sherron's warnings went unheeded and the results are there for all to see.

Case VI: Satyam – Enron Replicated in India

In Jan 2009, when the world was reeling under the pressures of economic slowdown Satyam Systems cast a shadow over outsourcing firms in India, with Ramalingam's stunning confession of fraudulent accounting practices and fudging of figures. Employees too were shocked at these revelations. The company stocks plummeted and uncertainty soared. The morale of employees hit a low and performance took a hit.

Case VII: Private Educational Institutions in Mumbai - Lack of Transparency in Appointments, Increments and Promotions

These are incidents from educational organizations in Mumbai, as shared by ex-employees. In all instances, the Director/Head is empowered to take all day-to-day and some policy decisions on behalf of the Management. These 'leaders' champion the cause of ethical governance but many a time, their staff and colleagues are taken aback by the lack of transparency in decisions, minor and major, like leave sanctions, appointments, increments and promotions. Actions belie words, reducing these statements to mere lip service. The impressive talk at the time of interviews and offer coupled with the infrastructure convey messages of growth, independence and success to prospective employees.

There is no set procedure or policy explaining certain decisions that seemed, contrary to expectations, arbitrary.

The appointment letters showed discrepancy in the period of probation and positions offered. Some young recruits with hardly any experience and not even the required qualifications were offered probation of one year, and higher positions, while some others with post doctorate qualifications and experience were offered probation of two years and a lower position.

In another case a good performer was asked to resign, in spite of an excellent track record. The reasons could be either personal grudges or leader's insecurity. Whatever the case may be, employees derive negative messages from such actions.

Ex-employees revealed another case of the head slapping Grade IV employees (peons) for minor or no mistake. The language used was highly abusive and unparliamentary. This too, sent contradictory messages across all levels in the Institution.

In yet another incident, a female placement coordinator in an academic institution was instructed to go on a business visit after working hours, and show off her 'assets' to the HR Manager concerned.

In all these incidents, there was no direct source of reliable information where people could fearlessly ask questions. The employees have no forum for redressal of their grievances.

- Qualified and experienced professionals expressed dissatisfaction
- Increased attrition
- Dubious record of low ranking and high attrition
- Lowered morale and organizational efficiency
- Little or no response to advertisements for recruitments meet with little response

Case VIII: A Company Shuts Down

Situation

The offers in the appointment contract of a CEO. This is an example quoted by Narayan Murthy in 'The Essence of Leadership.'

He mentions a company that offered the CEO a brand new Mercedes, promised a monthly first-class air ticket for his mother, along with a cash bonus of $10 million and other benefits. There was no explanation or logic offered for such benefits.

Not surprisingly, this company has already filed for bankruptcy.

Unethical communication practices and lack of transparency in all the above cases have a negative impact on the organizations.

FINDINGS

The above cases confirm the hypothesis that successful leadership depends largely on transparency in communication. There is a definite correlation between the words and actions of leaders, and the results that follow in the organization. As seen from cases I to IV, Ritchey, Prof. Dhawan, Sam Walton and Stu Reed demonstrate that a leader's communication addresses not just the issue that is obviously confronting them, but also the latent issues that are left unsaid in the minds of the team.

Cases V, VI, VII & VIII show how actions and words of leaders have failed to meet the standards of transparency and justice. Contradictions send out negative messages across the board. This negativity percolates down the grapevine, and the results are the subsequent downfall of the leader or organization.

The Hay Group, a global management consultancy, further confirms this hypothesis in a study. They found that:

- Trust and confidence in top leadership was the single most reliable predictor of employee satisfaction in an organization.
- Effective communication by leadership in three critical areas was the key to winning organizational trust and confidence:

(a) Helping employees understand the company's overall business strategy.

(b) Helping employees understand how they contribute to achieving key business objectives.

(c) Sharing information with employees on both how the company is doing and how an employee's own division is doing - relative to strategic business objectives.

David Hanna in the book Leadership for the Ages identifies nine attributes that enable true leaders to succeed where many fail. Of these, at least three may be related to communication styles:

- Their ability to inspire trust and confidence in others
- They are great communicators
- They align their followers to deliver a different level of performance

Conclusions

From the above findings it can be concluded that communication from the leader has to be issue based rather than person specific and transparent. As Narayan Murthy says, 'Trust and confidence can only exist where there is a premium on transparency. The leader has to create an environment where each person feels secure enough to be able to disclose his or her mistakes, and resolves to improve. Investors respect such organizations. Investors understand that the business will have good times and bad times. What they want you to do is to level with them at all times. They want you to disclose bad news on a proactive basis. At Infosys, our philosophy has always been, 'When in doubt, disclose.'

'We must become the change we want to see in the world.' Leaders have to prove their belief in sacrifice and hard work. Such behavior will enthuse the employees to make bigger sacrifices. It will help win the team's confidence, help leaders become credible, and help create trust in their ideas.' – Mahatma Gandhi

Recommendations

- Leadership as a topic in the HR syllabus should also focus on ethical communication.
- Training programs for managers and leaders in transparent communication techniques would also be fruitful.
- The theoretical aspects of transparent leadership can be translated into concrete action by defining company policies to ensure open channels and forums for democratic exchange of ideas and implementation plans.
- Communication audits at internal levels would be effective in monitoring the processes.
- This paper highlights the success ratio of transparent leadership communication. A detailed research into leadership communication in Indian organizations is recommended for practical implementation of concepts and ideas.

References

- **Balasubramanian S,** (2007) *The art of business leadership – Indian Experiences,* Sage Publications. USA.

- **Kalam. APJ Abdul,** (2005) *Wings of fire*, University Press. India.
- **Hanna David P,** (2007) *Leadership for the ages*, Jaico Books. Mumbai
- **Yuki Gary,** (2007) *Leadership in organizations,* Pearson Education. UK
- **Stuart B.E, Sarow M.S, Stuart L.,** (2007) *Integrated business communication in a global marketplace,* Wiley-India Edition. India.
- **Wallace Peter & Zinkin John,** (2006) *Corporate governance – Mastering business in Asia,* Wiley-India Edition. India.

Internet Sources

- **Guthrie Philip.** (June 2007). Ethical communications – An oxymoron in practice? [On-line] Retreived on 16 July 2008, fromhttp://www.senatecommunications.co.nz/ethical _communications_an_oxymoron_in_practice.php
- **Kalam APJ Abdul**. (April 2008). *A leader should know how to manage failure.* India@Wharton. [On-line] Retrieved on 10 July from knowledge@wharton.upenn.edu/india
- Case Study: Reed Stu. (2007). EXCEL Award. IABC International Conference. *Leadership in communication series.* [On-line] Retrieved 10 July 2008 from http://www.iabc.com/ awards/leadership
- **Murthy Narayan.** (Jan. 2005). *The essence of leadership*[On-line] Available http://www.rediff.com/money/2005/jan/ 04spec.htm
- **Clark Donald**. (May 2008). *Concepts of leadership*. Big Dog's Leadership Training. [On-line] Available http:// www.nwlink.com/~Donclark/leader/leadtrn.html
- **Salvatico Robert**. (2006). Enabling transparent leadership: A small business manager's perspective. *Journal of management development.* Vol. 25 [On-line] Retrieved on 16 July, from http:/ /www.emeraldinsight.com/10.1108/02621710610708658

- **Karper Erin & Neyhart David** *APA formatting and style guide*. Edited by Brizee Allen June 2008. [Online] Available.
- owl.english.purdue.edu/owl/resource/560/05/http://www.time.com/time/nation/article/0,8599,194927,00.html
- http://www.forbes.com/2009/01/07/satyam-raju-governance-oped-cx_sb_0107balachandran_print.html

10

Reproductive Health Awareness Among Tribal Women Through Folk Ways

Ms. Jagrati Vadnerkar
Dr. Rameshwari Pandya

"Folk art is a highly effective medium to educate people about the health programmes" - Robert Blake

On the basis of above mentioned studies, it is ensured that the use of folk media to reach the common people in the process of change and development of the country individually in reproductive health areas widely acceptable.

Reproductive Health

Reproductive health is defined by WHO as a state of physical, mental, and social well-being in all matters relating to the reproductive system at all stages of life. Reproductive health implies that people are able to have a satisfying and safe sex life and that they have the capability to reproduce and the freedom to decide if, when, and how often to do so. Implicit in this are the right of men and women to be informed and to have access to safe, effective, affordable, and acceptable methods of family planning of their choice, and the right to appropriate healthcare services that enable women to safely go through pregnancy and childbirth.

Folk Media

According to Forcucci (1984), "folk media is with us since the dawn of history". The broad general definition of "Folk media" is that it is "media of the 'folk' or "of the people". (Nettl & Myers 1976, Forcucci, 1984).

- Folk means people in general or mass. Folk includes the culture which already exists or is present and which is not new. It means whatever the culture or tradition people have their attitude, beliefs, values, skills, thinking etc.
- Any medium when used to give knowledge, information and entertainment for a specific purpose it becomes media.

Compiling two definitions it can be said while using cultural folk things which already exists to provide knowledge and information to the people then it becomes folk media.

Reproductive Health Awareness is a holistic approach to reproductive health incorporating many important aspects such as body awareness, self-care, gender, sexuality, and interpersonal communication.

The most important period in the lifespan of women is reproductive health period, which starts from menarche and ends with menopause. Between these periods, she passes from multifarious activities like pregnancy, childbirth etc. this condition of women are based on various social as well cultural aspects. Most of the reproductive health problems arise in this period only. These problems are determined by the knowledge and awareness of women in regards to their reproductive health matters and the general practices prevalent among the women. Without reproductive health, freedom, and appropriate knowledge, women cannot fully exercise their fundamental human rights. Yet around the world, the right to health, and especially reproductive health, is far from a reality for many women. The main sufferer in the context is the women and especially they who live in a very far - flung areas or remote areas who are more likely to it are Tribal women. The Indian society is a complex social system with different caste classes' creeds and tribes. The high rate of illiteracy added to the inadequacies of mass media and the other necessary services to reach almost 80% of people who resides in village or in outreach areas. There are around 636 schedule tribe categories in India.

Even though they have a rich culture they are socio-economically disadvantaged and marginalized "Tribes in India, who constitute 15 per cent of the geographical area and nearly 8 per cent of the population, are truly disadvantaged and marginalized population of our country. Every 12th women in India belongs to a schedule tribe community. Thus improving the health status of the tribal woman becomes an important developmental goal. Tribal have a far less health modernity, as compared to the rest of the population. Their own beliefs, illiteracy, poverty, non-access to scientific information contribute to this low Health Modernity status. Obviously it might lead to maternal as well as child mortality. Similar crude births practices were found to exist in other tribal groups National Family Health Survey (1998-99). Many of the programme and policies made by the government and other concern institution but suspect mass media prove too glamorous impersonal and unbelievable in context with the tribal women living in village areas' could not only see and here but also even touch. Many health aspects were there to literate people (especially women reproductive health aspect), has remained untouched.Basic maternal and child health (MCH) care, from both public and private sources, has been grossly neglected in India. MCH services, which are practically the only special program for women, receive a mere 2 percent of the national health budget. In fact, with less than 1 percent of the gross domestic product currently allocated for health services, there is a large gap between health needs in India and the public infrastructure intended to serve them. The number of health workers and the infrastructure available for women, even the existing limited services are inadequate and of poor quality. Added to this deficiency is a bias favoring rural areas in health care delivery (Duggal, Ravi 1995). The situation is due to poor socio-economic conditions, non-availability of trained health personnel in tribal areas and traditions surrounding marriage and childbirth. Eighty-five percent of deliveries in rural areas take place at home and most of the communities rely on a dai (traditional birth attendant) or relatives for delivery care (National Family Health Survey-2(1998-99).

Subramanayam says that it is needful to the human society to improve knowledge and for knowing the new innovations and modern technology. Recognizing the need for sensitive and affordable health care for women in small towns, rural and mainly urban areas. Schubert (1997) concluded in a study that, the early years of CARE's family planning and reproductive health program stressed modern methods of contraception and providing services. However, new opportunities to address reproductive health awareness and natural family planning are emerging. Coordination and collaboration with sectors such as food and nutrition, children's health and natural resources management, together with more sophisticated ways to assess need and reach communities with information, have resulted in more people being reached than ever before with appropriate options and opportunities for reproductive health awareness and care. Creative combinations of interpersonal communication and mass and folk media are being used to disseminate information about reproductive health. While strategies are being designed and implemented on the basis of the need. Program impact is assessed and examples are given from India, Peru, and Nepal.

Yahaya (2004) assessed the knowledge on HIV/AIDS awareness through folk music and community outreach drama in Nigeria. According to him, in focus group discussions, almost all the discussants attributed their awareness of HIV and AIDS and related reproductive health issues to the drama and folk music (played in live performances and later recorded on audio tapes). In the discussions, drama seems to enjoy relative popularity on preference rating of the two sources compared to music. About two - third (74%) of the discussants highly preferred the drama sketches compared to about one - third (33%) who preferred music. The probable explanation for this finding with particular reference to this study area and the intervention programme could be the live performances by the main actor - Ndayagi (a popular radio actor) in the drama during outreach programmes. Seeing Ndayagi in live drama scenes and performance during this period undoubtedly increased people's belief, association, and understanding about the topic selected.

Folk media, being the media of the people, have been with them for centuries and have become a part of life. Folk media always have their own languages so it represents their true culture so they understand it well as they easily associate with the gesture, music and rhythm. This characteristic of folk media develops familiarity.

Tribal Women and its Correlation with Reproductive Health and Folk Media

Tribals have their own culture and social life and thus are important in India. With culture they also have their own folklore, folk songs, dances etc. Almost all tribal communities possess rich mythologies, folk tales, stories which illustrate their affinity and relationship with tradition and traditional characters. With traditions they have their own general beliefs. Heath status of the tribal population is marked by all the negative features that one may find in morbidity and mortality. Poverty, illiteracy, malnutrition, lack of personal hygiene, unsanitary conditions and absence of health education, poor mother and child health services and poor coverage of the national preventive programmes have been found responsible for the poor health of the tribal communities. To them mass media prove too glamorous impersonal and unbelievable in context with the tribes' could not only see and here but also even touch.

Besides poor coverage, the tribal communities have their own systems of medicines, dispensed through the medium of shamans, herbalists and witchdoctors, which also act as a barrier in healthcare programmes. Finally some specific reproductive health practices mostly prevalent in the Indian tribal communities such as home as a safest place for a child birth, unhygienic and unhealthy practices during menstruation, improper care during and after pregnancy of a women, etc. are largely located in the tribal hinterlands.

Tribal development means as overall development of rural areas social, economic, political and cultural - so that the people are to lead a pleasant life. Agriculture plays the most important and decisive role in rural development. Infect, nobody can deny this fact that most of the population 'People of India' project shows that there is extent of sharing of culture in most of the tribes and non-tribes now. The percentage of joint families is higher among the tribals and most of them are engaged with agriculture and related activities as their main occupation. There are exceptions and some educated tribals have opted for nuclear families.Himalayan range of Jammu and Kashmir (a tribal dominated area) organized a campaign with the focus of HIV/AIDS awareness. The tribes are being imparted knowledge about the ways and means to prevent the dreaded disease.

The Tribal Research and Cultural Foundation have launched a fourfold programme throughout the State with special focus on the tribes of Gujjars and Bakerwals. This was in view of lack of knowledge among people about deadly diseases and sexually transmitted infections.

What makes the initiative unique is the fact that the programme is in Gojri, the language of nomad Gujjars.Various mass communication techniques such as the use of folk poetry, posters and folk theatre with indigenous settings are being employed. Folk artistes, story-tellers, folk painters and theatre performers have been associated for the purpose. Javaid Rahi, national secretary of the Foundation told The Hindu that he hoped that the folk media is a powerful tool to spread knowledge to counter the threat of deadly diseases. He said "tribal Gujjar doctors" will educate the nomads about health care and the programmes launched from time to time. Hence folk media has relationship with tribal areas and also is a means to create awareness among them. The government of India has implemented specific programmes for the healthcare development of the tribal communities and there have been encouraging results. However, much is required to be known in the area of tribal morbidity and traditional systems of medicines. To consider tribal women's reproductive health awareness through folk media will be an attempt to being together the advance reproductive aspects and their health development aspect (in terms of knowledge of reproductive health), on one hand, and of traditional cultural heritage in the form of traditional systems, on the other.

No communication strategy would be complete unless it included the folk media, which must rank alongside the more commonly accepted channels of communication.

Why Using Folk Media For Reproductive Health Awareness

- Folk media support by any extension worker, opinion makers, and religious leaders with close involvement in the reproductive health programme greatly influences the behavior and response patterns of women of the tribal communities.
- This serves to tribal communities to be attentive towards the quality and coverage of women reproductive and its related health services, including referral care.

- An extension worker, a researcher, any NGO or a social work organization could spread widely the messages of the meaning of reproductive health care, family planning, reproduction, reproductive tract infections, and sexually transmitted diseases and so on.
- The involvement and enthusiastic participation of above individuals or organization will ensure dedicated involvement of tribal women in the use of folk media for awareness. As many of researches have already been shows that every tribal community has their own culture as well as their own belief. More of the use of folk media will develop more understanding among the tribal women of their community. The use of all folk media will enhance its acceptance throughout the tribal women of society.

Apart from all the above mentioned points the students from Faculty of Journalism and communication from The M S University of Baroda organized a campaign on to protect the environment. They felt that The need to protect our environment, cautioning people not to be influenced by the media hype and the current political scenario in the country, featured in the folk media presentation. The programme, Jhalak, had a glimpse of all the known art forms of the country, including bhavi, puppetry, and tamasha. Students also used the medium of theatre to reflect the present political crisis in the country. The script and the characters were from Mahabharata and the students dressed traditionally as the characters of the epic. Students used the folk form of puppetry to show how one's psyche was affected by the media. However, this time around students did not use the traditional puppets, but puppets of Bollywood stars Shahrukh Khan, Kajol and Rani Mukherjee. Citing the example of Bollywood blockbuster Kuch Kuch Hota Hai, they conveyed how Kajol won over Shahrukh by being herself and not getting affected by media.

Use of Folk Media in Changing Behaviour

Soloman says that Non formal methods of educating people always bring changing behaviors. The function of folk media is consistent with Bandura's social learning (cognition) theory, which states that most behaviors are learned through modeling. This theory explains that vicarious learning from others is a powerful teacher of attitudes and behavior. Bandura believed that individuals learn not only in classrooms but also by observing role models in everyday life, including characters in movies and television programs. Accordingly, folk media performers are role models from whom people learn. The various types of folk media are used as primers that provide the basis for residents of rural communities to discuss and diagnose their socio cultural and health situations and that enable them to take steps to find solutions to those problems. The role of folk media further subscribes to Rogers's communication and innovations theory, which explains how an innovation can be sustained within communities or groups of people after it has been adopted by the leadership of that community or group.

Classification of Folk Media

Traditional forms of expression were identified by some researcher. The classification covering the performing arts and the visual arts of folk media included music, song, drama, skits, puppet shows , poetry, speech, sounds, gesture, gossip, jokes, proverbs, painting, certain printed literature, sculpture, handicrafts, costuming, patterning and colouring of material and use of head-gear. Symbolic meanings may often be an important consideration in use of any one or combination of these forms of expression and therefore the thought-processes behind selection of forms assumed significance.

Way to use Folk Media for Awarenes

There are some ways to using folk media for the awareness among tribal women, and are always helpful because still the use of it has a significant effectiveness on their perception level and for enhancing their knowledge level also.

- Ways to disseminate information about reproductive health are being broadened to include creative combinations of interpersonal, mass and folk media, whether it is an informal one-to-one counseling session with flipcharts, a community mobilization event, a multi-media campaign, or any combination thereof.

- Likewise, the target audience need not always be the women of reproductive age, not should the RH messengers always be the medical and public health professionals.
- What is critical in all of these instances is to craft strategies based on appropriate research and need, continuously monitor progress, refine approaches as necessary, track results and evaluate the process and impact of interventions leading to behavior change. The challenge is not insignificant, but the rewards to be reaped through the improved programs are clearly worth striving for.
- However, new and fresh opportunities to address reproductive health awareness and natural family planning are now emerging as important options. In these programs, coordination and collaboration with other sectors such as food and nutrition, children's health and natural resource management, combined with more sophisticated approaches for assessing need and reaching communities with information, has resulted in more people being reached than ever before with appropriate options and opportunities for reproductive health awareness and care.

There are examples of CARE projects from India, Peru and Nepal where activities which feature working across development sectors and engaging communities to address their individual and collective RH needs are featured. Ways to disseminate information about reproductive health are being broadened to include creative combinations of interpersonal, mass and folk media', whether it be an informal one-to-one counseling session with flipcharts, a community mobilization event, a multi-media campaign, or any combination thereof.

Status and Function of Folk Media for Reproductive Health Awareness

- As an intrinsically valuable form of popular entertainment or artistic expression it is worth preserving and developing the knowledge of tribal women in reproductive aspects for its own sake.
- It is a means of changing values, attitudes and norms in order to provide a proper climate for social and economic progress by improving their reproductive health also.
- It is a method of promoting certain behavior acts or patterns. The aim is to get people to perform specific acts to achieve objectives of national policy and programmes which are actually running for them either by the government or by any other organization for their reproductive health developmental aspects.
- It is a channel for conveying information about available techniques and facilities which tribal women may use to solve their related problems.

The above purposes, it was noted, are not necessarily in compatible with each other. Certain media may not be appropriate for certain purposes and certain purposes may not be achieved by employing particular folk media, or any folk medium. It is therefore important to evolve criteria both for selecting media and for selecting messages that pass through them.

Advantages of Folk Media

- Traditional media come from the people and antecede the mass media; their appeal has historically been both functional and aesthetic. Whether of roughly-hewn folk origins or of classifiably rigid moulds, they have always served to entertain, educate to reinforce existing ideas or ideologies or to change existing values and attitudes.
- Being close to people at the local level, these channels are potentially useful in the service of social concerns, as

determined by local, provincial or national authorities themselves.

- They are, moreover, abundantly present in areas where mass media technology has not been fully or effectively developed to capture sustained interest at local, provincial or national levels. Folk media are personal forms of entertainment and communication.
- This is important because behavioral changes are most easily brought about by personal interaction. These forms of art are a part of the way of life of a community and provide acceptable means of bringing development issues into the community in its own-terms.
- They are capable of reaching intimate social groups, thus making use of already established communication networks in the audience.
- These forms of entertainment evolved as grassroots expressions of the values and life styles of the people, dealing with values as well as information. These features are significant for development, planners in the field of population, since it is rapidly becoming apparent that something more than information is necessary to bring about the behavioral changes involved in the adoption and continued practice of health and Family Planning.
- Another advantage of the traditional media is that they attract people who might not attend an educational meeting. With skill, new content might be added to the old forms which are already familiar and dear to the people. Finally, unlike mass media programmes, produced for large and often diverse audience, the folk forms can use familiar dialects for the most intimate and local communication at the village level.
- Folk media rather deal with values that relate to family life, such as the status of women, conjugal relationships, education and standard of living. Folk media can be seen as part of the social fabric of the community, while they

could reinforce relevant social changes that are already occurring (or bc used directly to introduce new ideas), folk forms should not be used for propaganda.

- Some of the advantages of traditional folk media are that they do not require large capital investments and there is not a dependence on expensive communication technologies that are liable to break down. Traditional media can be used "live", and are likely to have the greatest impact when audience members can interact with the performers and artists and even participate. Alternatively, they can be coupled with other media such as radio and television.

The only Limitations, on the other hand, included the dangers in "overloading" certain traditional channels with too many "messages" of an instrumental nature. Channels could only be loaded according, to their capacity and with respect, in particular to cultural, religious, or other sensitively integral elements. Sociologists and anthropologists could help planners define these sensitive factors affecting such limitations.

Some Criterias For Selection And Use of The Folk Media in People's Lives:

How frequently and extensively are emotional or artistic expressions? This would indicate the Vitality of the tradition in which they reset. What is the usual size and composition of audience attracted in terms of age, sex, educational, economic and social groupings? What is the importance of the functions performed, in a framework of prevailing social needs and values?

- Examination of religious or social functions attributed to the medium should be made so as not to distort its special role.
- It would determine whether the medium has an age or individuality (in which case positive identification of audience with actor can be the agent of change), or whether it is entirely non-individual. It has sometimes been found that certain messages can be best expressed without the

personalities of, actors in evidence during performance, as in puppet show, mask presentations and giant figures.

- It should be noted, whether a particular medium or any aspect of its traditions and features could be used by or extended to, mass media presentation. If so, is this desirable in relation to both a medium and the message?
- Are the required resources, talent, materials, texts, available for extensive utilization of the medium?
- Does the selected medium have entertainment value and or artistic appeal?
- Is it unique enough to prove a valuable communication channel?
- Is the form of the proposed medium flexible enough to incorporate a sufficiently broad range of content materials, such as family planning and other developmental messages?
- Is the medium sufficiently versatile to reach varied audiences? To properly assess this criterion, the country must be in a position to assess the range of traditional media and their suitability for audiences according to local and provincial make-up.
- Is the selected medium, relevant to the intended audience?

If all the folk media will be selected on the basis of above mentioned criteria then it will be goal oriented.

SUGGESTIONS

Some suggestions can be given to improve the knowledge level of the tribal women as well as to increase the use of folk media are as follows:

- One week training can be organized in needy tribal areas, related to reproductive health awareness, so it may be helpful to get good reproductive health.
- A campaign or a health camp can be organized with the use of folk media like drama, nautanki, tamasha etc. so that the necessary messages can be spread effectively to the tribal women. It will also be useful to develop

understanding regarding different aspects reproductive health.

- Use of folk media is also a source of great entertainment with its appropriateness and it brings women closer to each other, hence a collective, participatory and strengthened approach can also be developed among them.
- Combination of folk media like puppet show, munadi, folk dance and folk songs altogether will have a significant impact over the education of tribal women, hence this increment in knowledge will sustain throughout their life.
- By using folk media a major problem of reproductive health concern can be solved to great extent in terms of knowledge gain among tribal areas.

CONCLUSION

There is no end to this interesting matrimony between tribal women and folklore. With this it can be concluded that the role of folk media on the tribals of any settlements in specific and in general is much useful then the other area. The residents of the road side villages are more exposed to outside when compared with that of the interior tribals.

The extension of folk media use to the interior tribals definitely bring them to the main stream, when they come into contact with the essential knowledge of the reproductive health area, they try to change their attitude in the direction of the most aware communities. The role of media in the tribal development process has wider scope to create awareness among them in their related aspects. Though they have belief in that, so the extension agents, the village leaders, the political leaders have to take up this challenging task in order to elevate them into the equals than being to kept aside. The interior tribals should be brought into the mainstream instead of keeping them in isolation.

Majority of the tribals are still ignorant about the reproductive health concerns and related programme actually running for them. Because lack of information and improper motivation. Many agencies, NGOs and academic institutions (working for reproductive health and tribal women) have found it profitable to use folk music, folk elements, and folk functions along with an appropriate choice of languages. This folk media can create awareness and make them to participate fully in the ongoing development programmes and in turn they get the opportunity to contribute for nation development.

References

- **Duggal, Ravi,** (1995) 'Our health costs little,' in Our Lives, Our Health, ed. Malini Karkal. New Delhi: Coordination Unit, World Conference on Women-Beijing.
- **Forcucci, Samuel L,** (1984). A Folk Song History of America: America through Its Songs. Englewood Cliffs, New Jersey: Prentice-Hall, Inc.
- **Handoo, J,** (1998), Folklore in Modern India - language in India' Central Institute of Indian Languages.
- Health and Population, CARE, Atlanta, Georgia 30303, USA. Pub Med Index for medicine.
- **Indian Express Vadodara,** (1999) Using folk media to send across a message Monday, February 14-15.
- **Kumar H,** (2006), Folk Media and Rural Development Indian Media Studies Journal • Vol.1 • No. 1. July-Dec.
- **Monali Ramesh Panchbhai,** (1997), Health of Indian Tribal Women SHPT School of Library Science, SNDT Women's University, India, Jun-Sep13(2-3):355-61.
- National Council For Science and Technology Communication (NCSTC), Ministry of Science and Technology, Department of Science and Technology, Annul Report 2007-2008.
- **Schubert , J, Pillai, G and Thorndahl R,** (1998), Breaking the mold: expanding options for reproductive health awareness: the CARE experience Journal of Contraception, Jun-Sep;13 (2-3):355-61
- **Solomon P et al,** (2001) Using Folk Media in HIV/AIDS Prevention in Rural Ghana, American Journal of Public Health October: Vol 91, No. 10

- **Subramanyam V and Rama Mohan. K.R,** (2006). Mass Media and Tribal Life: A Study in Visakha Agency Area of Andhra Pradesh, Department of Anthropology, Andhra University, Visakhapatnam Andhra Pradesh, 8(2): 75-81.
- **Suman S and Asari V G** Reproductive health care of women in rural areas: an exploratory study in Nilgiris District in Tamil Nadu. The journal of family welfare January 1997 pp. 49-55.
- **The Hindu** (2008), AIDS awareness campaign to focus on J&K tribes.
- **Thirumalai S, Mallikarjun B and et al** (1997), "Strength for Today and Tomorrow" Jun-Sep;13(2-3):355-61.
- **Thirumalai, S, Mallikarjun B and Laxmi C** (2004), "strength for today and tomorrow" May Volume 4:5.
- **Yahaya. M. K,** (2004), "Center for Communication and Reproductive Health", EE4 Conference: Maddy Semaar Soul City Institute for Health and Science, Dubai.

11

Non-formal Education Through Red Ribbon Club

Dr. Jagdish Solanki

"Civilization is a race between education and catastrophe."

Today society is increasingly becoming complex in multiple spheres of human life. The problems are perceived in the areas of technology, medicine, economics, human behaviour and health etc. When life and learning become more complicated we cannot live our life, unless we educate ourselves in non-formal, formal or informal ways.

Informal education:

- Works through, and is driven by, conversation.
- Involves exploring and enlarging experience.
- Can take place in any setting.

The present world situations offer education with a new challenge. When formal education has failed to reached to all, the fate of non-formal and informal education is at stake. Generally, non-formal or informal education offers mature understanding, develops an attitude of acceptance, love and respect and people learn to react to causes not the symptoms. Further, it helps people to acquire necessary skills to achieve the potential of the people and help the people to understand the dynamic society. In the domain of informal education, various human needs are fulfilled mainly physical needs, the growth urge, the security, need for new experiences, affection and recognition etc. The incentives for adult learning through education are multiple. People want to gain health, time, improved security, praise from others, comfort, increased enjoyment, amusement etc... They want to be sociable, up-to-date, and creative. They want to express themselves, collect/acquire and finally they want to save time, money, worry, doubts, risk, embarrassments etc.

Generally informal education would seem to be the area of vocational training, creativity, music, art, literature, personal adjustment, social adjustment, leisure time skills and home-making.

The purpose of non-formal education?

The very purpose of this education is to produce individuals who are effective members of the society to which they belong and to develop intellect, character, appreciation and physical wellbeing of each individual. Non-formal education tends to emphasize certain values. These include commitments to:

- Work for the well-being of all.
- Respect the unique value and dignity of each human being.
- Dialogue.
- Equality and justice.
- Democracy and the active involvement of people in the issues that affect their lives.

Non formal educators: attend to the vast range of opportunities that arise in everyday settings for learning, look to relationships and processes - and how these can be made more fulfilling, express certain, compelling, concerns - for democracy, justice and respect for others.

Informal education's central form - conversation - carries these, value people's experiences and feelings, work in ways that help people to deepen their understandings and commitments and to act on them. In daily life we all act as educators from time to time. But there is also a need for specialists - educators who are skilled in, and committed to, working with people in everyday situations so that life can be more fulfilling and all can share in its fruits.

The methods which are used for Non formal education are:

- Lectures
- Question-answer sessions
- Discussions – Leader- member centered and focus group discussion
- Project
- Laboratory
- Apprenticeship
- Demonstration with visual aids
- Individual investigations
- Motion pictures
- Film strips
- Exhibits
- Radio and television
- Recordings
- Models
- Charts and blackboards
- Pageants
- Field trips
- Role playing
- Leadership techniques
- Buzz sessions

The clubs, groups, forums and conferences have also become very effective tool of informal education in 21st century.

Concept of Red Ribbon Club

Vision

Red Ribbon Clubs (RRC) are envisaged to instill among all the stakeholders, including students in the educational institutions values of service, develop healthy life styles, and increase access to safe and adequate quantities of blood to all the needy by promotion of Regular voluntary blood donation.

Apart from this, RRC also aims at harnessing the potential of the youth by equipping them with correct information on mental health, Substance abuse, nutrition and reproductive health and building their capacities as peer educators in spreading messages on positive health behavior in an enabling environment.

Objectives

The specific objectives of the programme are:

- To instill life skills into youths to live better and healthier life.
- Increasing the capacity of the education system in teaching, training of various basic health aspects and helping the adolescents and youths for achieving positive health
- To ensure that every college going youth in the state is equipped with conceptual knowledge about various basic health aspects which he may possibly encounter during his life.
- To motivate youth and build their capacity as peer educators and change agents by developing their skills on leadership, negotiation, and team building.
- To promote voluntary non-remunerated blood donation among youth.
- Promote Regular voluntary blood donation by young people and increase access to safe and adequate quantities of blood.
- To develop essential skills to cope up with the adverse conditions pertaining to health specifically, supporting young people.

- To know their healthcare needs better.
- To develop and reinforce life skills that enables them to protect themselves from various health hazards
- To dispel myths and clarify misconceptions regarding various health issues and events.
- And to find out a way where they can identify various health problems and can fight them out

Basis Strategies of Red Ribbon Club Programme

The programmes are implemented through Non Governmental Organization in coordination with Universities' trained RRC In charge / Programme Officers (Lecturers) and peer educators.

Non Governmental Organization staff would train the nodal teachers and peer educators with initial support from trained resource persons

These sessions are based on five issues those are as follow;

Five important Health issues for Health Promotion

1. Healthy Life Style and Stress and Strain free Environment
2. Drug Addiction,
3. Blood Donation Promotion,
4. Life skill Development and good eating habits.
5. Reproductive & Sexual Health including RTI/STI and HIV/ AIDS,

The sessions are participatory and seek to address the concerns of youths on growing up through role-play, brainstorming and discussion. They also address myths and misconceptions that young people have about health and reply to queries of youths by using the Question Box.

Role of Principals in Red Ribbon Club Programme

- Formation of Red Ribbon Club advisory committee in college.
- Selection of two lecturers (Preferably one male and another female) for Red Ribbon Club.

- Oversee and participate in the implementation of Red Ribbon Club Programme, including development of youth interactive programme, implementation, and evaluation of activities.
- Provide technical support to NGO and RRC in-charge/ Programme Officer to develop youth friendly and youth focusing IEC materials.
- Facilitate NGO representatives in implementing RRC programme effectively.
- Establishment linkages with other health services to increase assess of youths to them.
- Support in developing capacity of faculty to understand adolescents /youths' mental, reproductive and sexual health Problems and provide students enabling environment to cope with them.
- Motivate students to donate blood regularly.

Role of Programme Officers (Lecturers) in Red Ribbon Club Programme

Principal will identify two lecturers from every college for Red Ribbon Club Programme as Programme Officers/ Incharge RRC (preferably one male and one female). She / he is the teacher at the Institution designated as NSS Programme Coordinator, who should also be given their responsibility of the RRC in the capacity of Programme Officer. In the institutes where NSS is not available the head of such institution and advisory committee will be requested to designate one of the teachers as Programme Officer for RRC.

The Programme Office will work closely with the RRC/ NGO to reach out to RRC members and other youth in the institution through RRC volunteers.

Role of In-charge Red Ribbon Club

- Responsible for overall coordination, planning, implementation, supervision and management of RRCs in the college.
- Help creating a supportive and enabling environment in the institutions for formation of RRC

- Supporting and facilitating the formation of RRC in the college/educational institutions.
- Ensuring the Red Ribbon Clubs are established in the colleges under his/her jurisdictions in close coordination with NGO/RRC Coordinator.
- Support the RRC coordinators to identify and establishment of Red Ribbon Clubs in colleges.
- Organize and facilitate sensitization training for Peer leaders in close coordination with NGO/RRC Coordinator.
- Liasoning with the positive networks and other government/non-government organizations in the region for facilitating the activities of the RRC.
- Serving as resource person to impart technical knowledge on youth related issues to RRC members and peer educators by youth friendly methods.
- Facilitate to develop new IEC material (plays, songs, posters, slogans etc.)
- Assess the need of capacity building and conduct capacity building exercises accordingly on regular basis for Peer educators whenever needed.
- Facilitate the monthly meeting of Red Ribbon Club.
- Organize class room sessions on five issues. The student groups will be trained on issues relating to Life Skills, promotion of voluntary blood donation, Nutrition, mental health and Reproductive health which leads them to adopt healthy life styles and behavior change.
- Facilitate the activity like; Meetings, Debates, Competitions, Blood Donation Camps, etc. as per schedule.
- Build the capacity of Red Ribbon Club members and provide technical support. Provide necessary support to NGOs and Red Ribbon Club to organize their regular activities.

Role of Peer Leaders in Red Ribbon Club Programme

- Gain in-depth knowledge about Life Skills, promotion of voluntary blood donation, Nutrition, mental health and Reproductive health issues.

- Mobilizing resources for the Club's activities.
- Producing innovative BCC (Behavior Change Communication) materials - slogans, jingles, posters, logos, handbill messages, songs and plays, etc.
- Actively participating in competitions and community outreach programs inside and outside the campus.
- Orienting the new comers about the objectives and activities of the Club and contribute to the sustainability of the Club.
- With developed life skills and leadership qualities, performing the role of peer educators to heighten the Life Skills, promotion of voluntary blood donation, Nutrition, mental health and Reproductive health perception and instill negotiation skills among the youth
- Promoting VBD among the students and participate actively in blood donations.
- Sensitizing the youth regarding the rights of PLHWAs.
- Facilitate the monthly meeting of Red Ribbon Club on 1st Saturday of every month.
- Facilitate the activity like; Meetings, Debates, Competitions, Blood Donation Camps, etc. as per schedule.
- Increase the involvement of students in RRC.
- Popularize the RRC in college.
- Motivate the students to donate blood regularly.
- Establishing linkages of RRC with NGO.
- Disseminating information related to Life Skills, promotion of voluntary blood donation, Nutrition, mental health and Reproductive health among Peers
- Mobilize the RRC members and college student for meeting and other activities.

Operational Framework at Institutional Level

- At the organization level, organization organizes the advocacy and sensitization meeting of principals to aware the Principals/HODs about the vulnerability of youths towards Life Skills, promotion of voluntary blood donation, Nutrition, mental health and Reproductive health and need and concept of Red Ribbon Club (RRC) Programme. Apart from this organization will seek the permission for the formation of RRC in the institution. Once the head of the institution approves the RRC formation, permission to meet student leaders will be sought in order to explain the concept and importance of RRC.

- An orientation workshop at the university level is organized whereby two lecturers (Preferably one male and one female, those are associated with youths' different programmes and having interest to work with youths) from each college/ institution will be oriented on the RRC scheme. The date for the same can be decided in consultation with the head of the institutions, considering that it does not interfere with the educational schedule of the Institution. The workshop will conclude with the inauguration of RRC. The local VIPs may be invited and the inauguration will be presided over by the Head of the Institution.
- After imparting the training to lecturers a meeting is organized at every institution/college level. Whereby the RC along with Programme Officer of the institution (an NSS Officer) and student leaders will contact and mobilize as many students as possible from all departments (not only students enrolled with NSS but also from the entire strength).Volunteers may also be selected at this stage.
- Pamphlets, brochures and related IEC material will be distributed before and during inauguration of RRC. All IEC material will be supplied by GSACS in the State and Programme Officer will be responsible for its timely procurement.
- Screening of Life Skills, promotion of voluntary blood donation, Nutrition, mental health and Reproductive health related films etc. should be undertaken during the

orientation and inauguration on RRC. Such films could be procured from GSACS.

- When the youth participating in the programme appear to be absorbed and motivated distribute the membership forms for voluntary enrolment in RRC. The format for the same is provided in
- The signed forms should be collected and the names of the youth should be entered in the Membership Register. Red Ribbon Club Coordinator with support of Programme Officer will be responsible for regular updating of the Register/forms.
- The strength of the club can vary from 10 to 500 voluntary members.
- The activities of the RRC must be youth oriented, innovative and interactive that should generate active participation of youth and at the same time should provide them with healthy edutainment.
- Establishment of linkages with government Departments/ NGOs for increasing the access of youths to RTIs/STIs Treatment, Counseling and Testing Services, Condom and PLWHA care and support services.
- Organize Positive speaker bureau (PSB) in colleges to dispel myths and misconceptions and reduce discrimination against PLWHA.
- Class room sessions on five issues. The student groups will be trained on issues relating to Life Skills, promotion of voluntary blood donation, Nutrition, mental health and Reproductive health which leads them to adopt healthy life styles and behavior change.
- Two activities like seminar, competitions, rallies etc.
- Arrange information kiosk and other interactive activities in colleges.
- Voluntary blood donation camp will be organized.
- Establish/Enriching Information centers in the institutions.

- Visit to ICTC/ART Centers and other health related services.
- Best peer leader will be honored with an award each at college, university and state level.

Need of Red Ribon Club

Today there is an increasing need of creating Red Ribon Clubs because of many reasons. Youth is a back bone of the society who decides socio, economic, political and cultural health of the society. Thus Red Ribbon Clubs for imparting Non-formal education to Youths prepares solid grounds for its emergence.

How health issues of youth influence the overall development of an individual

- Result into lesser job opportunities
- Affect the economic status of the family while investment of health concerns Will have serious impact on the economy and development of nation as a whole
- increase substantially
- Affected the overall progress of the family-socially and economically

Reaching early to the youth will be more effective

- Health behaviour that will last long into adulthood can be strongly influenced
- Gender norms and roles, notions about responsible sexual behaviours and awareness of such issues can be shaped
- Positive life style can be encouraged
- Teaching does not have adverse impact, it always enriches human beings

Youth programme will make the difference

- To avoid harmful behaviour like drug use and irresponsible sexual practices
- Help adopt self-control as a best option to lead a healthy life

- Prevent early marriage and pregnancy
- Preserve resources invested on negative health outcomes

Youth and vulnerability

- They are different cognitively and emotionally
- They may lack the ability to use abstract thought to project their actions
- They have unclear understanding of consequences of their behavior
- Youth may not readily associated emotional issues with puberty and are often unable to express their feeling
- Mostly concerned about issues of puberty and body image and developing interest in relationship with opposite sex
- Some may be especially concerned with masturbation
- Myths regarding body growth and physiological change

CONCERNS AND ISSUES OF YOUTH

Psychological concern of youth

- As a part of growing up, adolescents redefine their relationship with parents, peers and members of the opposite sex. Adult have expectations from them and do not understand their feelings.
- Adult do not respect their right to choose with dignity and participate in decision making process.
- Adult need social skills for building positive and healthy relationship with others including peer of opposite sex. They need to understand the importance of mutual respect and socially defined boundaries of every relationship.
- Self-awareness helps youth to understand themselves and establish their personal identity. Lack of information and skill prevent them from effectively exploring their potential and establishing positive image.
- Adolescent girls are brought up with several stereotype gender roles. Boys build their 'egos' to assume masculine

roles. "suffering in silence" is seen as a virtue among woman and girls

- Adolescent find it difficult to resist peer pressure. Some of them may yield to there pressure and tale on to experimentation at greater risk.
- Aggrieve self conduct; unsafe sexual behavior and drug use involve greater risks with regarded to physical and mental health.
- The experiment with smoking and milder drugs often leads to switching over to hard drugs and addiction in later stage.
- The risk of contracting HIV and getting involved in anti-social Behavior are serious consequences of drug abuse

Health Concern of Youth

- Misconception about menstruation, masturbation and nocturnal emission cause stress.
- Social norms and inability to share their concern with other make it even more stressful.
- The widening gap in communication between adolescent and parents especially on reproductive and sexual health is matters a great concern.
- Services provided are judgmental and do not ensure confidentiality.
- Adolescents seeks information from their peer groups who are also ill informed and some fall prey to quakes.
- Fear and hesitation prevent them from seeking knowledge on preventive methods and medical help if suffering with RTIs and STIs.

Social Concern of Youth

Early marriage has far reaching consequences in terms of their development, fertility rate and reproductive health. Cultural norms may encourage early child bearing, posing risks to both infants and mother. If girls who are not fully developed become pregnant, they can experience damage to their reproductive tracts, delays or obstructed labor, ruptures in the birth canal and increased risks of maternal mortality

SVADES: An Experiment of Red Ribbon Club About SVADES

Svades (Society for Village Development in Petrochemical Area) is a collective endeavor that binds the industry and rural community together towards effective socio-economic development in the rural areas surrounding industry. It is indeed a unique example of unified action in the corporate sector to contribute to the progress of rural community, their development and social up-liftment. Svades is registered under the Societies Act, 1860, as a voluntary organization set up by the giant public and private sector industries in the Nandesari area of Vadodara Taluka, in the state of Gujarat, India. Participating industries are:

IPCL (Indian Petrochemical Corporation Limited)
IOCL (Gujarat Refinery)
GSFC (Gujarat State Fertilizer Company Limited)
GACL (Gujarat Alkalies and Chemicals Limited)
GIPCL (Gujarat Industries Power Company Limited)
SABIC
Deepak Nitrate Limited
Bayers ABS Limited
Ashok Organic Limited

SVADES works in 16 Panchayats comprising of 40 villages, which covers a total population of around 1,80,000. It is backed by the financial assistance of its member industries, community contribution, national and state level funding agencies, and also district, state and central governmental grants.

Approach

- Need based, practical and collaborative
- Involving the community at all stages of development, during the planning as well as execution, along with NGO's, government and participant industry conducting through village surveys

- Ascertaining and understanding the needs of the villagers through meeting and personal interactions
- Motivating the community to provide both monetary and human resource to execute the plans
- Active involvement of the community during the implementation stage, integrating the programs with the governmental initiatives.

Svades has been entrusted with the responsibility of forming Red Ribbon Clubs in the Vadodara City and near by villages of Vadodara Taluka District with an objective to bring awareness about the activities of Red Ribbon Club SVADES, believes that leaders can be made through the right training imparted to them. This is the basic feature of the Peer Leader Training Program of the RRC program of SVADES. They are also made aware of the responsibilities to carry out on their shoulders to train their peers about the awareness of HIV, AIDS and the other areas covered in the areas of health. Thus the role of the peer leaders in creating awareness about RRC in areas of health in general and HIV AIDS in particular is highlighted by SVADES :

SVADES provides awareness about how one can be infected by HIV and what are the preventives measures one can take to protect himself/ herself form the disease. Medical professionals are invited to give brief overview of the history of HIV and its current status in the country.

The other aspects covered by doctor are as follows:

- Evolution of HIV and its stages of treatment till now.
- Statistics of HIV infected people in India and on a global scenario.
- Revision in terms of awareness in the publics.
- Various age groups and sections of societies being affected.
- Chemical composition of the HIV virus and its peculiarities.
- Fluids of the body being contaminated by HIV.
- Fluids of the body not being contaminated by HIV.

- Pictorial representation of the ways in which the disease is contaminated.
- How HIV affects the immune system.
- Course of HIV infection.
- Symptoms of the disease.
- Diagnosis and counseling for the patient.
- STD scenario in India and in other countries.
- Factors responsible for STD.
- Groups vulnerable to STD.
- Preventive measures for STD.
- Impact of STD on females.
- AIDS prevention techniques.
- Facilities at hospitals.

As a part of RRC discussions on various types of leaderships like autocratic, democratic, charismatic and institutional are held. The significance of youth being selected as leaders is also given importance. Then there are discussions of essentialities to practicing leadership. The ones stated and explained were as under:

- Discipline in behavior
- Commitment towards ones work
- Curiosity to know more
- Cooperation to work with others
- Communication skills

The youth is imparted with the skills of how to go about doing things through planning, organizing, listening and implementing and evaluating the events and projects.

With the objective of helping the leaders to evaluate themselves, in relation to their external environment, workshops are held to impress upon the concept of self evaluations and self appraisal with reference to health issues.

Students are helped to evaluate themselves so that they come to know where they lack and can know what to learn. They are also trained on the themes namely awareness and Knowledge, Communication abilities and skills, Effective leadership, Sensitivity and empathy, Emotional maturity.

The youth are informed about the field of HIV and AIDS, sex and sexuality, STD/STI, drug and substance abuse, smoking drinking and its consequence, food and nutrition, stress management and leadership. The pragmatic approach is followed to impart nonformal educations by RRC by dividing groups into parts to perform a group task where they have to define what a leader is and what his special qualities are. Each group has a leader to represent the idea of the group. They are aided with charts and markers to put down their ideas to present it to the group. The emphasis is to remove the aspect of fear of speaking in public and also to improve the communication skills of the individuals.

Screening of movies Videos of experiences of PLWHA's and members of AP+ are also shown to the participants.

RRC covers talks about Smoking and its side effects and significant facts about smoking i.e. one cigarette reduces one's life by 11 minutes, every 6.5 seconds someone dies due to the ill-effects and illness caused by smoking. Smoking trends amongst women seem to be on a rise. A discussion is also held regarding ill-effects on pregnant women.

Further RRC also covers areas of alcoholism and blood donations for enhancing health awareness.

"WHAT WILL YOU DO NEXT?" is also the theme on which RRC offers non-formal education by incorporating management functions namely Planning, Organizing, Staffing, Directing, Coordination, Reporting, Budgeting.

Thus SVADES as a NGO with a vision ,mission and result orientation contributes a lot in providing nonformal education by establishing RRCs as a part of its initiative in collaborations with various faculties and colleges of universities, government youth programes namely National Service Scheme and schools with active support of governmental and corporate resources.

References

• SVADES brochure, Vadodara 2009.

- Gujarat State AIDS Control Society catalog, Ahmedabad.
- Population Reference Bureau.
- National AIDS Control Organization, Ministry of Health and Family Welfare, Govt. of India.
- Informal adult education -MALCOLM S. KNOWLES, Association press, New York.
- Fieldwork Experiences of MHRM Students.

12

Spirulina as a Nutritional Supplement for Adolescent Girls Health

Dr. Anjali Dewan

Malnutrition is a serious problem in India as millions of children die with it every year[1]. The Govt. of India has identified chronic protein energy malnutrition[2] in children as a major nutritional problem of public health importance and micronutrient deficiencies of iron, iodine and vitamin A[3]. The discovery of spirulina marked an important breakthrough in tackling the problem of malnutrition. It is a blue green micro algae, which is considered as food for the future because of its amazing ability to synthesize high quality concentrated food than any other algae[4]. Spirulna has a unique blend of nutrients that no single plant source can provide. It provides 65-70 percent proteins, 8-14 percent of carbohydrates, vitamins such as â-carotene, thiamine, riboflavin, niacin, vitamin B_6, folic acid, biotin, vitamin C, vitamin E, iron, calcium, phosphorus. The objective of the present study is to find out the impact of spirulina supplementation on dietary, clinical and morbidity status of adolescent girls.

Materials and Methods

Selection of Subjects

A sample of 200 adolescent girls of age between 13-15 years belonging to urban areas of Shimla were selected by random sampling technique and equally divided into two groups Experimental (E) and control group (C).

Dietary Survey

A complete record of the food intake of each subject was kept by 24 hour recall method for three consecutive days using both before and after the supplementation. Nutritive value of the diets was calculated with the help of the Nutritive value book. The Nutriguide software programme[5] was also consulted. The amount of nutrients supplied by Spirulina were added to the total nutrient intake of the subjects of Group E.

Clinical Examination

The respondents were clinically examined for the nutrient deficiency symptoms with the help of a doctor. Nutrient deficiency symptoms of the respondents were assessed as per the method described by Jelliffe[6] both at T_1 and T_2.

Morbidity Status

Morbidity status was assessed through medical history and clinical examination. The respondents were asked if they were suffering from common illnesses like viral fever, malaria, diarrhea, common cold and cough etc. during past six months both at T_1 and T_2.

Supplementation

Spirulina powder in the form of 'Dabur Sunova' capsules were bought from the market for supplementation. Two capsules (1gm.) were opened and thoroughly mixed with 35 gm. of wheat besan ladoo and supplied daily to the subjects if Group E for six days a week for a period of two months.

Statistical Analysis

The results obtained were statistically analyzed using student t-test, coefficient of correlation and chi-square (÷²) test to see the effect of spirulina supplementation on dietary and health status of the adolescent girls.

Results and Discussion

The demographic information of the adolescent girls in the present study revealed that the majority of the subjects (78.5%) in both the groups belonged to nuclear families and had 3-5 family members. It was observed that more than half the subjects in both the groups had both parents educated. 68% of the subjects were vegetarian in both the groups.

Table 1 Type of family of the Adolescent girls

Group	*Nuclear family*	*Joint family*
Experimental	86	14
Control	71	29
Total	157	43

Type of family of the Adolescent girls

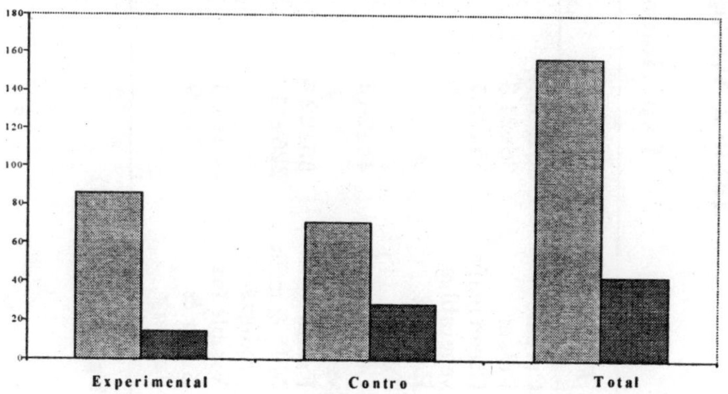

Fig. 1

Table 2 Average daily food intake of the Adolescent girls

	Experimental group		Control group			
Foods (gm.)	T_1	T_2	T_1	T_2	*RDA*	*t-value*
Cereals	301±30.4	310±21.3	314±29.6	323±16.8	430	1.71
Pulses	36±21.3	41±18.7	40±26.4	39±23.2	70	1.12
Green leafy vegetables	35±28.1	48±13.8	38±19.2	39±20.1	75	2.97*
Roots & Tubers	50±15.2	75±21.2	67±23.4	69±27.4	75	0.21
Other vegetables	44±26.4	53±19.2	46±22.5	49±24.9	75	1.28
Fruits	55±22.6	71±21.6	67±21.9	68±26.5	30	1.31
Milk & milk products	225±41.1	245±39.2	212±42.8	216±32.6	250	0.03
Visible fat	42±4.6	46.8±3.5	42±7.5	43±7.3	25	2.76**
Sugar & Jaggery	25±7.9	36±6.2	29±8.2	33±6.4	30	4.32**

**- significant (pd"0.01)

Fig. 2 Average daily intake of foods of Adolescent girls

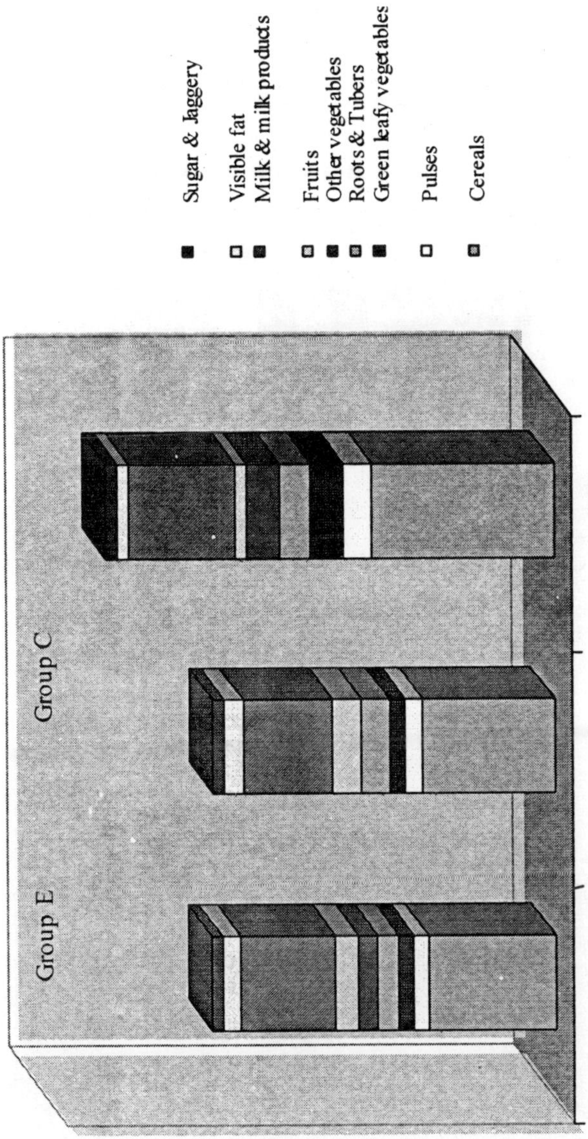

Intake of various food groups in Group E and Group C before supplementation with Spirulina

Fig. 3 Average daily intake of foods of Adolescent girls

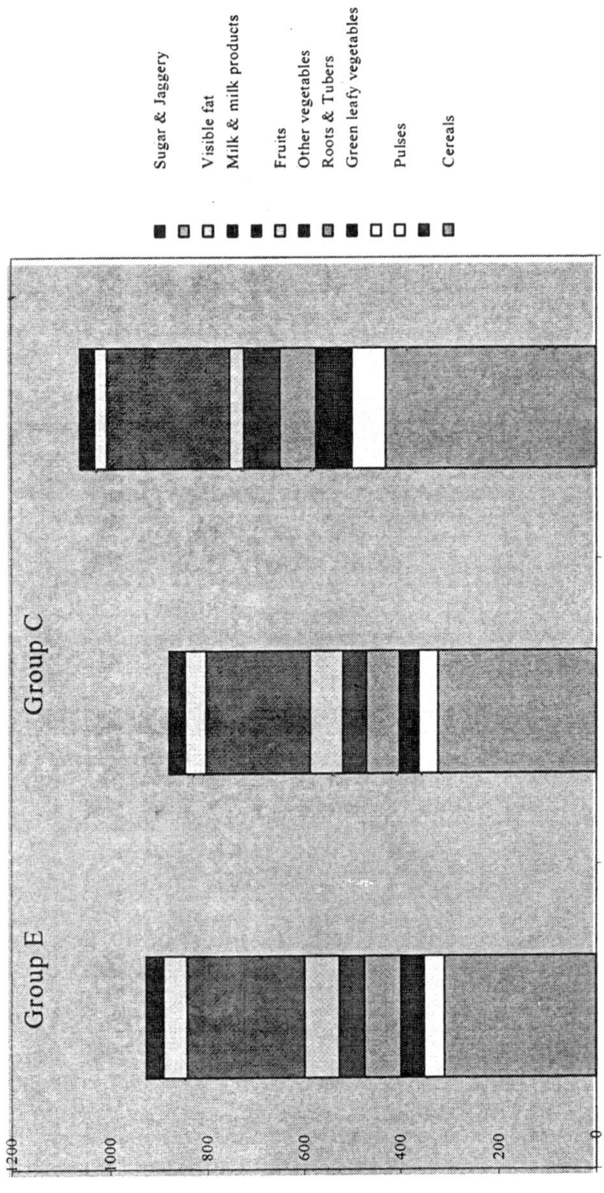

Intake of various food groups in Group E and Group C after supplementation with Spirulina

Dietary intake by the Adolescent girls

The data in Table 2 showed that mean intake of cereals by the respondents of E and C group before supplementation (T_1) was 301±30.4 and 314±29.6 gm. and after supplementation (T_2) was 310±21.3 and 323±16.8 gm. respectively. There was an increase in cereal consumption due to supplementation because of increased intake of wheat in the form of ladoo, used for supplementing spirulina. The average daily intake of pulses by respondents of E and C group at T_1 was 36±21.3 and 40±26.4 gm. and T_2 was 41±18.7 and 39±23.2 gm. respectively. The average intake of pulses increased due to the presence of gram flour in the ladoo. The intake of pulses was much below the RDA[7]. The diet was deficient in the intake of green leafy vegetables in both the groups. The consumption of T_1 being 35±28.1 and 38±19.2 in group E and C respectively. A significant (pd"0.01) increase in the consumption of green leafy vegetables was found in both the groups as they were easily available at low price during the months of March-April. The subjects did not meet the suggested intake of 100 gm. as per ICMR recommendations as most adolescent girls disliked green vegetables. A higher intake of roots and tubers, other vegetables, fruits and visible fat was observed in both the groups. The consumption of milk and milk products was marginally adequate in both the groups at $T_{1,}$ the values being 225±41.1 and 212±42.8 gm. in group E and C respectively. The average intake of sugar and jaggery among respondents of E and C group at T_1 was 25±7.9 and 29±8.2 gm. and at T_2 was 36±6.2 and 33±6.4 gm. respectively.

Clinical Signs of Nutrient Deficiencies

The adolescent girls were observed for various clinical symptoms of diseases due to nutritional deficiencies as shown in Table 3 and Figure 4 and 5. Paleness of skin was more pronounced in most of the respondents in both the groups. Pale conjunctiva was also observed in 46 percent of the subjects in

Table 3 Clinical symptoms of nutritional deficiencies in Adolescent girls

	Experimental group				Control group			
Clinical signs	*Number of subjects*	*%*	*Number of subjects*	*%*	*Number of subjects*	*%*	*Number of subjects*	*%*
Eyes: Pale conjunctiva	46	46	21	21	30	30	28	28
Skin: Pale	15	15	6	6	18	18	16	16
Lips: Angular stomatitis	10	10	-	-	6	6	6	6
Gums: bleeding	5	5	-	-	3	3	3	3
Teeth: Mottled Enamel	28	28	7	7	12	12	12	12
:Dental caries	58	58	10	10	45	45	43	43
Fatigue	40	40	3	3	15	15	15	15
Anorexia	17	17	4	4	8	8	8	8

Fig. 4 Clinical Symptoms of nutritional deficiency diseases in Adolescent girls before supplementation with Spirulina (T_1)

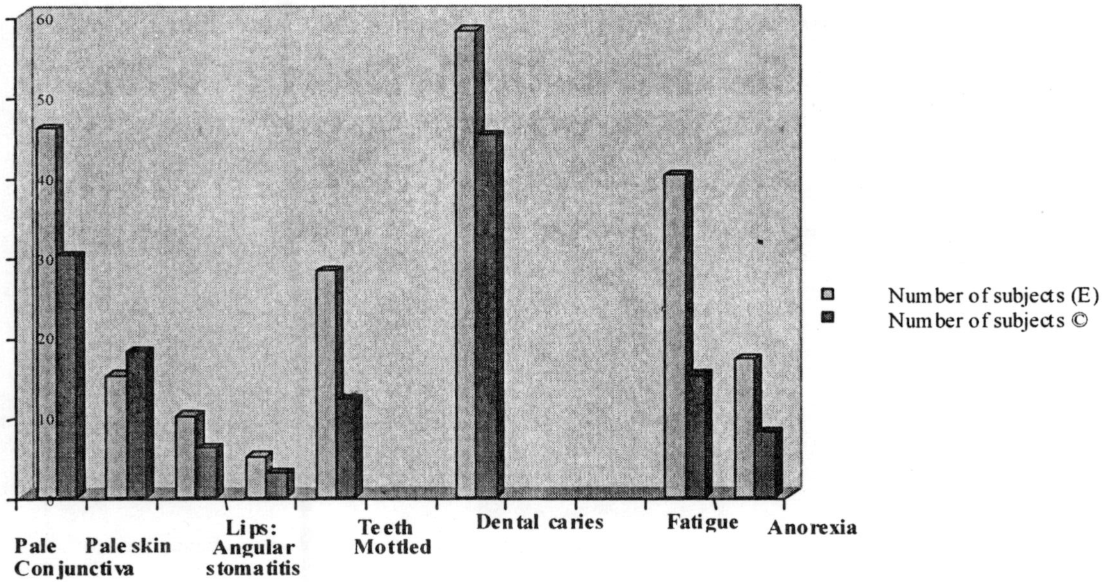

Symptoms of various nutritional deficiency diseases

Clinical Symptoms of Nutritional Deficiency in Adolescent Girls after Supplementation with Spirulina (T_2)

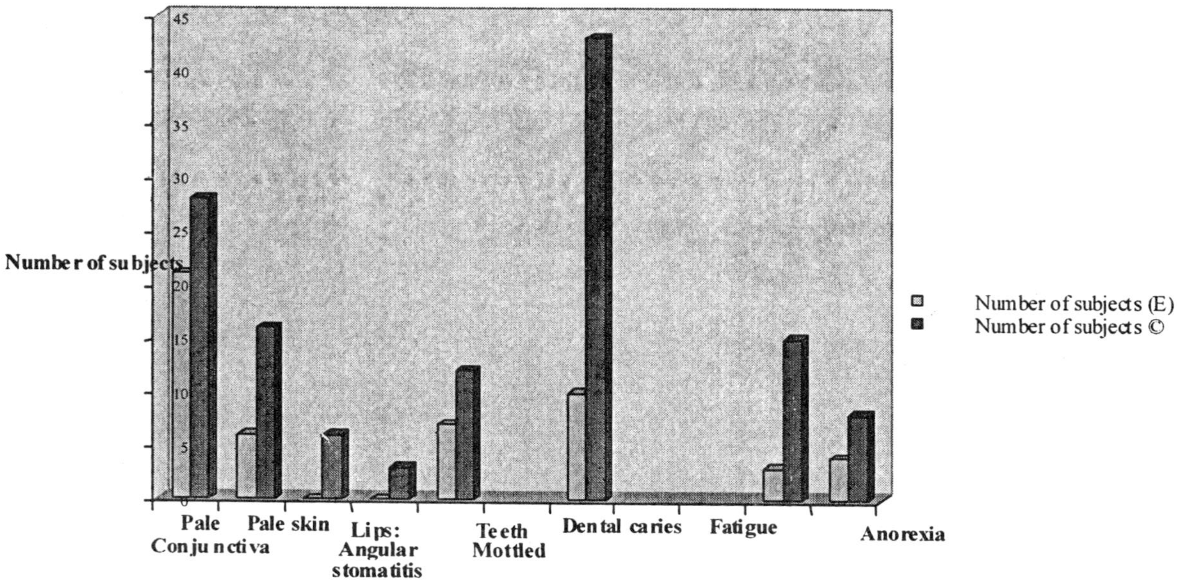

Symptoms of various nutritional deficiency diseases

group E at T_1 which decreased to 21 percent at T_2. Angular stomatitis, which is a sign of B-complex deficiency, was observed in only 10 percent and 6 percent respondents in E and C groups respectively. The condition remained the same for group C during the entire study period but none of the respondents in group E showed these signs at T_2. Dental caries were observed in 58 and 45 percent of subjects in E and C groups respectively. Irregular brushing of teeth, poor oral hygiene and excessive eating of sweets were the possible reasons for high incidence of dental caries in both E and C groups. But the carious lesions decreased to 10 percent in group E at T_2 though the rate of formation of caries remained the same in the case of group C at T_2. The data collected showed that the clinical signs of nutritional deficiency diseases were more marked in group C as compared to Group E at T_2 showing positive and supplementing effect of spirulina. It has also been reported by Sheshadri and Jayam[8] that as a result of supplementing the diet with 1 gm./day of spirulina of preschool children, there was a decrease in the B-complex deficiency symptoms.

Morbidity Status of the Respondents

Morbidity status of respondents is presented in Table 4 and Figures 6 and 7. Measles had the maximum prevalence among subjects belonging to group E while Viral fever had highest prevalence in group C at T_1. Common cold was observed in 31% and 15% in subjects belonging to group E and group C respectively. Diarrhoea was found in 19% and 28% in subjects belonging to group E and C respectively. Typhoid was also present in a number of respondents. Prevalence of common diseases like common cold and cough, diarrhoea, measles, chicken pox, typhoid showed a marked decrease in respondents of group e at T_2 which was due to spirulina supplementation as it is a good source of phycocyanine which enhances body's immunity to fight against diseases. According to Venkataraman[9], spirulina consumption results in improvement of general health and protection against common ailments.

Table 4 Morbidity status of the Adolescent girls before and after supplementation with Spirulina

	Experimental group				Control group			
	T_1		T_2		T_1		T_2	
Diseases	*Number of subjects*	*%*	*Number of subjects*	*%*	*Number of subjects*	*%*	*Number of subjects*	*%*
Viral fever	20	20	19	19	31	31	30	30
Malaria	26	26	25	25	16	16	15	15
Diarrhoea	19	19	9	9	28	28	27	27
Common cold and cough	31	31	11	11	15	15	15	15
Measles	42	42	8	8	13	13	12	12
Chicken Pox	11	11	1	1	9	9	9	9
Typhoid	15	15	2	2	10	10	9	9

Fig.6 Morbidity status of the respondents before supplementation with Spirulina

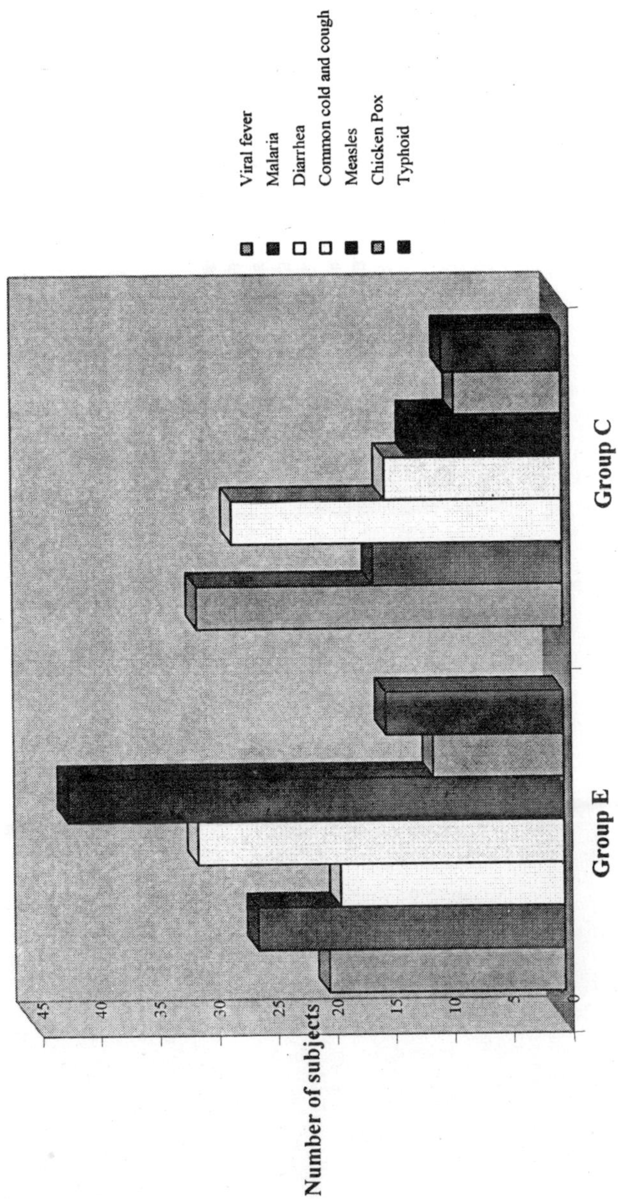

Various non nutritional diseases

Fig. 7 Morbidity of respondents after supplementation with Spirulina

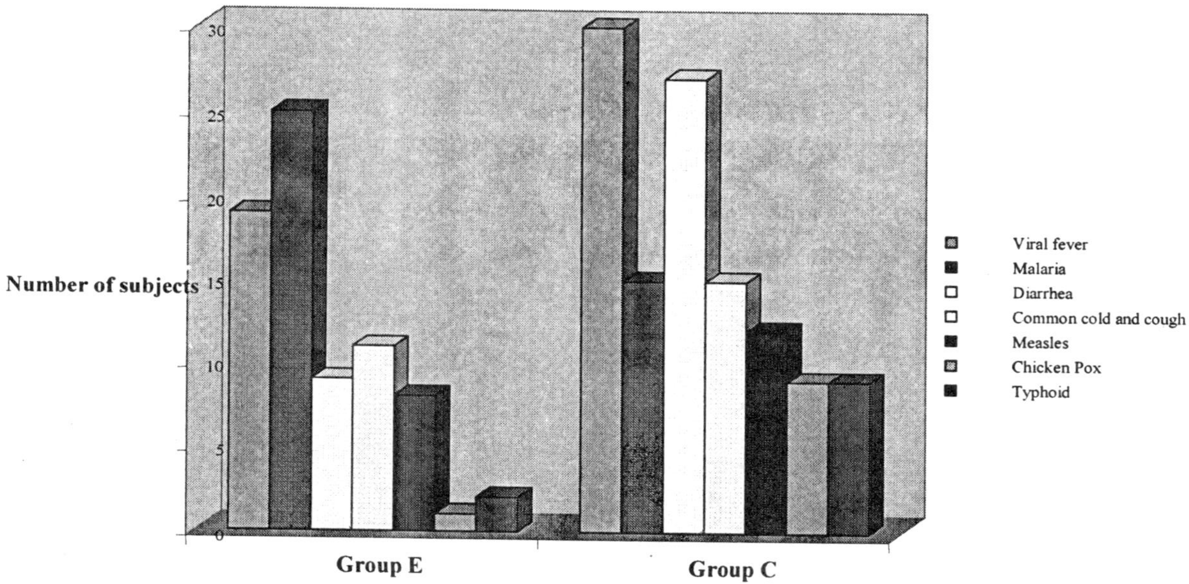

Various non nutritional diseases

Conclusion

The result obtained from this study showed that the diets consumed by the subjects in both the experimental and control groups were deficient in cereals, pulses, green leafy vegetables but was high in fats and sugar and jaggery as compared to ICMR recommendations. The adolescent girls were not eating properly and there was also skipping of meals. An improvement in the health and nutritional status of the subjects in group E as compared to group C at the end of the study clearly shows the beneficial effect of including spirulina supplementation. Spirulina is a good source of â-carotene, vitamin E and pigments like phycocyanine, other carotenoids which enhance the immunity of the body against diseases. Hence, Spirulina can be taken as a health food safely for supplementing the diet of adolescent girls. It is important that together with supplementation with spirulina, nutrition education should be imparted to the mothers as well as the adolescent girls to emphasize on the consumption of cheap, nutritious foods like sprouted and fermented foods in their daily diet.

References

- **Gopalan, C., Sastri, B. V. and Balasubramanian, S.** (ed.) (2004) Indian Council of Medical Research. *Nutritive Value of Indian Foods,* National Institute of Nutrition, ICMR, Hyderabad.
- **Jeliffe, D.B.** (1966). *The Assessments of Nutritional Status of the Community*. World Health Organization, Geneva.
- **Muratee, S.** (1993) Spirulina-The Wonder Algae: Mohan, Ram, M (ed.). Nutrition, A Quarterly Publication of National Institute of Nutrition, Hyderabad.
- **National Nutrition Policy** (2005) Govt. of India, Dept. of Women & Child Development, Ministry of Human Resource Development, New Delhi.
- **Sheshadri, C.V. and Jayam** (1993). Large scale nutrition supplementation with spirulina algae, MCRC, Chennai,

Monograph series on engineering of photosynthetic systems, Vol. 36.

- **Song, W.O., Mann, S.K., Sehgal, S., Devi, P.R., Gudam, S. and Deokorale, M** (1992). *Nutriguide: Asian Indian Foods,* Nutritional Analysis Computer Programme, Michigan State University, U.S.A.
- **The Ninth Five Year Plan,** (1999) Govt. of India, Financial Express
- **Venkataraman, L.V.** (1993). Spirulina: Global reach of Health care product, Elvess Biotech Consultancy Pvt.

Yojana,(1999) Yojana Bhavan, Sansad Marg, New Delhi, Vol.5: 43.

13

Gender Mainstreaming and Empowerment of Women

Dr. Shobha Rani

Women's rights and issues have always been a subject of serious concern of academicians, intelligentsia and policy makers. From pastoral society to contemporary information and global society, the role of women has changed drastically. The process of industrialization, modernization and globalization has shown deep impact on the roles and responsibilities of women. It has been widened and attained new definition and perspective where women also share the financial responsibilities along with their traditional role of housewives in both cities and villages.

The last decades have witnessed some basic changes in the status and role of women in our society. There has been shift in policy approaches from the concept of 'Welfare' in the seventies to 'development' in the eighties and to 'empowerment' in the nineties. This process has been further accelerated with some sections of women becoming increasingly self-conscious of their discrimination in several areas of family and public life but, despite all their progress, practically all women across the board are still subjected to exploitation, atrocities and violence.

This affects the women who work as agricultural labour and also those cosmopolitan women who inhabit our cities.

The Constitution of India aims at securing justice-social, economic and political, equality of status and of opportunity to assume the dignity of the individual and unity and integrity of the Nation. Specific provisions to achieve these objectives have been made in part III and part IV of the Constitution.

The Constitution has taken due care of the interest of women and has laid emphasis on equality of men and women. Economic interest of the women have been secured both in provisions relating to Fundamental Rights and Directive Principles.

Article 14 guarantees equality before law and equal protection of the laws to all persons including women. Article 15 prohibits any discrimination against women in any field of life. Rather, it desires and protects special provisions for women. It implies that special provisions for their benefit may be made by the state and these will not be treated as discrimination against men Article 16 guarantees equality of opportunity for all citizens in matters relating to employment or appointment to any office under the state. It specifically prohibits discrimination on the basis of sex.

In part IV of Directive Principles of the State Policy also provide for the protection of economic interest of women in the country. Article 39 provides for securing of adequate means of livelihood to men and women equally, equal pay for equal work for both men and women.

Article 39 A requires that the state shall secure that the operation of legal system promotes Justice, on the basis of equal opportunity and shall provide free legal aid to ensure that opportunities for securing justice are not denied to any citizen by reason of economic or other disabilities. Article 41 provides for right to work and public assistance. Article 42 requires securing of just and human condition of work and maternity relief living wages and conditions of work to ensure decent standard of life are desired by article 43.

Besides, these Fundamental Rights and Directive Principles another important Constitutional provision which requires specific attention in Article 51 A (e) which lays down a Fundamental Duty of every citizen. It requires the renouncing of practices derogatory to the dignity of women.

Women and the Five Year Plans

Women's development began mainly as welfare oriented programmes in the First Five year plan (1951-56). The Central Social Welfare Board (CSWB) set up in 1953, undertook a number of welfare measures through the voluntary sectors.

The second Five Year Plan (1956-61) organized women into Mahila Mandals to act as focal points at the grass root levels for development of women.

The third, fourth and other interim plan (1961-74) accorded high priority to education of women and introduced measures to improve maternal and child health services, including supplementary feeding for children and nursing mothers etc.

In the Fifth plan (1974-78), there was a shift in the approach for women's development from welfare to 'development' to cope up with several problems of the family and the role of women. The new approach aimed at integration of welfare with development services.

The Sixth Five Years Plan (1980-85) was a landmark in the history of women's development as it received recognition as one of the developmental sectors and was included in the Sixth Plan Document as a separate chapter for the first time in the history of development planning. It adopted a multi-disciplinary approach with a three pronged thrust an health, education and employment.

In the Seventh Plan (1985-90), the developmental programmes for women continued with the major objectives of raising their economic and social status and to bring them into the mainstream of national development. A significant step in this direction was to identify/promote the beneficiary-oriented programmes for women in different developmental sectors which extend direct benefits to women.

The Eighth Five Year Plan (1992-97), which was launched in 1992, promised to ensure that the benefits of development from different sectors do not bypass women. Therefore, the flow of benefits to women in the three core sectors of education, health and employment would be monitored with a greater vigil. Women must be enabled to function as equal partners and participants in the developmental process. This approach to the Eighth Plan marked a shift from 'development' to 'empowerment' of women. In order to meet both the increasing and challenging needs of women and children, there had been a progressive increase in the Plan outlays over the period of last four developmental decades. The outlay of Rs. 4 crores in the First Plan (1951-56) had gone upto Rs. 2000 crores in the Eighth Five Year Plan (1992-97).

'Empowerment of women' as agents of socio-economic change and development became one of the nine specific objectives of the Ninth Plan (1997-2002). The Plan envisaged primarily to ensure that benefits flow to women from all the general development sectors and emphasized on (1) reservation of not less than 1/3rd seats for women in the parliament and State Legislative Assemblies; (2) convergence of existing services, resources, infrastructure and manpower in women specific and women-related sectors; (3) adoption of special strategy of women Component Plan (WCP) to ensure that not less than 30% of funds/benefits flow to women from other development sectors; (4) organizing women Self Help Groups as a major process of empowering women; (5) high priority to reproductive child health care; (6) universalizing on-going supplementary feeding programme; (7) ensuring easy and equal access to education for women and girls; (8) elimination of gender bias in all educational programmes: (9) free education for girls up to college level including professional courses: (10) promoting skill development amongst women in modern upcoming trades etc. Some special initiatives taken during Ninth Plan included launching of an externally aided scheme of Swashakti (1998) for socio-economic empowerment of women through self reliant self help groups, instituting Street Shakti Puraskars (1999), setting up of a Task Force under the Chairpersonship of Deputy Chairman, Planning Commission to review existing women-specific and women-related legislations (2000), adoption of National Policy for Empowerment of Women (2001), celebration of the year 2001 as Women's Empowerment Year, recasting of Indira Mahila Yojana as Swayamsidha (2001), launching of Swadhar (2001) to extend rehabilitation services for women in difficult circumstances etc.

'Empowerment of Women' as Agents of Social Change and Development was continued in the Tenth Plan. Towards this a Sector- specific 3-Fold Strategy was adopted based on the National Policy for Empowerment of Women (2001).

The National Policy on Women 2001, which informed the 10th five-year plan, articulated a series of goals towards women's empowerment. The objectives of this Policy include (1) Creating an environment through positive economic and social policies for development of women to enable them to realilze their full potential (2) The de-jure and de-facto enjoyment of all human rights and fundamental freedom by women on equal basis with men in all spheres - political, economic, social, cultural and civil (3) Equal access to participation and decision making of women in social, political and economic life of the nation (4) Equal access to women to health care, quality education at all levels, career and vocational guidance, employment, equal remuneration, occupational health and safety, social security and public office etc. (5) Strengthening legal systems aimed at elimination of all forms of discrimination against women (6) Changing societal attitudes and community practices by active participation and involvement of both men and women. (7) Mainstreaming a gender perspective in the development process. (8) Elimination of discrimination and all forms of violence against women and the girl child; and (9) Building and strengthening partnerships with civil society, particularly women's organizations.

In the context of the preparations of the 11th Five Year Plan (2007-2012), the Planning Commission constituted a Steering Committee on the 'Empowerment of Women and Development of Children' under the Chairmanship of Dr. Syeda Hameed, Member, Planning Commission with the following Terms of Reference.

The female population of the country rose marginally from 48.1 per cent of the total population in 1991 to 48.3 percent of the total population in 2001. In absolute numbers, this implies an increase by 89.4 million from 407.1 million in 1991 to 496 million in 2001. the growth rate of female population for the 1991-2001 decade was 23.08, slightly higher than the male. Population decennial growth rate of 22.26. The expectancy of life at birth has been rising steadily for women and is higher than the male life expectancy. However, demographic imbalances between men and women continue to exist, even worsen, in certain regions.

The 11th plan approach to gender equity has Five key elements:-

1. The recognition that women are not a homogenous category for planned intervention. Official directives must be issued to WCD programmes as well as women-related programmes in other Ministries to reach women across multiple axis of deprivation (gender, class, caste, community, marital status, geographic location etc.), to monitor implementation and collect disaggregated data along these multiple axis. The double deprivation of particular categories of women (SC,ST women, Muslim women, single women/widows, and women in conflict zones like the north-east and J&K), in addition to being

addressed through general programme interventions, have to also be addressed through a range of special, targeted and/or pilot interventions.

2. The recognition that only inclusive development of all categories of women can ensure holistic national development toward the millennium development goals.
3. The recognition that both inter-sectoral convergence as well as targeted, exclusive women-focused planning (through the Ministry of WCD) are necessary to achieve inclusive development towards the social, economic and political empowerment of women.
4. The recognition that for interventions in favour of women to have a sustained, long term, incremental impact beyond individual five year plan periods, they have to be four-pronged- (i) to provide women with basic entitlements such as food security, health and education, (ii) to address the reality of globalization and its impact on women by prioritizing economic empowerment and mainstreaming women in new and emerging areas of the economy (iii) ensure an environment free from all forms of violence against women-physical, economic, social, psychological, and (iv) ensure the participation and adequate representation of women at the highest policy levels, particularly in Parliament and Assemblies.
5. The recognition that permanent institutional mechanisms, such as a Women's Knowledge Commission or alternatively a permanent (Inter-Ministerial) Standing Committee on Gender, with 50% participation of civil society gender experts, must be put in place to include women's participation, experiences, capacities and knowledge into the process of development planning, formulation and administration across all sectors. There must be mandatory representation of qualified women in all Planing Commission Steering Committees.

The following five-fold strategy will be followed by 11th plan:

1. Economic empowerment, with special focus on women in agriculture and on the effects of globalization;
2. Social empowerment and engendering social change;
3. Political Empowerment – to facilitate entry and effective functioning of women in Parliament, PRIs and in premier government services;
4. Strengthening mechanism for effective implementation of women related legislations;
5. Creating institutional mechanisms for gender mainstreaming and strengthening delivery mechanisms for effective implementation of women-related programmes.

It is clear, that since independence a lot of developmental planning and action were undertaken but none of these policies have been the ultimate solution to the problems that beset women's lives.

The mere provision of constitutional and legal rights does not ensure that women will get equal opportunities. For instance, the question of reservation for women in parliament has become a bone of contention between men and women. Instead of feeling honoured to offer women seats in parliament, men feel threatened by them. They feel that their territories are being encroached upon.

There is no denying the fact that due to governmental policies and affirmative actions, there has been positive impact on the socio-economic status of women as well as the girl child. Significant strides have been made in increasing life expectancy and decreasing infant and maternal mortality rate. Enrolment rate of girls in primary schools and total female work participation have also gone up over a period of time. But, still the situation is alarming and a lot needs to be done to improve the status of the girl child and the Indian women.

INDICATORS OF GENDER DEVELOPMENT

- Gender Development Index (GDI) value (2007)- 0.594
- GDI value as a percent of HDI value (2007) - 97.1

	Years	*Female*	*Male*
Life expectancy at birth	2007	64.9	62.0
Adult literacy rate (% aged 15 & above)	2007	54.5	76.9
Combined gross enrolment ratio (%)	2007	57.4	64.3

INDICATORS OF GENDER EMPOWERMENT

- Seats in parliament (% held by women), (2008)-09
- Earned income, ratio of female to male, (2007)-0.32
- Women in ministerial positions (% of position), (2008) -10
- Administrators and managers (% women), (1997)-2.3
- Professional and technical workers (% Women), (1997)-20.5

Half of the total population in India is Women. Majority of Women live in rural areas and belong to small, marginal or landless families. Researches have shown that there is significant contribution of women in the field of agriculture and in terms of working hours duration women are contributing comparatively more than men. The participation of women in agriculture is 78 percent as against 63 percent participation of men. Out of the total women workers in India (About 9 crore) 25 Percent women are farmers, about 32 percent are farm labourers and 2.0 percent are engaged in animal husbandry, fisheries and forestry. Thus, about 50 percent women workers are classified as farm labourers and about 70 percent agricultural work are being done by women only. Rest are engaged in other industries such as household industries, Trade and tourism, Transport and communication, Manufacturing and Mining etc.

Moreover, several farm activities traditionally carried out by men are also being undertaken by women as men are pulled away into higher paying employment. Thus rural India is witnessing a process i.e. 'feminization of agriculture' due to the migration of men from rural areas to town in search of paid employment. Rural women are much more over-burdened than men owing to their multiple-occupations. Researches on women in agriculture have revealed that on an average women work for 15-16 hours a day.

The enormous amount of recent literature, conferences and workshops on gender issues in development clearly indicates that the distinction between the roles of women and men is critical to agricultural production. Rural women in particular are responsible for half of the world's food production and produce between 60 and 80 percent of the food in most developing countries. Women sow, weed, apply fertilizer and pesticides, harvest and thresh the crops. In the livestock sector, women feed and milk animals, while raising poultry and small animals such as sheep, goat, etc. Also, once the harvest is in, rural women provide most of the labour for post-harvest activities, taking responsibility for storage, handling processing and marketing. Yet, despite their contribution to global food security, women farmers are frequently underestimated and overlooked in development strategies.

According to one of the ILO report, "women are 50 % of word population, do 2/3rd of world's work hours, receive one-tenth of women's income and own less than 1% of world's property". Therefore, there is a lot to be done for the women's equity and justice so that their dominant role in the economic development is not underestimated.

Yet it is precisely livelihood in agriculture that has tended to become more volatile and insecure in recent years and women cultivators have therefore been negatively affected. The income they earn is not commensurate with the task they perform. The government's policies for alleviating poverty have failed to produce any desirable results, as women do not receive appropriate wages for their labour. There is also significant amount of unpaid or non-marketed labor within the household. The increase in gender disparity in wages in the urban areas is also quite marked as it results from the employment of women in different and lower paying activities. They are exploited at various levels. They should be provided with proper wages and work at par with men so that their status can be elevated in society.

Rural women confront lack of access to land, credit, training, extension and marketing facilities. For social and economic reason, women's constraints are even more pronounced. Consequently, the development of technologies specifically tailored to women-specific occupation and the involvement of women in technology development and transfer have received inadequate attention.

It is common practice to direct extension and training services primarily towards men. A recent FAO survey showed that female farmers receive only 5 percent of all extension services worldwide and that only 15 percent of the world's extension agents are women. Since women often lack access to land, or to other collateral with which to obtain credit, extension services, unintentionally, bypass women.

In the Panchayati Raj system, however, women have been given representation as a sign of political empowerment. However, their power is restricted, as it is the men who wield all the authority. Their decisions are often over-ruled by the government machinery. All this shows that the process of gender equality and women's empowerment still has a long way to go and may even have become more difficult in the recent years.

Gender discrimination, rooted in law and custom, is pervasive and impedes socio-economic development. It is gender that differentiates the roles, responsibilities, resources, constraints and opportunities of women and men for which precise gender information is the need of the day. The division of labour between genders still remains poorly understood. Therefore, there is a lot to be done for the women's equity and justice so that their dominant role in the economic development is not underestimated.

Gender mainstreaming is "the process of assessing the implications for women and men of any planned action, including legislation, policies or programmes, in all areas and at all levels. It is a strategy for making women's as well as men's concerns and experiences an integral dimension of the design, implementation, monitoring and evaluation of policies and programmes in all political, economic and societal spheres so that women and men benefit equally and inequality is not perpetuated. The ultimate goal is to achieve gender equality". Gender Mainstreaming is a process rather than a goal. Efforts to integrate gender into existing institutions of the mainstream have little value for their own sake. We mainstream gender concerns to achieve gender equality and improve the relevance of development agendas. Such an approach shows that the costs of women's marginalization and gender inequalities are born by all.

Gender analysis is recognized worldwide as an important aspect in the design, implementation and evaluation of development projects. It is the most critical step towards gender-responsive planning and programming. It involves the collection and analysis of sex- disaggregated information. It examines the differences, commonalties and interactions between women and men. It also examines women's and men's specific activities, conditions, needs, access to and control over resources, and access to development benefits and decision-making.

The methodology of gender analysis encompasses the following core issues:-

- **Women's and men's role** Who does what, with what resources? Paying particular attention to variation within sub-groups of women and men eg. Elderly women, adolescent girls, men from urban areas etc.
- **Factors that shape gender roles and the gender division of work** Depending on the circumstances,

traditions and institutions that shape gender roles represent constraints and/or opportunities for women and men and are critical to designing culturally appropriate programmes and projects.

- **Access to and control over resources and opportunities, and their systems of distribution** Understanding the mechanisms and rules by which the resources and benefits are distributed is important to assess the situation and determine the cost effective entry point for action.
- **Access to and participation in decision making processes** How are decisions taken concerning women's and men's lives and those of their families?
- **Men's and Women's practical and strategic needs and interests** Given their respective roles, who needs what for what purpose?

Gender Budgeting is a dissection of the Government budget to establish its gender- differential impacts and to translate gender commitments into budgetary commitments. It looks at the budget from a gender perspective to assess how it address the needs of women in the areas like health, education, employment, etc. Gender Responsive Budgeting initiatives provide a way of assessing the impact of Government revenue and expenditure on women. Thus they can contribute to achieving the objectives of gender equality, human development and economic efficiency. It is necessary to recognize that women are equal players in the economy whether they participate directly as workers or indirectly as members of the core economy. To that extent, every policy of the Government fiscal, monetary or trade, has a direct impact on the well being of women. Thus, it is not adequate to analyze in detail, allocation of resources for a few sectors of the economy which are traditionally considered as women related. The analysis has to cover every rupee of public expenditure. It has to cover the way schemes are conceptualized and how women friendly they are in implementation and targeting of beneficiaries. When gender equality considerations are incorporated into policy making, the concerns and needs of both women and men become integral part of the design, implementation, monitoring and evaluation of policies and programmes in all sections of society.

Strategic Framework of Gender Budgeting Activities

The Ministry of women and child Development has drawn up a Broad Framework of Activities or action areas for gender mainstreaming, as written below:

- Quantification of allocation of resources for women in the Union, States and Local Administration budgets and expenditure thereof.
- Gender Audit of policies of the Government – monetary, fiscal, trade etc. at the Centre and State levels.
- Impact assessment of various schemes in the Union and State budgets.
- Institutionalizing the generation and collection of gender dis-aggregated data of cost of delivery of services.
- Consultations and Capacity building.
- Review of decision making processes to establish gender equity in participation.

Strategies for Mainstreaming Gender

- A comprehensive support system has to be evolved with a view to enabling women to perform their duties and responsibilities. Such a system may be in the form of awareness generation and training, necessary for decision-making at different levels. In other words, the effective management and development of women's abilities, interests, skills and other potentials are of paramount importance for mobilization and development of human resources.
- Steps should be taken to make women aware of financial and technical assistance available to them under government and non-government schemes.

- Education for rural women should give importance to income earning, activities. The process of "learning by doing and earning" would certainly empower rural women.
- The emergence of self-help groups is a welcome development. The groups would provide a permanent forum for articulating their needs and contributing their perspectives to development.
- Women-oriented projects need to be given priority even under limited budget to help develop rural women. Enterprises which are familiar to rural women should be encouraged. Importance should be given to locally available raw materials and training needs.

Male workers can be trained to work more closely with women in settings that are culturally acceptable, such as women groups.

- Innovative credit programmes using non-traditional forms of collateral and local institutions (women groups) can ensure that women are able to obtain access to credit.
- Identifying the right training and extension needs of women is one of the most important step in initiating any development programme using participatory approach.
- Giving women farmers more access to meetings, trainings, exposure visits and demonstrations, organizing training programmes based on the needs of the women.
- Technologies to reduce energy and time spent, particularly the household and farm production activities. Extending the technological innovations such as weeders, paddy threshers, winnowers, sprayers, harvesting tools, parboiling units, maize shellers, dal making machines etc will reduce the burden of women.
- Increasing the biomass production to meet fuel needs, plantation of fast growing fodder in common lands and developing mechanism for sharing the fodder helps women in saving lot of time and devote this time for income generating activities.

- Where severe fragmentation exists, collective farming should be encouraged by women.
- Active women can be selected, trained and they should be provided with inputs and credit to practice the improved technology. Their fields/units can be used as demonstration plots for training other women.
- Appointing female supervisors and Subject Matter Specialists and recruiting more women extension workers from the rural areas and training them.
- Making better use of male extension agents; Change the stero-typed attitude of male agents with regular gender sensitization courses; Increasing awareness of gender roles; Developing skills in use of language and communication to suit women.
- Provision of creches for children of women workers/ farmers. This will enable girls to go to school.
- Provision of proper health care support for girls and women.

Our greatest resource is the human resource. We should make efforts to mobilize this resource for creative endeavour. There is a great need to translate the concept of equality into a social reality by enabling women to join the mainstream. The empowering strategies need to be further strengthened to make them effective and result- oriented. Only then shall we be able to ensure a happier and better tomorrow.

References

- **Annual Report,** (2006-07), Department of Women and Child Development, GOI New Delhi.
- **Azim, Shaukath,**(2001). Gender Empowerment-Where Does India Stand? Social Welfare, New Delhi.
- **Government of India** 'Fourth World Conference on Women, Beijing (1993) Country Report, Government of India, Department of Women and Child Development, Ministry of Human Resource Department, New Delhi, 1995.
- **Human Development Report,** (2009) New Delhi.

- **Indu Grover,** (2004) Gender Theory & Development, HEL Project, CCSHAU, Hisar.
- **Kant,S.K,** (2001), Women's Empowerment and Mutual Co-operation in theFamily, Social Welfare. New Delhi.
- **Mitra, Jyoti,** (1997), Women and Society – Equality and Empowerment, Kanishka Publishers, New Delhi.
- **Samanta, R.K,** (1995). Women in Agriculture: Perspective, issues and experiences , M.D Publications Private Limited. New Delhi
- **Singh, D and Ansari, N.A.** (2008) The Empowerment of Indian Women with reference to Five Year Plans, Kurukshetra
- **UNESCO'S** Gender Mainstreaming Implementation Framework (GMIF) for (2002-07).

14

Women and Information Technology: A Critique

Prof. Parimal H Vyas
Ms. Priti Nigam

Breaking the Stereotype, Indian society has transformed from an agrarian society to an industrial society, and is further moving towards information led, knowledge driven society. The concept of formal education after independence introduced new modes of thinking, aspirations and ambitions for both men and women. All these transformations created a transition in the culture, society and role taking of men and women in India to a large extent. However, the approach of Indian society to women's employment has through out been dualistic because of the contradictory images of women held by women, men and society.

India is a multifaceted society where no generalization could apply to the entire nation's various regional, religious, social and economic groups. Nevertheless, certain broad circumstances in which Indian women live affect the ways they participate in the economy. Though, specific customs vary from region to region within the country, there are different standards of behaviour for men and women that carry over into the work environment. (John E. Dunlop and Victoria A Velkoff, 1999).

The Constitution of India provides legal equality for men and women of this country, however, social and economic equality is yet to be achieved. It guarantees several rights for Indian women viz., equality before Law for Women; the State to make any special provision in favour of women and children; the State to direct its policy towards securing for men and women equally the right to an adequate means of livelihood as well as equal pay for equal work for both men and women, the State to make provision for securing just and humane conditions of work and for maternity relief, and not less than one-third including the number of seats reserved for women belonging to the Scheduled Casts and Scheduled Tribes of the total number of seats to be filled by direct election in every Panchayat to be reserved for women and such seats to be allotted by rotation to different constituencies in a Panchayat.

Women and Techonolgy

No one would make the argument that megapixels are masculine or that gigabytes have a gender. But, as gadgets and websites become an integral part of everyday life, a high-tech world that has been largely built and engineered by men is getting the feminine touch. Digital cameras, cellphones, and online social networks appear unisex but social scientists argue that every product is hardwired in subtle ways that reflect the cultural assumptions of its makers. In a technology world that has been dominated by men, a growing number of companies have now realized that feminizing their products essentially, by putting style and functionality on an equal footing with power and speed is good for business.

Traditionally, women have not been thought of as the first audience for most tech firms, But, women is the original early adopters. She has not only brought some of the earliest machines such as Television, the Telephone, and the

Radio into the home, but has made smart use of Automation in her daily chores, and were gatekeepers for the (www.usabilitynews.com).

Educational and Occupational Profile of Women in India

The position of Indian women has considerably changed from the birds in a cage situation. Attempts have been made to empower women in India and she has made significant strides in all fields, although their number remains insignificant. Women are certainly more likely to be working outside the home than ever before.

Between 1950s and the end of the 1990s, the proportion of women aged 20 to 59 who were in the labour force increased from around one-third to one-half. In many cases, women's participation has increased at the expense of men. It has been now recognized that education and career are not only the right of women, but a key factor that contributes to the economic and social development of a nation. Although, the participation and contribution of women in many professions is not very significant, it is gradually increasing, as noted earlier in the section. Higher education facilitated women's entry into gainful employment. In the early and middle of the 20th century, that is in the 1940s and 1950s only women from the lower classes sought outside jobs. The middle and the upper class women stayed home caring for their children and attending to their domestic chores. Gradually, women from these classes also started joining the workforce, which to a considerable extent is the result of higher education among the girls (Stanley Jaya Kumar, G, 1994). Women's increasing participation in the modern professions is also remarkable. Women have risen to high ranks in a wide range of professions (Aruna Asaf Ali, 1991).There has been a transformation from job orientation to career orientation to professional orientation among women. **Better access to education, changing societal attitudes although, slow and favourable Government policies has**

facilitated the entry of women into varying field. There has been a clear shift in the thinking pattern of women regarding formal work as integral part of their life space. Both income generation and career have become equally significant (C V Madhavi, 1994).

As per 2001 Census, 54.16 percent of female are literate with 72.99 percent being urban female and 46.58 percent rural female. In the year 2001, nearly 7,929 colleges for general education and 2223 engineering and professional colleges were enrolled 36.9 percent of women in higher education. **The disparity between male literacy and female literacy has constantly been at 25 percent for more than four census periods between the years 1961 to 1991** (M Kalaiselvi Geetha and Dr. R Krishnamurthy, 2002).

The literacy drive coupled with Information and Communication Technology (ICT) access has made Indian women to attain certain degree of cultural and economic independence to take their own decisions. However, women represent a large untapped source of talent. Unfortunately, there seems to be an under representation of women in technology field. One of the most significant barriers to women entry into the IT field or their rise in high technology businesses has little to do with gender. Instead, it has a lot to do with education. Their representing the Science and Technology (S&T) fields remains low, with women being present mostly in the natural sciences.

This low visibility is reproduced in the S & T workforce, where women represent only 7.7 percent of scientists and engineers, technicians at 9.5 per cent, and auxiliary personnel at 17 percent (UNESCO, 1997).

As large number of Indian women lack basic education, more advanced and specialized IT education is out of reach. At present, IT education is offered in Degree Programmes in Engineering Colleges and Universities and in Diploma and Certificate Courses. **It is being seen that women**

pursue their studies in humanities and business rather than in IT related fields. In India, the participation of women in engineering was negligible till the early 1980s. It is only since the 1990s that their enrolment has shown an increasing trend as seen in table 1.219. This movement began first in the Southern States, and has gradually spread to other parts of India (PP Parikh & SP Sukhatme, 2004).

An Overview of it Sector Worldwide and India

Information Technology (IT) is the study, design, development, implementation, support or management of computer based *information systems*, particularly software applications and computer hardware. It deals with the use of electronic *computers* and *computer software* to *convert, store, protect, process, transmit,* and *securely retrieve information*. It encompasses many aspects of computing and technology. It is a general term that describes any technology that helps to produce, manipulate, store, communicate, and or disseminate information. It is the branch of technology concerned with the dissemination, processing, and storage of information, esp. (www.rediff.com).

The IT sector provides basically the root services that is Networking; Software Installation; System Integration and Operating system (OS) Development. ITES-BPO segment constitutes the supporting services such as Customer Care; Finance, and Human Resource Development, Engineering Design; Simulation; Animation and Research and Development activities. ITES-BPO segment thus has a tremendous scope to grow further, in contrast to the IT Services sector, which has limitations in growth (Vipan Kumar, 2003).

The development of the Indian software industry had a slow and hesitant start in the mid-1980s, and then captured in the 1990s. In the year 2000, the software industry of India generated revenue of US $5.7 Billion, with US $4 Billion from exports. India's software exports represented 10.5 per cent of

India's total exports in the year 2004-2005, and recorded a growth of $200 Billion in the year of 2008-2009. (www.iimcal.ac.in).

The IT sector of India is one of the fastest growing segments of Indian industry. Its major achievements include viz., the development and tremendous success of the software industry, large-scale computerizations and Internet usage, IT-based automation in various industries, and development of supercomputer technology. It has ushered India into an era where various services can now be delivered remotely. Time and distance barriers have been dismantled as software companies provide customer interaction services, help desks, medical transcription, translation, localization services, data digitization; legal databases, data processing, back office operations, digital content development, remote network management and specialized knowledge services to both domestic and foreign customers (www.planning commision.nic.in). The Planning Commission's approach to the Eleventh Five Year Plan has emphasized to concentrate on ICT services towards faster and more inclusive growth by aiming at increases in (a) the tele-density in comparison with other countries; (b) rural tele-density compared with urban through private sector, and mobile telephone expansions; (c) Internet connectivity for Text, Data and Image communications, and (d) larger and speedy connectivity through wireless technology and on Fiber Optic Cables (www.blonnet.com).

The Ministry of Information Technology were to set up 100 Million Internet connections in the year 2008 and 01 Million Internet-enabled IT Kiosks/Cyber Cafes were to be established across India to facilitate implementation of citizen-based e-Governance applications and to provide easy access of information. The Government of India decided to set up the Ministry of Information Technology in October 1999 as the Nodal Ministry for all initiatives in this area. It had planned to achieve a target of US $50 Billion in Software exports in the year 2008 (www.cosmoc.org).

According to a study undertaken by the IMRB (Indian Market Research Bureau), a mere 30 per cent of businesses in India have the means to access the Internet at their premises (P. Subba Rao, 2001).

IT services form the largest segment of the world-wide spends on technology products and related services. The India domestic IT and ITES market is expected to cross Rs. 2, 00,000 Crores in the year 2012 compared to Rs. 90,014 Crores recorded in the year 2007. IT market grew at 22.4 per cent in the year 2007. IT sector market size is estimated at over US$1.5 trillion. Software and IT-BPO services accounted for over 70 per cent of the total market size in the year 2007.

As per the NASSCOM Report, 2005, size of Information Technology/Information Technology Enabled Services (IT/ITES) Industry in India was to the tune of US$ 36 Billion dollar while it employed about 1.3 Million people. By the year 2010, IT/ITES sector is set to grow to $ 60 Billion, and would employ about 2.5 Million persons. Spending on Engineering and R&D excluded above estimated US$780 Billion. Spending on IT services was estimated at US$470 Billion growth of 5.9 per cent over US$ 444 Billion in 2007. In the year 2007, the spend on IT outsourcing was estimated at over US$ 170 Billion, which was 36 per cent more than in the year 2006 (www.gujaratIndia.com).

During 1960s to 2000, the IT industry sold $40 Trillion of hardware, software and services and, aims to sell more than $15 Trillion by the year 2015. The total numbers of jobs in the emerging countries were expected to equal to those in the developed countries (www.IDC.com).

According to Internet World Stats With more than 3.6 Billion people, Asia is approximately 54 per cent of the world's population. But, only about 10per cent of them are online. USA lead with an online population 153.4 Million followed by China with figure of 86.8 Million Internet users and figure were for Japan with 53.6 Million, Germany 32 Million, the UK 30 Million, and India was ranked at the eight places. Internet users outside USA accounted for 80 per cent of the world's online population.

The growth rate for Internet penetration in India is staggering. The country's Internet population has grown 700 per cent since 2000, and there's still plenty of room for it to expand. Internet penetration in India has witnessed a dramatic growth and her Internet population grew at 33 per cent, making IT Sector as one of the fastest-growing sector of India in terms of Internet users. According to Internet World Status Report, as on March 2008, there were 60,000,000 Internet users in India, reflecting penetration of 5.2 per cent penetration of Internet. (www.Internetworldstats.com/asia).

According to the I-Cube 2008 jointly undertaken by IMRB International and IAMAI there were 3.3 Million active Internet users in rural India as on March 2008.With figure of 250 Million urban population in India, 82 per cent of Internet users were amongst literate and only 31per cent were English-speaking. However, out of 77 Million (38 per cent of 205 Million), 84 per cent were found as PC-literate. India has an online Internet community of 40 million a steady rise from 5 million in 2000. (www.zonkerala.com).

According to I-Cube 2008, a survey conducted jointly by IMRB International and Internet and Mobile Association of India (IAMAI), India had 45.3 million active Internet users and 62.5 Million claimed internet users in September 2008.

Active internet users are those who have used Internet at least once in the last one month, while claimed users also include those who have used Internet sometime but not in the last one month. Urban users continue to dominate internet use contributing to 42 million of the 45.3 million active Internet users.

The number of claimed Internet users in urban India in September 2008 was 57 Million compared with 48 Million in September 2007, recording a less than 10 per cent growth (www.alootechie.com). The Government is trying to reduce barriers and a monthly broadband subscription can cost as little as 199 rupees, or about $4.50 (www.dailyreckoning.com).

Broadband penetration in India is still 0.2 per cent as compared to 19.3 per cent in the US. Consumer e-Commerce Market segment in India was estimated to be Rs. 7,080 Crores (1770 Million US $) which is still small as compared to the average growth rate for the year 2008-2009 projected as 30 per cent (www.hellogiri.com). There were 13.54 Million Internet subscribers at the end of March 2009 as compared to 12.85 Million at the end of December 2008 showing a growth of 5.30per cent.

One of the opportunities that the growth of the Internet has provided is the ability for Internet users to browse commercial products shown on Internet, and in some cases to place an online order using a personal computer. Online communication like e-mail and Chat are the two most common purposes behind accessing the Internet followed by Information Search. With the increase in the use of the Internet, e-Commerce applications such as online bill payment, online ticket booking have gained more popularity.

The results of the AC Nielsen online Consumer Opinion Survey demonstrated that approximately 10 per cent of the world's population which showed figure of more than 627 Million people shopped online at least once. Europe and North America showed highest number of online shoppers, with Germany, Austria and the UK that topped the list, with at least 95 per cent of online shoppers. In Asia pacific region, South Korea and Taiwan were ranked as highest, with figure of at least 90 per cent of online shoppers.

There are many drivers for online shopping in India, such as access to information and communication; rising PC penetration; and the proliferation of cybercafés showing figure of more than 1, 26,000 in India. In one of the study jointly conducted by the IAMAI and IMRB International, that covered around 65,000 individuals from 16,500 households surveyed in 26 different cities across the India. Average time spent on Internet, in terms of minutes per week, shown an increase with the increasing age of Internet user, it showed that the older population spent more time on Internet as against the younger Internet users who are considered to be more Internet-savvy.

While, the school going children spent an on average of 322.3 minutes a week on Internet, the College going students spent an on average of 433.2 minutes per week, and the older men spent an on average of 580.5 minutes a week. **Working women spent 535.3 minutes per week while women non-working women spent an on average of 334.5 minutes per week on Internet** (www.iamai.co.in).

The Growth of it Sector in the State of Gujarat

The Information and Communication Technology (ICT) Sector in the State of Gujarat has been projected to receive investments up to US$3.7 Billion by the year 2011. Its turnover grew from US$ 60 Million in the year 2005, and expected to reach figure of to US$2.4 Billion in the year 2010-2011.Software Exports recorded a growth rate of 107.3 percentage to reach US$134 Million in financial year 2006-2007 as compared to that of financial year 2005-2006. Information Technology-Enabled Services (ITES), and IT Hardware Industry is the focus growth areas of Gujarat's IT industry (www.gujaratIndia.com). With 4.93 per centage population of India, it contributes about 16 per centage of the India's Manufacturing GDP. It has excellent physical infrastructure and has made rapid strides in the field of IT and e-Governance. IT sector in Gujarat employs about 15,000 persons. However, Gujarat is yet to realize its true potential in IT/ITES sector. (Government of Gujarat, Science and Technology Department, November, 2006).

ITES viz. Knowledge Process Outsourcing (KPOs) and Business Process Outsourcing (BPOs) are the fastest emerging sectors in the State of Gujarat. The IT/ ITES sector turnover was expected to grow from US$60.98 Million in the year 2005 to US$2439.02 Million in the year 2010-2011. The ICT Sector is projected to witness investments of up to US$3658.54 Million by the year 2010. Global sourcing of technology related services was estimated to grow by about 30 per cent to reach figure of US$ 70 to 76 Billion in the year 2007.

A comprehensive IT Policy 2006 – 2011 was released by the State Government of Gujarat with a vision to endeavor for rapid expansion and growth of knowledge based economy in the Gujarat State. It has envisaged attracting investments in the IT sector by promotion of urban based IT infrastructure, enhancement in employing supply of skilled manpower and promotion of IT and related industries to it (www.gujaratbusinessIndia.com).

Proportion and Participation of Indian Women in it Sector Of India

Strong fundamentals of a large talent pool, sustained cost competitiveness and an enabling business environment can help India sustain her position as the most preferred sourcing destination. India's young demographic profile, complemented by a vast and growing academic system continues to add to its pool of educated talent.

There is no other country such as India that offers a similar mix and scale of human resources. While some gaps in talent suitability still exist, it is being adequately addressed through strong provider-level initiatives with focus on skill development. Around 12.32 Million registered online women users were found in India during the year 2005-2006, showing of 4 per cent against when compared with figure of 11.85 Million of the year 2004-2005. It showed that in India the number of women browsers had increased while the number of men browsers had declined by 4 per cent showing figure of 26.18 Million (www. juxtconsultant.com). The number of women online Internet users in India crossed the figure of 12 Million mark but they still continued to be substantially outnumbered by their male counterparts with figure of 26 Million as on December, 2007 (www.phyorg.com). The ratio of women in IT services in India to rise steadily in the coming years due to a variety of reasons.

More and more women are entering professional engineering streams such as computer sciences and electronics. **The Indian women in the IT fields are very committed and they acquire software skills quite fast just like the men. The male-female ratio in IT services in India is expected reach the 50: 50 mark in a near future** (www.rediff.com).

The IT sector in India has created employment opportunities in areas such as telecommunications, banking, shopping, education, health and business. The high end firms undertake software products, R&D, turnkey solutions and strategic technical alliances. The professionals employed in this area are engineering graduates, mostly Ph.Ds and post-graduates with technical multi-skilling. The middle end firms undertake development of software packages, offshore services, and alliances for market access. This category of job demands engineering graduates who are geographically mobile and possess managerial skills. The export end firms undertake onsite services, maintenance and implementation, alliances with labour contractors, etc.

The current trend in employment of women in Information and Communication Technology (ICT) work arena is with a gender ratio (female: male) varying from a best level. The growth of Information Technology in the country during the last two decades has opened up a plethora of opportunities which saw growing number of women take up employment in the IT industry. According to NASSCOM, by the end of the decade, women will account for 45 percent of the country's total IT workforce as compared to 14 percent in 2003 (ChenMay Yee, 2000).

The ratio of women in IT services in India is rising steadily, whereas the percentage of women IT workers in the US has been declining. 24 per cent women were found as software professionals in IT companies of India. This ratio is reversed in the ITES-BPO sector where the ratio of men to women is 31:69.**IT majors in India are hiring more and more women.**

To illustrate, Infosys has employed 8,262 women employees showing male to female ratio as 76: 24. Wipro Technologies also has a similar women employment record where the ratio of women employees rose to 21.22 per cent in April 2005 compared to 18.75 per cent in April 2004.

The Data Quest survey revealed that though women make up about 20 percent of the IT work force in India, only a few women reach the position of CEO's. The number shrinks as one move up the hierarchy. At the senior levels women constitute merely 6 percent of the workforce. IT is an industry where women shall stand shoulder to shoulder with the men. There are six primary myths that prevails provide us an answer with regard to invisibility and lower proportion and participation of women in IT industry worldwide listed out as flows (Linda Wirth, 2002).

- **Myth 1:** Women are Emotional while tech is strictly logical. As a result, Both do not go together.
- **Myth 2:** Men are Good at Maths and Machines while Women have No Clue about it.
- **Myth 3:** Men are the providers while Women are Nurturers.
- **Myth 4:** Technical Women are Unattractive, Arrogant and Abnormal.
- **Myth 5:** Women can not do it Because they are made that way: the Divine or the Evolution Argument.
- **Myth 6:** Women are not as Good at Visualizing as Men, and hence, do not make Good Engineers.

One therefore needs to get answer of following questions.

- What is it that keeps Women from making it to the top rung of authority in the India's IT Sector?
- Is it the IT sector that has not recognized and rewarded women well enough for their efforts?

Women and it Sector of India: A Critique

Women have entered high skilled jobs in IT in developing countries. This has happened particularly in countries where national policies have promoted Science & Technology education and where young women entered these fields. Technological innovations and the increasingly globalized economy have created job opportunities for women particularly in the service sectors. As IT sector remains a leading player in the industry, women have come to play a major role in the growth of this sector. The IT sector in India has created employment opportunities in areas such as telecommunications, banking, shopping, education, health business. Internet has generated new job areas like the design, maintenance and management of websites on the World Wide Web. Though women are better represented in the IT sector, they have not assumed significant role and status (Dr. Suriya, 2003).

Women tend to be well represented in Software Programming but not in Hardware Design, Operating Systems or Computer Maintenance. An analysis of the gender situation in the stratified nature of the software development activities high value added and low value added activities, showed that a largest segment of women were clustered in the low-end jobs; while a smallest segment of women were found at the higher end which reflects the gender divide in the IT industry?

Despite being a new field in most developing fields, gender inequities that are well established in other sectors of the labour force are already being replicated in the IT Sector. Although, one finds slow and gradual change in the profile of the workforce of the IT companies in India are experiencing changes. The study conducted by Center for Organization Development, Hyderabad, the gender specificity and women in the field of IT aimed at to investigate the policy implications to promote more women into the IT sector and to higher levels of management.

The Government of India has already launched programmes and policies to address the significant obstacles girls and women face in Indian Society to improve women's status. The Ministry of Education offers formal and informal education programmes for women and girls working in collaboration with Non-Government institutions. The Department of Women and Child Development has devised plans, policies and programmes for enacting and amending legislation, guiding and coordinating the efforts of both Governmental and Non-Governmental Organizations. It has also implemented programmes in the areas of welfare and support services, training for employment and income generation, awareness generation and gender sensitization. It has created working women hostels and crèches to better address the mobility constraints being faced by women working in IT sector of India. To illustrate, the State of Andhra Pradesh has reserved 33 percent of seats in all higher education institutions to encourage women for enrollment in advanced IT education programmes. Two extensive studies on women engineers that were undertaken by the Indian Institute of Technology (IIT), Mumbai found that from 1951 to year 2001, there was nearly a 50 fold increase in the intake capacity which is a sure sign of growing literacy amongst women (UGC, 1999).

Following their urban counterparts, large number of rural women too is opting for computers as a career option. To illustrate, training programmes conducted by Pune Zilla Parishad clearly showed that out of total applicants, near 25 per cent of women have opted for raining related to computers. It created self-employment and entrepreneurship initiatives among the womenfolks. Out of 2,465, more than 500 women opted for training courses in computer and information technology. The department is also initiating talks with various societies and state corporations for arranging loans for these

Besides IT Courses, the women have also opted for Fashion Designing, Beauty Parlour, Food Processing and Leather Works. The courses in fashion designing recorded the highest attendance of more than 600 women following beauty parlour courses. More than 500 women have undergone training for beauty parlor courses. Adding to this, near about 40 women from tribal areas opted for Ayurvedic Medicine Courses (www.timesofindia.indiatimes.com).

It is therefore highly essential women would require qualitative, cost-effective and need-based education with easier access, availability and affordability for learning and sharpening her communication, conceptual, technical, and managerial skills. It shall call for Integration of work and family life coupled with well-informed collaborative effort on the part of all the stakeholders that affects concerns, commitment, creativity and counseling of women in India.

Epilogue

With the evident growth of IT in India, more women will enter in to the Indian It Industry. It is being assumed that Indian IT companies will be forced to address the women related issue more directly to make them work more comfortably. IT Industry has the potential to offer varying type of jobs and opportunities to women. But, women cannot do it themselves. The IT Policy of the Government of India & the State of Gujarat must take Gender into account for providing an enabling work environment and opportunities to women on those jobs that that women can fill.

Women's ability to work is significantly influenced by the availability of childcare, flexible work hours and maternity leave (Alfred Sloan Institute, February 2002).Organizations and institutions therefore need to take certain specific steps to recruit, develop and retain women professionals to achieve her socio-economic balance. Community-based women's organizations have been instrumental in the process of enabling women to cross the so-called digital divide and become confident users of ICTs. With women's empowerment as a key objective, it can use technology to successfully build personal confidence and self-esteem that has had wider implications in women's lives. Social attitudes and cultural biases are mainly identified as crucial factors discriminating against women and holding them back from attaining higher level jobs. We need to make effective use of complementary strategies in management, covering areas such as training, networking, mentoring, review of recruitment and promotion, family friendly policies, awareness raising, positive action, recognition of women's increasing economic role and contribution (Martha Fetheroff Loutfi, 2002).

The holistic new ICT technologies are powerful tools for women to overcome discrimination, achieve full equality, well-being and participation in the decisions that determine their lives and the future of their communities. It would be a highly valuable reference tool for policy makers and development leaders, so that appropriate steps can be taken to mainstream the gender dimension in all areas of technology development, incubation and adoption.

The valuable role of women can certainly play as one of the major contributors in the economic growth outside the family in India. In this context it would be interesting to explore the field of Information Technology and the role of women in Information Technology in India. (UGC, 1999).

References

- **Aruna Asaf Ali,** (1991) The Resurgence of Indian Women, Radiant Publishers. New Delhi.
- **C V Madhavi** (1994) Women Entrepreneurs in India, in (ed) Khair Jahan Sogra, Women in Management.
- **ChenMay Yee,** (2000) High tech Lift for India's Women, The Wall Street Journal, November1.
- **Indira J Parikh** (1992): Women in Management in India, were reading in the first workshop on Role Effectiveness for Women Executives, October 12 –17,Hyderabad, Centre for Organization Development.
- **Information Technology**; Department of Science and Technology; Government of Gujarat; Available at (www.gujaratIndia.com)
- **John E. Dunlop and Victoria A Velkoff** (1999) Women and the Economy in India, International Programs Center, US Census Bureau, The Official Statistics.

- **Linda Wirth** (2002), Women in Management: Closer to Breaking Through the Glass Ceiling, in Martha Fetherolf Loutfi (ed) Women, Gender and Work: What is Equality and How do we get there? ILO Rawat Publications, Jaipur.
- **M Kalaiselvi Geetha and R Krishnamurthy** (2002), Women and Information Technology in India, in The First Annual Conference on Women in Information Technology – WIT 2002 Proceedings, August 29 & 30, p. 44.
- **Martha Fetheroff Loutfi** (2002), Women, Gender and Work: What is Equality and How Do We Get there, ILO, Rawat Publications, Jaipur.
- **P. Subbarao.** (2001),The Next Generation: IT Industry; Journal of Computer-Mediated Communication; Vol. 34; No. 19,
- **PP Parikh and SP Sukhatme** (2004), Women Engineers in India, Economic and Political Weekly, January 10, 2004.
- **Stanley Jaya Kumar, G** (1994), Changing Directions in the Status and Role of Women In India, in (ed) C. Chakrapani and S. Vijaya Kumar's book Changing Status and Role of Women in Indian Society, M D Publications, New Delhi.
- **UNESCO** (1997) Statistical Yearbook 1997.
- **Vipan Kumar** (2003); Nistad news; Information Technology; Vol.2; No.3; 2003;

Webliogrphy:

- www.rediff.com
- www.gujaratIndia.com
- www.gujaratbusinessIndia.com
- www.planningcommision.nic.in
- www.altassets.com
- www.ciol.com
- www.cosmoc.org
- www.IDC.com
- www.iipa.com
- www.Internetworldstats.com/asia
- www.eetIndia.co.in
- www.juxtconsultant.com

- www.iamai.co.in
- www.phyorg.com
- www.usabilitynews.com/news/
- www.timesofindia.indiatimes.com/
- www.zonkerala.com/articles/internet-users-india.htm
- www.alootechie.com/content/45-million-active-internet-users-india-survey
- www.dailyreckoning.com.au/internet-india/2007/01/11/
- www.hellogiri.com/india-internet-users-trends-market-penetration-and-future
- www.trak.in/tags/business/2009/07/15/india-telecom-report-internet-broadband-services

15

Capacity Building of Rural Women Through Self Help Groups

Dr. Anu Kathuria, Prof. Savita Singal
Prof. Shashi Varma

India has been a welfare state ever since its independence and the primary objective of all governmental endeavors has been the welfare of people. Over the years, it has been realized that a sustainable strategy of poverty alleviation should be based on increasing the productive employment opportunities for economic development, increased participation of people in rural development programmes, decentralization of planning, better enforcement of land reforms and greater access to credit. The fundamental objective of economic development is to bring about rapid and sustained improvement in the quality of life by improving the living standards of the people. Central to this goal is the rapid growth in income and productive employment. Investment in people and capital is equally important if the country has to foster an environment which encourages full utilization of human resource, labor and material in a most productive manner.

Situation of Women

India being an agrarian country, its women form the backbone of agricultural operations wherein 70 to 80 % of field work is performed by women. However, women's situation remains plightful, especially in the context of rural society. The reason for this being illiteracy among women, poverty, early marriage, male domination in the family and less opportunities to come forward. Coupled with all these, social conventions and gender ideology deprive them of the access to and control over the resources which would enable them to increase their productivity.

Initiatives taken under 5 year Plans for Human Resource Development of Women

From the very beginning of independent India's development planning process, one of the main issues has been that of providing equal status to women. The stress of the **First five year plan (1951-56)** was on promoting education of women through enrolling large number of girls in schools. The **Second five year plan (1956-61)** emphasized the need for promoting girl's education through educating parents, making education more relevant to girl's needs. **The Third five year plan (1961-66)** continued to lay emphasis on the welfare aspect. The only mention of women in industry is the reference that introduction of 'Amber *Charkhas*' for *khadi* spinning created employment opportunities for women. In the **Fourth five year plan (1969-74)**, the work of Social Welfare Board and granting assistance to voluntary organizations dealing with welfare of women were emphasized. The first serious attempt to better women's lot was done by way of appointing a committee on status of women in India during 1971, the report of which in 1974 (Towards Equality) finally led to preparation of Perspective

Plan for Women (1988-2000 A.D.). **Fifth five year plan (1974-79)** claimed to provide an alternative strategy for National Development so far as upliftment of women and their emancipation was concerned. **The Sixth five year plan (1980-85)** was a milestone in women's development, as a separate chapter on "Women and Development" was included in the plan. Setting up of women cells at district levels for improving women's participation through self-employment was suggested. The **Seventh five year plan (1985-90)** recommended the need for women's corporations at state level for promoting employment through skill training with equal participation of central and state governments. The **Eighth five year plan (1992-97)** took Human Resource Development of women as one of the major thrust areas. National Commission for Women (1992) and *Rashtriya Mahila Kosh* (1993) were set up as a part of the integrated approach to empowerment of women. National Policy for Empowerment of Women was prepared in 1996. Today there are 27 programmes involving 6 ministries and 8 departments which focus on women upliftment and income generating activities. The **Ninth five year plan (1997-2002)** had goals for overall development of Indian women so as to make her capable of entering the 21st century with a lot of self-confidence. The plan proposed 30 per cent representation for women in public sector, and free education for girls' up to college level, besides setting up of a Development Bank for women entrepreneurs. The Plan laid emphasis on **promotion of Self Help Groups (SHGs)**. The **Tenth five year plan (2002-07)** made a major commitment towards empowering women as the agent of socio-economic change and development. Based on the recommendations of National Policy for Empowerment of women, the plan suggested three fold strategies for empowering women through social empowerment, economic empowerment and gender justice. To fill gap of rural urban divide, the allocation of funds for rural development programmes has been hiked to Rs.76,774 crore in the **Tenth five year** plan from Rs.42,874 crore during Ninth five year plan.

Self Help Groups, Micro Finance and Human Resource Development

The concept of SHGs and micro finance was first introduced by Mohammad Yunus of Bangladesh in 1976 who got the Noble Prize for the said innovation. Since then, micro credit has been recognized as a key strategy for addressing the issues of poverty alleviation and women's empowerment. Micro finance through SHG has become a ladder for the poor to bring them up not only economically but also socially mentally and attitudinally and above all to help them break through the strong hold of exploitative money lenders. Easy access of poor to credit is the biggest need of hour rather than cheaper rate of interest. The experience of micro finance shows that the poor are bankable and that poverty alleviation is possible without subsidies. Micro finance provides opportunity to the poor for getting sufficient amount of credit easily to start any income generating activity or to meet emergent needs.It is felt that for illiterate or poor rural people, individual effort is too inadequate to improve their fate. This brings about the necessity for organizing them in a group by which they get the benefit of collective perception, collective decision making and collective action for common benefits. Thus, Self Help Group is a small, economically homogenous group of poor people, voluntarily formed to save and contribute to common fund, to be loaned to its members as per the group decision.

Objectives of Self Help Groups

(a) To inculcate saving habits among poor to meet their financial requirement.

(b) To evolve supplementary credit strategies for meeting the credit needs of poor.

(c) To build mutual trust and confidence between the bankers and the poor.

(d) To encourage banking, both on the thrift as well as credit dealings.

Organizational setup of Self Help groups

Self help group comprises of three office bearers i.e. President, Secretary and Treasurer. These office bearers are generally known as group leaders. Apart from these office bearers, other women members of SHGs are defined as SHG members. SHG consists of 10-20 members.

SHGs differ in the degree of cohesiveness. The extent to which members are knit together depends on their strength of interpersonal attachment and communication. Group cohesiveness is an important indicator of how much influence the group as whole has over the individual members. Cohesiveness causes more harmonious behaviour among group members. Its conduct and way of functioning is decided by the members themselves who have equal opportunities to express their views in any of decision taken by the group. The core funding of SHG group is internal saving mobilized by its members. The group also maintains proper accounts of their saving and lending (micro-credit) in a transparent manner.

Bank linkages of Self Help Groups

As per the guidelines, SHGs are allowed to open saving bank account in the name of the SHG. Following formalities are required while opening the account:

- Copy of rules / regulations of the SHG
- Copy of resolution authorizing office bearers to operate the account on behalf of the group.
- Photographs of office bearers
- Introduction of any saving account holder known to the group or NGOs, Government department officials, Sarpanch etc.

Financing of Self Help Groups

To receive loan from the bank, SHG should fulfill the following conditions -

- The group should have been in active existence for at least six months

- The group should have attained affinity / cohesiveness / homogeneity
- The group should have successfully undertaken savings and credit operations from its own resources.
- The groups should maintain proper accounts / records
- The group formation should reflect genuine need to help each other and work together.
- The SHG and its members should determine purpose for which loan is required. The credit should cover not only consumption and production loan for various farm and non farm activities of the poor but also include their other credit needs such housing and shelter improvement.

Capacity building of SHG members through training

Training is an important component of SHG. Constant inputs of training and capacity buildings are required to sustain SHGs. There are basically two types of training provided to the SHGs.

1. Training on SHG orientation which includes SHG formation and strengthening, book keeping, financial management and developing linkages with bank.
2. Entrepreneurial training which includes different types of trainings provided to SHG for initiating different home/ farm based micro enterprises.

Part 11 Research Work
Rationale for the Study

The concept of SHGs has brought out remarkable improvement in poverty alleviation, provision of self employment, and efficient utilization of local resources as shown by various studies. The said concept has gained momentum recently in Haryana with the hope to reap benefits of this concept. Haryana emerged as a separate state in the federal galaxy of Indian Republic on November 1, 1966 where 80% of its population is engaged in agriculture directly or indirectly. Since 1998, a scheme with an outlay of Rs.186.21 crore has been implemented in Haryana, named "Swashakti" which is known as a scheme for development and rights of rural women. Under this scheme, Self Help Groups (SHGs) are constituted with a view to provide grants so that women can uplift their standards of living. Co-ordination is built between SHGs and lending institutions so that economic resources can be made available to women for earning income, and subsequently raising the standard of living. It is hoped that by this way, women will also be able to establish their control over income and expenditures. Keeping in view the plight of rural women in Haryana along with their potential for the human resource development and economic contribution to family resources, the present research was planned to study the nature and functioning of SHGs in Haryana with a focus on socio-economic empowerment of its members.

Research Objectives

1. To do an exploratory study of existence and nature of SHGs.
2. To study the socio-economic working of SHGs.

Methodology

The study was conducted in Sirsa district of Haryana which was purposively selected because the researcher was well acquainted with socio-cultural traits and the layout of that area. Sirsa district is divided into seven blocks as shown in the map (Fig. 1). The list of villages under each block was obtained from Block Development Officer of respective block. One village from each of these seven lists of villages was selected randomly. Thus, seven villages from seven blocks were selected randomly for the study. Lists of all SHGs formulated in these selected 7 villages were procured from District Rural Development Agency (DRDA), Sirsa. Leaders of SHGs were selected as the respondents for conducting exploratory study of existence and nature of SHGs. Thus, the total sample comprised of 28 group leaders of SHGs from the selected seven villages.

In accordance with the objectives of the study, an interview schedule was prepared for in-depth study of the nature and existence of SHGs. Interview schedule was divided into two sections. First section comprised of the information pertaining to the nature and existence of SHGs while second part dealt with its socio-economic functioning. The interview schedule was duly pre-tested in a non-sampled village of Sirsa district. Based on the responses obtained during pre testing, modifications were incorporated to make the tool more suitable for data collection. Further, the data were collected by administering of the final interview schedule to the respondents personally by the researcher. The responses observed for each of the question in the interview schedule were suitably coded into a master sheet and tabulated. Appropriate statistical tools like frequency, percentages and averages were used to draw meaningful inferences as per the objectives of the study.

Results and Discussion

According to the objectives, the results have been presented under the following heads:

- Existence and nature of SHGs
- Socio-economic working of SHGs

Existence and Nature of Existing SHGs

The information pertaining to the formation of all SHGs along with their income generating activities in selected 7 villages was obtained from their group leaders and is presented in Table 1.

Number of SHGs**:** The findings revealed that a total of 28 SHGs were formed in selected 7 villages. Six out of twenty-eight SHGs were formed during 2004-05. However, majority of SHGs (17) were formed either during 2002-03 or between the year 2000 to 2001 (5). These groups were found to be operating at two different stages Nine SHGs were functioning at stage 1 i.e., they had formed their groups and started the activities of saving and internal loaning. They had also been sanctioned a loan of Rs. 25,000/- by the bank for the purpose of internal loaning among its members. The remaining nineteen SHGs were working at second stage i.e., they had already started income generating activities (IGAs) after receiving bigger loans from the bank for the same, ranging from 1.6 lacs to 3.2 lacs. Out of these 19 SHGs, 6 SHGs were such which had started IGAs after receiving the loan from the bank but had stopped the IGAs after some time due to several reasons viz. lack of profits (1 SHG), marketing problems (4 SHGs) and non- cooperation among group members (1 SHG).

Initiative taken in formation of SHGs: It was interesting to note that an NGO called 'Life Line Society' took the initiative in formation of 9 SHGs spread over 5 villages. Another 8 SHGs were formed on the initiative of group members while banks took the initiative in forming 6 SHGs (Table 1). The remaining 5 SHGs were formed on the initiative taken by government officials of District Rural Development Agency (DRDA), Sirsa.

Composition and size of SHGs: As many as 24 SHGs were 'female only' while only 4 SHGs were 'male only'. This may be due to emphasis of the government on empowerment of women through SHGs. The study is in line with findings of Dahiya *et al* (2002) who reported that 82 percent SHG members were 'women only'. As per the directions of the government, the minimum size of SHG should be 10 while the maximum size should be 20. It was found that all SHGs comprised of ten members each as the group members felt that the size of ten members was convenient for financial dealings and harmonious working.

Type of activity: Dairy was the most preferred activity among the SHGs as 10 SHGs were involved in this activity. Sheep rearing and vegetable growing were preferred equally by 3 SHGs each. The other income generating activities were surf making (undertaken by 2 SHGs) and *masala* making (undertaken by only one SHG). SHGs had not started any income generating activity yet as these self help groups were formed recently and were involved in saving and internal loaning only. These SHGs had opened their saving account in the bank.

Nature of work: Nine SHGs were performing their income generating activities as a group. These income generating activities were sheep rearing (3SHGs), vegetable growing (3 SHGs), surf making (2 SHGs), and *masala* making 1 SHG). Ten SHGs were performing their income generating activities individually as they were involved in dairy agri-business. It was concluded from Table 1 that all SHGs had a size of 10 members and majority of SHGs were 'female only' groups (24), functional (22), in second stage (13), formed during the year 2002-03 (17), and were involved in dairy agri-business (10) which was being practiced individually by the members of these SHGs.

Trainings

Scrutiny of Table 2 reveals details of the training received by members of SHGs.

Training received: Members of 20 SHGs had received training while 8 SHGs did not receive any training. The findings are contrary to the findings of Kataria (1995) who reported that 96 percent respondents had not received any training under DWCRA programme. This may be due to the time gap between the two studies. The government now is giving more emphasis on training for successful functioning of SHGs. However, the findings of the trainings of the present study are in line with findings of Mann (2005) who reported that 91.37 percent respondents had received one or the other form of training in Punjab.

Area of training: Ten SHGs had got training in dairy keeping, 4 SHGs were trained in vegetable growing, 3 SHGs were trained in sheep rearing, 2 SHGs were trained in surf making and only one SHG had got training in *masala* making.

Place of training: Maximum SHGs (12) had received trainings from the experts of CCS Haryana Agricultural

University, Hisar, on its campus. Six SHGs received trainings within the village from the experts of DRDA, Sirsa, while 2 SHGs were trained by DRDA. All these trainings were sponsored by DRDA.

Period of training: Nine SHGs were trained in their respective enterprises in the year 2003-04 while another 9 SHGs had received training in the year 2004-05. Only 2 SHGs were trained in 2002- 03.

Stipend during training: All members of the SHGs who had received skill training in their respective enterprise were satisfied with the trainings provided to them.

Conclusively, it can be said that out of a total of 28 groups, 20 SHGs had received training. Though all these trainings were sponsored by DRDA, none of the SHGs received any stipend during the training period. The duration of training for maximum SHGs (15) was 3-4 days and maximum SHGs (12) were trained at CCS Haryana Agricultural University, Hisar between 2003-05. All SHGs who had received training expressed satisfaction with the training provided to them.

Socio-economic working of Self Help Groups

The information pertaining to the holding of meetings, saving and internal loaning patterns, and bank linkages is discussed under this.

Meetings

Perusal of Table 3 gives description about the details of meetings conducted by SHGs

Interval of meeting: As many as 16 SHGs conducted group meetings monthly while 6 SHGs had their meetings on fortnightly basis. The remaining 6 SHGs were not conducting the meeting regularly as they had discontinued their IGAs.

Place of meeting: Eleven SHGs conducted meetings in the common area called '*Satsang Bhawan*' in the village, while another 10 SHGs conducted their meetings at the residence of group leader. Remaining 4 SHGs conducted meetings at *Anganwadi* center and 3 SHGs conducted meeting at the residence of the group secretary.

Time of meeting: It was found that 13 SHGs preferred to conduct meetings in the afternoon hours followed by 11 SHGs having their meetings in the forenoon hours. Only 4 SHGs had their group meeting in the evening hours. Members preferred afternoon hours as they are little free at that time from household responsibilities.

Attendance: It was observed that attendance in 19 SHGs was more than 90 per cent while attendance in 3 SHGs was between 70 to 90 percent. Only 6 SHGs had less than 70 per cent attendance in their meetings. This may be because of the discontinuation of their IGAs. However, findings reflect that majority of the members were interested in attending meetings regularly. Dahiya *et al* (2002) in his study of SHGs in Himachal Pradesh also reported that more than 90 percent attendance of members in their meetings.

Duration: Twenty four SHGs had their meetings for 1 hour duration. Out of the remaining 4 groups, 3 SHGs had meeting which lasted nearly 2 hours while one SHG continued the meeting for more than 2 hours duration.

It can be concluded from Table 3 that meetings of SHGs were conducted monthly by a vast majority of groups (16), at a common place in the village (11) and in the afternoon period (13). The attendance of members in these meetings was more than 90 percent for a vast majority of SHGs (22).

Saving Pattern

Table 4 highlights the saving pattern of members of SHGs.

Bank: It was observed that an equal number of help groups had open their saving accounts in Haryana Gramin Bank and State Bank of India (10 SHGs each). Remaining eight SHGs had opened their saving account in Punjab National Bank.

Regarding location of the branch of the bank, village 2, 3 and 4 had its PNB branches located outside the village. SHGs of village 6 and 7 were dealing with SBI branches (one located outside the village and one inside the village). Haryana Gramin Bank had its one branch in the village and one outside the village.

Person responsible for maintenance of saving records: For 15 SHGs, secretary of the group was found responsible for maintenance of saving records. For 7 SHGs, President of the group was found to be maintaining records while 6 SHGs took the help of their children for keeping records. This may be because of the fact that most of the group members were uneducated.

Utilization of saved money: A vast majority of SHGs (23) saved money for internal loaning within group members for meeting their day to day needs. Regular saving and internal loaning pattern was main criteria for the bank to sanction further loans for starting business. Members of 4 SHGs were also giving loan for meeting emergencies, only one SHG also reported utilizing their saved money to make common purchasing for its group.

Person responsible for bank transactions: Group secretary was found to be responsible for bank transactions in 18 SHGs while president was responsible for bank transactions in 10 SHGs.

On the whole, Table 4 reveals that SHGs were dealing mainly with Haryana Gramin Bank and State Bank of India for depositing saving at the rate of Rs. 50/- per member (15 SHGs). Internal loaning was practiced for day to day needs and for meeting emergencies of group members (4 SHGs). Group secretary was the person responsible for maintaining financial records (15 SHGs) and for making bank transactions (18 SHGs).

Internal loaning pattern of Self Help Groups

To be eligible for getting loan from the bank for IGA, SHGs are required to open a saving account in the bank and to indulge in internal loaning within the group successfully for a period of at least 6 months. The scrutiny of Table 5 reveals internal loaning pattern of SHGs.

Duration and amount of loan: Maximum SHGs (17) gave loans to their members for a period of 1-6 months. The remaining 11 SHGs gave loans for longer duration, i.e. 7-12 months. Members of only 3 SHGs were taking loan between Rs. 601 to Rs. 800/- from their saved money. The amount of loan for the members of 16 SHGs ranged between Rs. 401 to Rs. 600, while members of 9 SHGs were taking loans between Rs. 201 to Rs. 400.

Purpose of loan: Although the purpose of loan varied from one member to another, yet the most common purpose reported by the members of 15 SHGs was illness of family members. Education of children was reported as another reason for taking loan by members of 5 SHGs. Other reasons for taking loans were marriage in the family or visiting of relatives as reported by members of 3 SHGs each. Only 2 groups had taken loans for the purpose of house repairs.

Interest rate: Maximum groups (26 SHGs) charged 1% rate of interest on the loans given to the members while 1.5 % interest rate was charged by the remaining 2 SHGs.

Defaulters in the group: It was encouraging to find that there were no defaulters among as many as 22 SHGs. Only 6 groups reported that some of their members were defaulters in repayment of loans as they had not paid their loans for the last 3-6 months.

Briefly, it can be said that maximum SHGs gave loans to their members between Rs. 401-600 (16 SHGs), for a duration of 1-6 months (17 SHGs) for treatment of illness (15 SHGs), at 1% interest rate (26 SHGs) and there were no defaulters in a vast majority of SHGs (22).

Bank Loan

As per the government policy, banks sanction a loan of Rs. 25, 000 to SHGs after 6 months of opening a saving account in the name of the group and successful loaning among its group members. The group receives a subsidy of Rs. 10,000 on this amount. After one year of successful working and use of smaller bank loan, bigger loan of Rs. 3 lacs is sanctioned for starting the income generating activity. Subsidy of Rs. 1 lac is given to SHGs by the government on this loan. The details of the bank loan sanctioned to and received by SHGs are presented in Table 6.

Total loan sanctioned: An amount of 3 lacs each was sanctioned by banks to 14 SHGs, while 5 SHGs were sanctioned an amount of Rs 3.2 lacs each as loan for staring income generating activities. For the remaining SHGs, an amount of Rs. 25,000 had been sanctioned but it had not been released so far. These groups had been formed about one year back and were still in the first stage of their functioning.

Loan installments received: Although 9 SHGs were sanctioned a loan of Rs 25,000 each but none of these SHGs had received this amount till the time of data collection. Eight SHGs which had been sanctioned loan between Rs. 3.0 lacs to Rs 3.2 lacs, had received Rs 1.6 lacs each from the bank as the first installment of loan. Other SHGs had received the total amount of 3.0 lacs each and 3 SHGs had received an amount of Rs 3.2 lacs each as a loan for starting the income generating activities.

Rate of interest: It was surprising to note that a vast majority of SHGs (26) did not know the rate of interest charged by the bank on the loan amount given to them. Only 2 groups reported that the rate of interest may be between 9 to 12%.

Repayment of loan: All SHGs had to repay the installments on their bank loan on monthly basis. It is revealed from Table 6 that members of 13 SHGs were regular in returning their installments while members of 6 SHGs were irregular. Nine SHGs had not received any loan from the bank.

Amount of installments repaid: Out of 19 SHGs, who had received loans from the bank, 12 were returning loan in installments of Rs 5000/- per month (@ Rs 500/- per member) while 7 had been returning between Rs 7500/- to Rs 10,000/- per month (@ Rs 750/- Rs 1000/- per member) to the bank as loan installment. It can be concluded that most of the SHGs had been sanctioned loans between 3 to 3.2 lacs (19), out of which 11 SHGs had received full amount of loan while 8 SHGs had received only first installment of Rs 1.6 lacs each. Though maximum SHGs (26) did not know the rate of interest, but the pattern of returning loan was found to be regular on monthly basis for 13 SHGs.

On the whole, the exploratory study of the existence and nature of SHGs formed in selected villages of Sirsa district revealed that 28 SHGs were formed since the year 2000, out of which 6 SHGs had started the IGA after receiving the loan from the bank but at a later stage these groups had discontinued their IGAs mainly because of the marketing problems. Out of the remaining 22 SHGs, 9 groups were in the first stage of grading, for which the bank loan of Rs 25,000/- had been sanctioned but not released yet. Hence, these 6 SHGs had not started any IGAs so far. Only 13 SHGs spread over 7 selected villages were actually involved in some or the other IGAs.

Summary and Conclusions

The information pertaining to formation of self help groups in selected 7 villages was obtained from their group leaders. The study revealed that all SHGs had a size of 10 members and majority of SHGs (24SHGs) were 'female only' groups. Maximum SHGs were in second stage (13) while 6 SHGs had discontinued their IGAs due to problems like marketing and lack of cooperation among group members. SHGs were formed during the year 2002-03 (17) and were involved in dairy agri-business (10) which was being practiced individually by its members. Out of the total of 28 groups, 20 SHGs had received training. Though all these trainings were sponsored by DRDA, none of the SHGs received any stipend during the training period. The duration of training for maximum number of SHGs (15) was 3-4 days and maximum SHGs (12) were trained at CCS Haryana Agrgicultural University, Hisar between 2003-05. All SHGs who had received training expressed satisfaction with the training provided to them. Meetings of SHGs were conducted monthly by a vast majority of groups (16) at a common place in the village (11 SHGs) and in the after noon period (13 SHGs). The attendance of members in these meetings was more than 90 per cent for vast majority of SHGs (23).

SHGs were dealing mainly with Haryana Gramin Bank and State Bank of India for depositing savings at the rate of Rs. 50/- per member (15 SHGs). Internal loaning was practiced for day to day needs and for meeting emergencies by group members (4SHGs). Group secretary was responsible for maintaining financial records (15 SHGs) and for making bank transactions (18 SHGs). Maximum SHGs (16) gave loan to its members between Rs.401-600, for duration of 1-6 months (17 SHGs) for treatment of illness (15 SHGs) at 1% interest rate (26 SHGs) and there were no defaulters. Majority of SHGs had been sanctioned loans between 3 to 3.2 lacs (19) out of which 11 SHGs had received full amount of loan and 8 SHGs had received only first installment of Rs.1.6 lacs each. Though maximum SHGs (26) did not know the rate of interest, but the pattern of returning loan was found to be regular on monthly basis for 13 SHGs.

The findings of the study have forcefully revealed that inspite of government's large scale efforts, the number of SHGs formed in the villages was far from satisfactory. This has important implications for governmental officials and field functionaries for strengthening the formation of SHGs. NGOs need to work as liason officers between the government policymakers, field functionaries and SHGs to facilitate the smooth functioning of SHGs. NGOs and agricultural universities can also be helpful in monitoring the work of SHGs, imparting skill trainings and developing marketing linkages for facilitating their entrepreneurial activities.

Table 1 Formation of self help groups and type of income generating activities

Aspects	Selected villages V1	V2	V3	V4	V5	V6	V7	n =28 SHGs
	n = 7	N -2	N -2	n = 4	n = 3	n = 3	n = 7	
Number of Self Help Groups	7	2	2	4	3	3	7	28 (100.00)
Stage of SHG								
Ist Stage	3	-	1	1	2	-	2	9 (32.14)
IInd Stage Involved in IGA	4	1	1	2	1	2	2	13 (46.44)
Discontinued IGA*	-	1	-	1	-	1	3	6 (21.42)
Year of establishment								
Jan. 2004-Dec. 2005	3	-	1	-	1	-	1	6 (21.42)
Jan. 2002-Dec. 2003	4	2	1	4	1	3	2	17 (60.71)
Jan. 2000-Dec. 2001	-	-	-	-	1	-	4	5 (17.86)
Initiative taken in formation of SHG								
NGO	2	2	-	2	1	-	2	9 (32.14)
Bank	4	-	-	1	-	-	1	6 (21.42)
Group members	1	-	1	1	-	3	2	8 (28.58)
Government Official (DRDA)	-	-	1	-	2	-	2	5 (17.86)

(Contd.)

(Contd. Table 1)

Aspects	Selected villages V1	V2	V3	V4	V5	V6	V7	n =28 SHGs
	n = 7	N -2	N -2	n = 4	n = 3	n = 3	n = 7	
Composition of SHGs								
Female only	5	2	2	2	3	3	7	24 (85.71)
Male only	2	-	-	2	-	-	-	4 (14.28)
Size of the SHGs								
10 members	7	2	2	4	3	3	7	28 (100.00)
Type of income generating activity								
Masala making	-	-	-	-	-	-	1	1 (3.57)
Vegetable growing	-	-	-	-	-	2	1	3 (10.71)
Surf making	-	-	-	-	-	-	2	2 (7.14)
Dairy	4	2	2	1	-	1	-	10 (35.71)
Sheep rearing	-	-	-	2	1	-	-	3 (10.71)
Not yet started (SHG at stage 1)	3	-	1	1	2	-	2	9 (32.14)

(Contd.)

(Contd. Table 1)

Aspects	Selected villages							
	V1	*V2*	*V3*	*V4*	*V5*	*V6*	*V7*	*n =28 SHGs*
	n = 7	*N -2*	*N -2*	*n = 4*	*n = 3*	*n = 3*	*n = 7*	
Nature of activity								
Individual	4	2	2	1	-	1	-	10 (35.71)
Group	-	-	-	2	1	2	4	9 (32.14)
Not yet started	3	-	1	1	2	-	2	9 (32.14)
***Reasons for discontinuation (n=6)**								
Marketing problem	-	-	-	-	-	1	3	4** (66.66)
Lack of profit	-	1	-	-	-	-	3	4 **(66.66)
Non-cooperation among group members	-	-	-	1	-	-	-	1 (16.66)

Figures in parentheses indicate percentages. * Multiple response

Table 2 Trainings received by self help groups in selected villages

Aspects	*Selected villages*							*n=28 SHGs*
	V-1	*V-2*	*V-3*	*V-4*	*V-5*	*V-6*	*V-7*	
	n = 7	*n* = 2	*N* = 2	*n* = 4	*n* = 3	*n* = 3	*n* = 7	
Training received								
Yes	4	2	-	4	1	3	6	20 (71.42)
No	3	-	2	-	2	-	1	8 (28.58)
Area of training								
Dairy	4	2	-	2	-	1	1	10 (50.00)
Sheep Rearing	-	-		2	1	-	-	3 (15.00)
Vegetable Growing	-	-	-	-	-	3	1	4 (20.00)
Masala Making	-	-	-	-	-	-	1	1 (5.00)
Surf Making	-	-	-	-	-	-	2	2 (10.00)
Place of training								
CCSHAU, Hisar	3	-	-	-	1	3	5	12 (60.00)
DRDA, Sirsa	1	-	-	-	-	-	1	2 (10.00)
Within village	-	2	-	4	-	-	-	6 (30.00)

(Contd.)

(Contd. Table 2)

Aspects				*Selected villages*				*n=28 SHGs*
	V-1	*V-2*	*V-3*	*V-4*	*V-5*	*V-6*	*V-7*	
	n = 7	*n = 2*	*N = 2*	*n = 4*	*n = 3*	*n = 3*	*n = 7*	
Duration of training								
1-2 days	1	-	-	-	-	-	-	1 (5.00)
3-4 days	3	2	-	2	-	3	5	15 (75.00)
5-6 days	-	-	-	2	1	-	1	4 (20.00)
Period of training								
2002-03 (last 4-5 years)	-	-	-	1	-	1	-	2 (10.00)
2003-04 (last 3 years)	-	2	-	-	1	-	6	9 (45.00)
2004-05 (last 2 years)	4	-		3	-	2	-	9 (45.00)
Stipend during training								
No	4	2	-	4	1	2	6	20 (100.00)
Satisfaction with training								
Yes	4	2	--	4	1	3	6	20 (100.00)

Figures in parentheses indicate percentages.

Table 3 Pattern of meetings conducted by self help groups in selected villages

Aspects	*Selected villages*							
	V-1 *N = 7*	*V-2* *n = 2*	*V-3* *N = 2*	*V-4* *n = 4*	*V-5* *n = 3*	*V-6* *n = 3*	*V-7* *n = 7*	*n=28SHGs*
Interval of meetings								
Monthly	5	1	-	1	3	2	4	16 (57.14)
Fortnightly	2	-	2	2	-	-	-	6 (21.43)
Irregular	-	1	-	1	-	1	3	6 (21.43)
Place of meeting								
Anganwadi Center	-	-	-	2	1	1	-	4 (14.28)
SHG's President's residence	4	-	1	1	1	-	3	10 (35.72)
SHG's Secretary's residence	-	1	1	1	-	-	-	3 (10.72)
Common place in village	3	1	-	1	1	1	4	11 (39.28)

(Contd.)

(Contd. Table 3)

Aspects	*Selected villages*							
	V-1 $N = 7$	*V-2* $n = 2$	*V-3* $N = 2$	*V-4* $n = 4$	*V-5* $n = 3$	*V-6* $n = 3$	*V-7* $n = 7$	n=28SHGs
Time of meeting								
Forenoon (10 A.M.-12 A.M.)	2	-	2	2	1	-	4	11 (39.28)
Afternoon (12 A.M.-2 P.M.)	5	2	-	-	2	2	2	13 (46.43)
Evening (4 P.M.-6 P.M.)	-	-	-	2	-	1	1	4 (14.29)
Attendance in meeting								
More than 90%	5	1	2	2	3	2	4	19 (67.85)
70 to 90%	2	-	-	1	-	-	-	3 (10.72)
Less than 70%	1	-	1	-	-	1	3	6 (21.43)
Duration								
One hour	6	2	2	4	2	1	7	24 (85.71)
Two hours	1	-	-	-	1	1	-	3 (10.72)
More than 2 hours	-	-	-	-	-	1	-	1 (3.57)

Figures in parentheses indicate percentages.

Table 4 Saving pattern of self help groups

Aspects	*Selected villages*							
	V1 *n =7*	*V2* *n = 2*	*V3* *n = 2*	*V4* *n =4*	*V5* *n =3*	*V6* *n =3*	*V7* *n =7*	*n= 28 SHGs*
Bank associated								
State Bank of India	-	-	-	-	-	3	7	10 (35.71)
Punjab National Bank	-	2	2	4	-	-	-	8 (28.58)
Haryana *Gramin* Bank	7	-	-	-	3	-	-	10 (35.71)
Money deposited per member per month								
Rs. 50/-	3	-	2	2	3	-	5	15 (53.57)
Rs. 100/-	4	2	-	2	-	3	2	13 (46.43)
Person responsible for maintenance of saving records								
President of self help group	1	-	-	1	1	-	4	7 (25.00)
Secretary of self help group	6	1	-	3	-	3	2	15 (53.57)
Helper	-	1	2	-	2	-	1	6 (21.43)

(Contd.)

(Contd. Table 4)

Aspects				*Selected villages*				
	V1 *n* =7	*V2* *n* = 2	*V3* *n* = 2	*V4* *n* =4	*V5* *n* =3	*V6* *n* =3	*V7* *n* =7	*n*= 28 *SHGs*
Utilisation of saved money								
Making purchases for group	1	-	-	-	-	-	-	1 (3.57)
Internal loaning for daily needs	4	2	2	4	2	2	7	23 (82.14)
Internal loaning for emergencies	2	-	-	-	1	1	-	4 (14.28)
Person responsible for bank transactions								
President of self help group	1	1	1	-	2	4	1	10(35.72)
Secretary of self group	6	1	1	3	3	1	3	18(64.28)

Figures in parentheses indicate percentages.

Table 5 Internal loaning pattern of self groups in selected villages

Aspects	*Selected villages*							*n= 28 SHGs*
	V-1* *N = 7*	*V-2* *n = 2*	*V-3* *n = 2*	*V-4* *n = 4*	*V-5* *n = 3*	*V-6* *n = 3*	*V-7* *n = 7*	
Duration of loan								
1-6 months	4	2	2	2	2	2	3	17 (60.72)
7-12 months	3	-	-	2	1	1	4	11 (39.28)
Amount of loan								
Rs. 201-400/-	-	2	2	2	-	-	3	9 (32.14)
Rs. 401/-600/-	4	-	-	2	3	3	4	16 (57.14)
Rs. 600/-800/-	3	-	-	-	-	-	-	3 (10.72)
Purpose of loan								
Repair of House	-	-	-	-	-	1	1	2 (7.14)
Attending marriage in family	-	-	-	-	1	1	1	3 (10.72)
Visiting relatives	-	1	2	-	-	-	-	3 (10.72)
Illness of family members	4	1	2	-	2	1	5	15 (53.57)
Education	3	-	-	2	-	-	-	5 (17.85)

(*Contd.*)

(Contd. Table 5)

Aspects	*Selected villages*							*n= 28 SHGs*
	V-1* *N = 7*	*V-2* *n = 2*	*V-3* *n = 2*	*V-4* *n = 4*	*V-5* *n = 3*	*V-6* *n = 3*	*V-7* *n = 7*	
Interest rate								
1%	7	2	-	4	3	3	7	26 (92.85)
1 ½ %	-	-	2	-	-	-	-	2 (7.15)
Defaulters in the group								
Yes	-	1	-	1	-	1	3	6 (21.43)
No	7	1	2	3	3	2	4	22 (78.57)
If yes, since when								
3-6 months	-	-	-	-	1	1	2	4 (14.28)

Figures in parentheses indicate percentages.

Table 6 Bank loan sanctioned to self help groups in selected villages

Aspects	*Selected villages*							
	V-1 *N = 7*	*V-2* *n = 2*	*V-3* *n = 2*	*V-4* *n = 4*	*V-5* *n = 3*	*V-6* *n = 3*	*V-7* *n = 7*	*n=28SHGs*
Total loan sanctioned								
Rs. 25,000	3	-	1	1	2	-	2	9 (32.14)
Rs. 3.0 lacs	1	2	-	2	1	3	5	14 (50.00)
Rs. 3.2 lacs	3	-	1	1	-	-	-	5 (17.86)
Amount of loan received								
Nil	3	-	1	1	2	-	2	9 (32.14)
Rs. 1.6 -2.00 lacs	2	2	-	1	-	3	-	8(28.57)
Rs. 3.0 lacs	1	-	-	1	1	-	5	8(28.57)
Rs. 3.2 lacs	1	-	1	1	-	-	-	3 (10.72)

(Contd.)

(Contd. Table 6)

Aspects	*Selected villages*							*n=28SHGs*
	V-1 *N = 7*	*V-2* *n = 2*	*V-3* *n = 2*	*V-4* *n = 4*	*V-5* *n = 3*	*V-6* *n = 3*	*V-7* *n = 7*	
Rate of interest								
Known	-	-	-	2	-	-	-	2 (7.14)
Not known	7	2	2	2	3	3	7	26 (92.85)
Pattern of returning loan								
Regular	4	1	1	2	1	2	2	13 (46.42)
Irregular	-	1	-	1	-	1	3	6 (21.43)
Not applicable	3	-	1	1	2	-	2	9(32.14)
Amount of installment/ member								
Rs. 500/-	4	1	1	1	1	2	2	12(42.85)
Rs. 750/-- to Rs, 1000/-	-	2	1	3	1	-	-	7 (25.00)

References

- **Dahiya P.S, Pandey N.K, and Karol A,** (2002) Socio-economic upliftment of women through self help groups in Solan district of Himachal Pradesh. J. Agric. Development and Policy, 14 (1): 10-19.
- **Kataria K,** (1995) Generation and allocation of economic resources by rural women under DWCRA. M.Sc. Thesis, CCS Haryana Agricultural University, Haryana.
- **Mann S.K,** (2005) An analysis of self help groups for empowerment of rural women in Punjab. Ph.D Thesis, Punjab Agricultural University, Punjab.

16

Assessment of Informtion Level of Adult Women

Dr. Anjali Pattanaik

In respect of food production India is no more deficient in food grains. The report shows that India has a quantum jump from 50 million tones in 1951 to 176 million tones in 1991. But despite this increase in food production the food security of certain communities, like tribal, rural and slum is not guaranteed. Particularly women, the most vulnerable section, continue to face the basic problems such as economic and political inequalities, social discrimination, inadequate access to health care, and lack of adequate knowledge in nutrition for themselves and their families. The reverse sex ratio of 933 women per 1000 men (Census report, 2001) indicates the status of women in our society. India is considered to be a rural country where the women are suffering from ignorance due to illiteracy. The tribal situation in India is complex not only due to their tradition and customs but equally due to illiteracy. Thus, the problem of malnutrition due to ignorance is more prevalent among the mothers and children. Ignorance in respect of food values, food availability, and nutritional requirements of the family members lead to unequal distribution of nutrients and improper utilization of what is available in plenty (WHO/FAQ, 1965). In the above context the present project is an attempt to assess the level of knowledge, practice behavior and information need of women in tribal and rural communities with regard to health and nutrition care of mothers. However, the objectives formulated were:

- To assess information level and consumer media habits, a base line study to be conducted.
- To develop a strategy of low-cost media materials for effective nutrition education.
- To develop low-cost media materials on three major theme areas of pre-natal care such as food and nutrition, consumption of iron and foliate, and immunization
- To distribute need salient massages through media materials to impart education on these three major them areas.
- To assess final impact of low-cost media materials through end-line study.

Design

The study was confined to the adult women, (mothers and would be mothers), and the samples were selected randomly from tribal and rural settings (100 number from each setting). The tribal area was from Phulbani district and the rural area from Puri district of the Orissa state. The methodological approach was a combination approach of family survey, through which socio-economic profile and information level in respect of pre-natal care were drawn by using structured questionnaire; and focus group interview which were carried out with a selected group of community members to make the process participatory one.

In the next phase, a strategy was evolved and low-cost media messages were developed keeping in view the background information of the target community in general and their need saliency in particular, with regard to pre-natal care. The media materials like leaflets and posters were developed, pre-tested, finalized and distributed. Four social animators were selected from within the community and given orientation thoroughly in providing simulation, conducting focus group meetings and collecting feedback. The media messages were distributed in two phases. The posters were affixed in targeted places.

There was a gap of one month between both the phases of distribution of message materials. After the distribution of leaflets, focus group meetings were organized with selected members of the community to bring clarity to the messages. Finally, the evaluative assessment was worked out to draw a comparative conclusion between the base-line and end-line study. Critical ratio (CR) was computed to find out the significant difference between the base-line and end-line reports.

Discussion

Data analysis of background profile of the samples, as presented in Table – 1, reveals that the average monthly income of the samples of tribal and rural groups was Rs.1500 and Rs.2350/- respectively. Their educational background showed that more number of women were illiterate in tribal areas than rural areas, the level of education was better in rural areas than their counterparts in tribal settings.

Table – 1
Background profile

Particulars		*Tribal*	*Rural*
Family income per month (Average)		*Rs.1500.00*	*Rs.2350.00*
Education	Illiterate	67%	5%
	Primary	31%	72%
	Under Metric	2%	23%

Table – 2
Media Exposure

Media	*Tribal*	*Rural*
Radio	73%	72%
News paper	--	6%
TV	--	11%
Cinema	3%	9%
Theatre/Opera	35%	40%
Display	23%	17%

Communication media habits of the samples, as presented in Table – 2, depict that, majority of the samples were exposed to information through radio followed by theatre/opera, display and cinema, and none of the tribal had ever been exposed to TV and newspaper.

Thus, the above review of the background information was found conducive for the purpose of trying out the low-cost nutrition education strategy.

Base-line study (Table – 3) reveals that so far as knowledge aspect was concerned, in tribal area only 16 percent of women had full knowledge about food and nutrition, but none had full information about consumption of iron and foliate, and immunization during pregnancy, and a few had partial information. But in rural communities 23% of women knew fully about nutrition and only 3% of them had full knowledge about consumption of iron and foliate, and immunization. So far as practice behavior was concerned 11% of samples from tribal and 19% from rural areas had the practice of good nutrition, and only 3% of the rural samples had taken iron and foliate and immunization during pre-natal period.

Table – 4 depicts the end-line report which shows that 39% of tribal an 42% of rural women were able to gain full knowledge about nutritional care during pre-natal period, 24% of samples from tribal and 33% of sample from rural set ups were able to understand fully about the importance of consumption of iron and foliate, and immunization.

Table – 3

Knowledge and Practice Behavior- (Base-Line report)

	Knowledge						*Practice Behavior*			
		Tribal			*Rural*		*Tribal*		*Rural*	
	Fully	*Partially*	*Nil*	*Fully*	*Partially*	*Nil*	*Yes*	*No*	*Yes*	*No*
Food and nutrition	16%	23%	61%	24%	36%	40%	11%	89%	19%	81%
Iron and foliate	--	2%	98%	3%	20%	77%	--	100%	3%	97%
Immunization	--	2%	98%	3%	25%	72%	--	100%	3%	97%

Table – 4

Knowledge and Practice Behavior- (End-Line report)

	Knowledge						*Practice Behavior*			
	Tribal			*Rural*			*Tribal*		*Rural*	
	Fully	*Partially*	*Nil*	*Fully*	*Partially*	*Nil*	*Yes*	*No*	*Yes*	*No*
Food and Nutrition	39%	58%	5%	42%	48%	10%	16%	84%	36%	64%
Iron and Foliate	24%	59%	17%	33%	52%	15%	23%	77%	30%	70%
Immunization	24%	51%	25%	33%	53%	14%	23%	77%	30%	70%

So far as the practice behavior was concerned 16% of tribal sample and 36% of rural samples agreed to follow the information about nutrition 23% of tribal samples and 30% of rural samples were convinced to change their practice in respect of iron and foliate; and immunization during pregnancy.

The computation of critical ratio (Table – 5) of those cases who had acquired full knowledge and became convinced fully to practice the new information, shows that the results of baseline and end-line were significantly different in respect of all the three major attributes, except in one case where it was non significant.

Table - 5

Difference between Base-Line and End-Line Results

	TRIBAL				*RURAL*			
				KNOWLEDGE				
	Pre	*Post*	*CR*	*P<*	*Pre*	*Post*	*CR*	*P<*
Food and Nutrition	16%	39%	3.64	0.01	24%	42%	2.70	0.01
Iron and Foliate		24%	5.22	0.01	3%	33%	5.22	0.01
Immunization		24%	5.22	0.01	3%	33%	5.22	0.01
				PRACTICE				
Food and Nutrition	11%	16%	1.03	NS	19%	36%	3.96	0.01
Iron and Foliate		23%	5.09	0.01	3%	30%	5.14	0.01
Immunization		23%	5.09	0.01	3%	30%	5.14	0.01

Thus the observations of base-line and end-line study, focus group interview, and feedback of social animators depict that prior to imparting education, the tribal communities were found lack in knowledge in food and nutrition, iron and foliate, and immunization requirements during pre-natal period. They had also low positive attitude towards change in their practice behavior due to lack of awareness. They were strong believers of traditional practices. End-line report shows that they could develop high level of motivation and were found to be receptive to new information in changing their traditional practices. This was possible, as Ling has stated that "Life styles are no longer conditioned by climate and (traditional) culture. They are initiated as far as communication speeds information from one country to another" (Ling 1989:24). But they were found to be apathetic due to poor socio-economic condition. However their concern for pre-natal care increased with proper educational media exposure and became more adaptive. Knowledge and practice behavior of rural women revealed low positive attitude towards adoption of new practices, and they were very much uncareful about pre-natal care despite some knowledge pertaining to risk factors. They were more influenced by social taboos and misconception. But the impact of nutrition education showed that they were able to improve their awareness level by showing a positive attitude for adoption of better practices. Also they took more interest in clarifying their misconception through mutual sharing and interaction with social animators. However, some of the samples in rural areas were convinced to follow the new practice in their families. Report of Jayagopal (1988:144) shows that health education can be rightly imparted by audio visual aids, mass talks, group discussion and individual counseling. This method cerates awareness in the people to generate interest in them which amounts to motivation to adopt health care practices for the benefit of their own health.

Conclusion

In conclusion it can be stated that the implementation of base-line and end-line study proved media messages worked successfully due to the process of simulation and by making the process participatory. Thus the report of Parthasarathy (1987) on a study of adult learners and drop-outs, states that they were very much persuaded by the messages delivered by the media like Animator articulation, in changing their attitude and knowledge level but the use of radio for the purpose did not produce any change as it lacked visual support or due to vagueness in the delivery of message. The difference between Animator results and Radio results was significant. To touch the problem of lack of information, Government has to chalk out need based programmes and policies. The study revealed that poor health behavior and practices are due to multitude of factors. Thus, for a corrective step there is need for salient nutrition education, and accessible information should be dissemination among the needy women.

REFERENCES

- **Jayagopal, R,** (1988) Communication Technologies in Delivering Health Messages Social Justice in Health: Universities/College Role, Bhatia, SC (ed.), New Delhi, Indian Univ. Asso. For Continuing Education.
- **Ling, Jack. C.S,**(1989) The Media's Role, World Health, Jan-Feb. 24.
- **Parthasarathy, K,** (1987) Study of Persuasive Communication, Techniques and its Effects on Adult Learning at Selected Villages of Chinghpur District in Tamil Nadu Unpublished thesis, University of Madras.

WHO/FAO, (1965) Expert Group on Protein Requirements WHO, Geneva.

17

Vocational Education, Training and Rehabilitation of Persons with the Disabilities in a Technological Era

Prof. Sushil Kumar Goel

India, a beautiful land of different cultures, may be called a unique mosaic. India is a land of contrasts and inequality is increasing at a faster pace. The previous heritage of the great Indian tradition is an amalgam and harmonious blending of a wide variety of colourful cultures. Varied ethnicities, diverse languages and different religions are all orchestrated into the indigenous civilization of India. Thus, Indian society is a plural society and Indian civilization is a conglomeration of traditions. As such, it is difficult to take just one index for the Quality of Life (QOL) and work out a solution. In India, as throughout the world, QOL steers us toward person-centred planning, supporting people's needs and desires, and asking people what they think and how they feel. In today's changing political and economic climate in India, we all need to focus on QOL principles so that people with disabilities will lead fulfilling, self-directed lives (Goel, 2000).

India is a country with highly skilled people but does not provide adequate opportunities for vocational education and training particularly for PWDs. If adequate opportunities of vocational education and training are provided, he or she can be made self-earning, respectable and useful citizen who will enjoy the human rights like all other people. They have to go through very difficult path, undergo vigorous training and make sincerest efforts if the goal "Rehabilitation for All" is to be attained. Quality rehabilitation services at an affordable price are the need of the hour in India today. Innovative applications of modern engineering can go a long way in achieving the country's motto-rehabilitation for all-economically and effectively.

India is a country of diversity. On one hand, we have brilliant scientists, doctors, engineers, educationists and a professional education system that is comparable with the rest of the countries in the world. On the other hand, we are also challenged with the predicament of acute poverty, illiteracy, malnutrition, sickness, infant mortality and disability. India is on the verge of processing one of the strongest information and the telecommunication links like the satellite, ISDN, telephone lines, wireless loops and information technology like videoconferencing/teleconferencing/audio-conferencing that are now available in India provide an answer to the challenge faced by the Indian disability rehabilitation system today.

The rehabilitation of an individual will not be complete if we are not able to make him self sufficient, self-dependent and self-earning member of our society. We have to use modern tools, information technology and other hi-tech methods for imparting training.

Present Day India

After 60 years of planned development, we have reached a stage when we can claim to produce practically everything we need within the country. There has been tremendous progress in S & T within the country during the last six decades. India's progress in S & T has been accepted and acknowledged by all countries of the world. With such a wide spectrum that India is covering in S & T, the question often asked is, why should India remain an underdeveloped and poor country and why we have to face hard realities such as balance of payment shortage of energy, shortage of foreign exchange, growing unemployment and continuing poverty? Today, our country is underdeveloped due to lack of linkages between one type of expertise and the other. India has got some peculiar problems. It has about 6, 00,000 villages and about three-fourth population lives in villages. To quote the words of Mahatma Gandhi, "If the village perishes, India perishes too". India will be no more India, her own mission in the world will be lost. The rural development holds the key for our national development. CAPART (Council for People's Action and Rural Technology), major organization of the Government of India, set up for promoting rural development has recently initiated supporting disability rehabilitation programmes. This is a very healthy development and a positive step because nearly 80 percent of our handicapped population lives in the rural areas. Thus many traditional occupations being pursued by visually handicapped persons are likely to continue throughout the country. Looking back over the last sixty years, we find that employment market for the people with visual disabilities consists mainly of open employment, sheltered employment, self employment and employment in the disability field. The only way of reaching out to the millions of the unreached persons with disabilities in rural areas is by initiating CBR programmes.

Information Technology is another area which is developing very fast for the employment and empowerment for the disabled. Necessary technical expertise can be sought from

IITs, DST, DRDO, NASSCOM, NISTADS, and other IT companies. Computers have taken every conceivable field of operation today. Regular schools in metropolitan cities have begun introducing children to computers from as early an age as seven years. Children with visual impairment require more expensive special equipment and software in order to keep up with the present trend. Special schools as well as other organizations working for them have very little choice but to go for it.

Empowerment

Disability is an issue that concerns all of us; it can affect anybody, of any background, in any country, at any time. In India, disability has so far been perceived as a problem and not a priority. Disability is not a charity issue, but it is a rights issue. People with disabilities want to be treated like other citizens, with rights. They want to be treated equally and to participate as equal citizens in their communities. There have been major shifts in the perception of disabled people's rights, from charity to social development, from treatment to prevention, from dependency to empowerment, from humanitarian concern to human rights. Self-awareness and self-confidence are two key essentials of empowerment. These have to be coupled with a realistic acceptance of the disability and a belief in oneself. It follows that for an individual to become empowered, the person needs to acquire knowledge, develop skills, and be motivated. To be empowered means "our inner being-our unique self-is vested with power and inner strength. When we feel empowered, we can meet challenges with confidence. Once we are empowered we have personal power and control over our lives. We have positive self-images that are affirmed and sustained."

Information Services

The major problem is that persons with disabilities and their parents do not know their rights and empowerment is a new concept for them in India. Knowledge is power and we must empower them with adequate information services which they richly deserve. The advancements taken place throughout the country should reach the grass-root level. The biggest problem faced by the visually handicapped is the lack of awareness of the resources from where the services can be utilized. While talking about access to information, it is necessary to emphasize the right of handicapped people to receive information about services which have been designed especially for their use. Right to obtain information through all accessible channels is one of the recognized fundamental rights of all blind persons, as indeed of all citizens. In the age of S & T, the fresh information is being generated at an exponential rate and it has become extremely difficult to face the information explosion. In order that a visually handicapped person should enjoy full participation and equality in every aspect of his life, it is imperative that information should be communicated in the form accessible to him. The efforts in India have not been properly initiated for systematic storage, retrieval and dissemination of information about various occupations, job components, organizations for training and placement, etc for the handicapped, especially in the rural areas. The institutions for the handicapped are scattered in different sectors without having any system of network among them, they function unilaterally in most cases and also do not have proper facilities to the information needs of visually handicapped persons, research scientists and service professionals working in them to the extent required. Scientific research which is a vital need for economic and social progress of the country is much hampered in this situation. The formulation and implementation of National Information System (NATIS) in 'special education and rehabilitation" is the only way to ensure that all engaged in research and development have access to the information they need. Information is a basic resource and link between a variety of activities, intellectual and material, in the society, institutions and individuals. Access to precise and reliable information in the most convenient form is essential for national development and help to minimize the wastage of resources. Information is the key for empowerment of families and communities. This situation calls for increased cooperation of subject specialists and information specialists (Goel, 1985, 1990). Networks will go a long way to break up the barriers standing between information and their users. There is a tremendous amount of disability related information on the internet. In the advanced countries, there are many internet web sites for some specific disability groups and many agencies are providing information search and retrieval services in special education and rehabilitation. Developments in Information Technology like Online Computerized Databanks, Online Rehabilitation Databases, etc have given a boost to visually impaired. A synthetic speech output for the blind has been developed whereby a microcomputer can speak to its operator, avoiding the need to translate printed information into Braille. Auditory form is the most important means to have access to information through talking books, talking computers, talking word processors, stereo cassette recorders, wireless, etc. Voice Indexing Device will allow random access to the pages of a talking book. They have already developed many databases and information products in the field of special education and rehabilitation. In India also various network systems like DELNET, INFLIBNET, OPENET, etc and many internet web sites have been launched to provide indigenous online database services on different subjects, but there is hardly any information in the field of special education and rehabilitation in the Indian context. The author has highlighted various challenges and emerging concerns in information-based rehabilitation of visually handicapped in India (Goel, 2001).

Vocational Education, Training and rehabilitation

All children and adults need school education, and a large number of them require vocation education and training (VET) in order to become self–sufficient in life. The quality of vocational is very important, it should be need based and avilbale to them vary close to their doorsteps and it should be imparted by trained instructors in a very conducive environment. If a person is not provided VET and properly rehabilitated, he will become a burden on the family and also on the society at large for the whole life. Hence rehabilitation of PWDs is absolutely necessary form the humanitarian point of view and also from the national economy point of view. The salient features of the total rehabilitation program are identification, medical care, aids and appliances, VET and finally the job placement. VET is one of the important avenues in order to rehabilitate a PWD in the society.

Inclusive education should be available to PWDs at primary, secondary and higher levels. It is necessary to provide all types of education (special, integrated, formal, non-formal) to them in both rural and urban areas. Mainstreaming these children in social, cultural, sport and vocational education centres should be encouraged from the very beginning. Assistive devices should be provided for better efficiency and optimum functioning in day-to-day life. On-the-job training needs to be provided to them for their practical orientation.

Vocational rehabilitation centres need to be set up in the rural area also in order to train them near their place of living in the appropriate occupations. Vocational rehabilitation is a process that assists individuals with impairments to overcome their handicaps and try to reintegrate them into society into a job or vocation using their residual physical and intellectual capacities. Vocational evaluation procedures take many forms, ranging from tests for specific functions to more complex assessments. The major aims of rehabilitation are given a under

1. to develop form of communication (gesture, speech, typing and with sign or electronic aids).
2. to develop independence in the daily activities of eating, drinking, dressing, washing, toileting and general self-care.

3. to play and develop recreational activities.
4. to develop some form of locomotion and independent mobility which may include wheelchairs, electronic mobile buggies or driving motor vehicles.

A final step in community reintegration in return to work. Various programs can be designed to provide

1. vocational assessment
2. vocational training
3. placement into job in the community or sheltered work setting.

During the long recovery process, a person may be identified who can provide crucial coordination and social support. This role is filled by

1. social worker
2. vocational evaluator and socio-vocational counsellor
3. placement officer

The case manager serves

1. As a liaison between the patient, family and service provider
2. To maintain medical records
3. Arrange for medical visits, screen programs and facilities
4. To co-ordinate with financial and insurance matters, which are of critical importance in long term planning.

Regular vocational training with the help of trained instructors, vocational counselors, psychologists, occupational therapists and family members should be imparted at the institution as well as home. The future of PWDs can be reasonably achieved through teamwork and cooperation of people. The author has prepared "An Orientation Guide For Promotion Of Vocational Education And Training Among Persons With Disabilities" which would apprise the parents/ teachers / employers / community members/ teacher educators/ etc. about the strengths and assets of PWDs and will go a long way to create awareness among various sections of the society

(Goel 2005). The objective behind the document on VET has been to present a comprehensive picture of disability in a readily comprehensible, useful and supportive manner. This document will serve as an essential tool not only for professionals working in different areas of disability rehabilitation but to the policy planners and administrators as well. The author has completed another project entitled " Compendium of Scientific and Technological Developments For The Vocational Rehabilitation Of Persons With Disabilities." (Goel 2006). The main goal of this project was to coordinate, compile and develop a proper database of the aids and appliances for the education, training and rehabilitation of PWDs, especially in the Indian context. The Scientific and Technological Developments in the field of disability rehabilitation were scattered and no effort had so far been made to consolidate this voluminous information. The document entitled "A Database Of Vocational Education, Training And Rehabilitation Services For PWDs In India" provides an overview of the historic developments, approaches, innovations and the services on VET for PWDs in the Indian context. It not only provides rich knowledge and material for trainers, but it also provides a forum for future discussion in various training programs within the country.

Tele-Rehabilitation

There is an urgent need to have a nation wide tele-rehabilitation programme that will connect specialists in various fields of disabilities (speech pathology, audiology, ophthalmology, ENT, orthopedics, pediatrics, psychology, education, social work, etc.) with the rural communities through the internet. Tele-rehabilitation means rehabilitation from a distance i.e. the service provider and the recipients do not have direct contact with each other. Ability Foundation, Action Aid (India), Ann Foundation (NY), CBR Network, Directorate of Disability Welfare (Karnataka), Spastic Society, Bangalore, etc. have already taken a lead in this direction.

Technological Advancements

Technological aids certainly include computers, but it could also refer to a number of other types of device which enable individuals with disabilities to function more independently. Computers are an important type of technological aid because they open up so many exciting possibilities for writing, speaking, finding information, or controlling an individual's environment, though computers are not the only avenues to solving problems through technology. Many assistive technology projects are available in advanced countries and are mainly engaged in manufacturing of technology-based devices for PWDs. Sophisticated technological interfaces in the form of special keypads, touch screens, wireless sensors are all available with their resource directory. Most of these devices are not affordable to Indian masses. Hence our main aim should be to produce quality rehabilitation aids through internal sources so that Indian mass can use it with in an affordable price.

There is lot of technological advancement in our country. Still due to lack of integration of corresponding medical and technical knowledge, most of the existing designs are stil in a crude form. These technological interfaces are to be multimedia-based front-end to complex technologies. The software is to be designed to take care of a user-centered approach, which is compatible with the user's expectation, provides the user with flexibility and control, explicit structure, continuous and informative feedback, error prevention and correction, and on-line help. This will help the subject as well as the healthcare workers to use these interfaces with ease without realizing the complexities involved. The rehabilitation team should aim at interacting with industrial and development groups to help in arriving at ultimate production design.

It is to be noted that people are not handicapped by their disabilities but by obstacles or barriers in their living environment. In order to meet a compromise between affordable prices for an essential utility in any part of the country, we have to find means of designing and developing the existing technologies according to the requirement of our society. Skilled volunteer engineers, design technicians and health workers should integrate to make assistive aids so that greater independence could be achieved for any PWD.

In India, many organizations are now manufacturing aids and applications for PWDs. Today ALIMCO is one such leading organization which is the largest Artificial Limbs Manufacturing Unit in entire South Asia. Alimco was incorporated on 29th November 1972 and is a Non Profit Organization (A Government of India Undertaking) working under the Ministry of Social Justice and Empowerment.

Alimco is manufacturing 355 types of aids and appliances of various categories.

Different categories of product being manufactured

- Orthopedically handicapped
- Visually handicapped
- Hearing handicapped
- Special Purpose Tools & Equipments

Alimco is committed to manufacture and supply of pre fabricated components of prosthetic/ orthotic systems and other rehabilitation aids/assistive devices for orthopedically, visually and hearing impaired at reasonable cost and for promoting, encouraging and developing the availability, use, supply and distribution of these aids and appliances across the length and breadth to the country through continual improvement in progress and technology.

For artificial limbs, jaipur foot technology is famous all over the world. Bhagwan Mahaveer Viklang Sahayta Samiti (BMVSS) Jaipur works in the collaboration with hospitals and medical colleges. BMVSS has always tried to provide the best artificial limbs to the amputee who comes from far and wide to get their artificial limbs.

India has a very large population of the lower-limb amputees. About 80% of them live in rural areas. The functional, socio-economic and cultural requirements of the Indian amputees are different from the western world. The conventional lover limb prosthesis has got a foot-ankle assembly which requires to be covered and protected with shoes which are expensive and add to the cost of prostheses. Moreover, the replacement is a costly affair for a poor villager. It was not only the shoe but also the other aspects of the prosthesis which demanded some innovations.

The growing industrialization /urbanization of the third world countries and a global upsurge of civil wars, use of landmines, insurgencies and terrorism demand handling of unprecedented number of amputees who have to be provided with limbs at reasonable cost, in a short time, and which will suit with their socio-economic culture. The advantage of the "JAIPUR FOOT and LIMB" have made it the most versatile technology which has, so far, successfully addressed the above problems not only in India but also in many other countries.

Science and the Technology Development Projects in Mission Mode

The Govenrnment of India has launched a Science and Technology Project in Mission Mode on Application of Technology for the Welfare and Rehabilitation of the Handicapped, to address the need for adopting an end-to-end approach beginning with R&D and ending with gainful utilization by the poorest of people with disabilities (PWDs) in all parts of the country. This project has the objective of coordinating, funding and directing application of technology in the development and utilization of : (a) Suitable and cost effective aids and appliances, and (b) Methods of education and skill development leading to enhancement of opportunities for employment, easier living and mobility, communication, recreation and integration in society.

With a view to provide suitable and cost-effective aids and appliances through the application of technology and also to improve the mobility, employment opportunities and integration of the disabled in the mainstream, the scheme of Science and Technology (S&T) - Project in Mission Mode was launched in 1988.

Science and Technology Projects in Mission Mode represent a new approach aimed at ensuring that emerging inter-disciplinary efforts to have the potential meet large scale societal/national needs, and can fulfill their potential in a time-targeted manner. The emphasis is on an end-to-end approach covering Research and Development as well as technological, financial, administrative and management aspects. These projects concentrate on new scientific inputs, generation of new technologies and guiding these to large-scale use.

The objectives of such projects, are to coordinate, fund and direct application of technology for development and utilization of :

(a) Suitable and cost effective aids and appliances
(b) Emphasis on education and skill development leading to enhancement of opportunities for employment
(c) Easier living and integration in society.

The Government of India had launched for the first five years a coordinated program for developing aids and appliances for persons with disability. The financial assistance is provided on a 100 per cent basis.

Some interesting and innovative products, for the use of persons with disabilities, have been developed by organizations funded under this scheme. These are :

- Speech Synthesizer
- Inter pointing Braille writing frame
- Close Circuit TV with magnification facility
- Photo-voltaic charger
- Safety devices for agricultural machinery
- Feeding aids for children with cerebral palsy
- Multifunctional wheel-chair
- Electronic guide stick

- Telefilm for training of parents of mentally retarded
- Video films on safe use of agricultural machinery
- Microprocessor based braille embosser.

Assistance to Disabled Persons for Purchase/ Fitting of Aids/Appliances

The main objective of the scheme is to assist needy persons in procuring durable, sophisticated and scientifically manufactured aids and appliances that promote their physical, social and psychological rehabilitation. The scheme is implemented through centers run by the companies registered under Companies Act, registered societies, trusts or any other institutions recognized by the Ministry of Social Justice & Empowerment for the purpose. A large number of governmental and non-governmental agencies are engaged for the implementation of the scheme. Aids and appliances such as wheelchairs, crutches, calipers, hearing aid, Braille slates, etc. are given to different categories of PWDs. Indian citizens possessing a certificate from a registered medical practitioner can benefit under the scheme. PWDs in need of aids and appliances are given travel allowance subject to a limit of Rs. 150/- for visit to implementing agencies' center. The boarding and lodging expenses at the rate of Rs. 10 per day subject to Rs. 150/- per beneficiary are also admissible in cases where the income of such persons is up to Rs. 1200/- per month.

Assistive Devices for the Visually Impaired

Assistive devices for the Visually impaired can be divided into the following six categories: (i) Educational Devices (ii) Mobility Devices (iii) Vocational Devices (iv) Daily Living Devices (v) Low Vision Devices (vi) Psychological and Learning Aptitude Tests.

Visually impaired users face a great challenge when interacting with graphical user interfaces. Typically, they use software applications known as screen readers that turn the texts, events, and elements in applications and websites into synthesised speech. For example, when a user opens a new window in Microsoft Internet Explorer, a screen reader such as JAWS (Job Access with Speech) or Home Page Reader might say "new browser window".

Another AT for the visually challenged is refreshable Braille display, which may be used as an alternative to screen reader. These devices convert screen text into Braille and display the Braille on a number of cells comprised of independently controlled pins. When editing and reviewing text, refreshable Braille displays can be much better to work with because a vision-impaired user can easily reread characters on the same line and check spelling. Screen readers are capable of reading words character by character, but the process of moving backwards in text to review and then moving forwards can be cumbersome. Despite their potential advantage, refreshable Braille displays are less common due to their higher cost.

In addition, a Braille embosser converts computer-generated text into embossed Braille output. Braille translation programs convert text scanned in or generated via standard word processing programs into Braille, which can be printed on the embosser. The results on thick paper are the individual dots that constitute Braille characters.

However, choice of appropriate hardware and software will depend on the user's level of functional vision. Put another way, it relies on the intensity of impairment. For example, low-vision users can use hardware such as large monitors, adjustable task lamp, Copyholder, closed circuit television, modified cassette recorder, and scanner to improve visibility. Moreover, this can be helpful to people who have difficulty reading or seeing self-voicing applications such as talking web browsers.

Devices could be procured from organizations/institutions where appropriate rehabilitation services are provided. To mention a few (i) National Institute for the Visually Handicapped (NIVH) Dehradun and their branches (ii) National Association for the Blind (NAB) Louis Braile Memorial Research Centre, Mumbai – their branches (iii) Blind People's Association, Ahmedabad.

Here are some of the following devices which may be used for children with visual impairments :

Audible Flying Disc
Audio Calculator
Audio Spirit Level
Automatic Drink Measurer
Braille Educational Kit
Braille on Magnetic Cassette
Braillink's Word Processor
Closed Circuit T.V.
Colour Tell Machine
Computerized Travel Aid
Electric Sewing Machine
Electronic Compass
Env/Inland Letter Addresser
Kurzweill Reading Machine
Laser Cane
Meganote Taker
Mowat Sensor
Notex
Paperless Brailler
Path Sounder
Pen-Pencil Writing Frame
Perkins Brailler
Rain Alert
Raised-Line Copier
Safety Device
Slate and Stylus
Sonic Guide
Sonic Weighing Balance
Speech Synthesizer
Tactile Image Generator
Taj Brailler
Talking Book
Talking Bus Stop
Talking Clocks
Talking Wrist Watches
Telebraille
Telesensory

Although hearing impaired individuals encounter less accessibility than the visually challenged do, they face tremendous difficulty in terms of learning, job access and social inclusion. These are due to the traditional way of learning.

Assistive Devices for the Hearing Handicapped

However, computer technology has emerged as blessing to the hearing impaired. As computer prompts such as spoken messages and beeps can be misunderstood or go unnoticed by hearing impaired individuals, this problem is solved through the use of tools that produce visual warning when the system plays a sound and/or display captions in place of a spoken message. Light signaller alerts the computer with light signals. This is useful when a computer user cannot hear computer sounds. As an example, a light can flash alerting the user when a new e-mail message has arrived or a computer command has completed.

In addition, hearing impaired person can use TTY/TDD (Telecommunication Device for the Deaf), which is an electronic device for text communication via a telephone line, telecare, closed captioning, teletext and multimedia projector to address accessibility problem. Moreover, newer text-based communication methods such as short message service (SMS), internet relay chat (IRC) and instant messaging have also been accepted by the deaf as an alternative or adjunct to TDD.

Listening Devices: Hearing aids, FM transmission and amplification devices and audio loops are special types of equipment that help people with hearing impairments and make better use of their residual hearing.

Telecommunication Devices: Keyboards with screens or printers connected to telephones take advantage of vision to improve communication for people with hearing impairments. Computers, fax/modems and e-mail are recent developments in this rapidly changing area.

Techno Talk: People who have difficulties in speaking have the right to express themselves. One of the primary areas of focus is the use of technology for the development of communication tools. Indian Institute of Cerebral Palsy (IICP), Kolkata has taken some initiatives, which have resulted in the development of voice output devices and specially designed software, which can enhance communication skills of children and adults. Technology places a vital role in supplementing educational skills with the use of different software with adaptive hardware, such as special access switches. It further facilitates written communication and enhances leisure skills with multimedia, internet, games, and drawing. Some of the communication aids developed by IICP are : 'My Stamp Book', 'Kathamala', 'Indian Symbols for Picture Communication', Sanjog', etc. 'My Stamp Book' includes a collection of 850 culturally appropriate picture symbols which are categorized for easy searching with multiple pictures of frequently used symbols and a detailed index helps to locate the symbols. Kathamala let to the development of 'voice output communication aid' (VOCA). Communication competence and participation can be enhanced with the use of a VOCA. 'Indian Symbols for Picture Communication' is a tool comprising 1650 indigeneously developed pictures for facilitators, helping them to design communication displays. 'Sanjog' is a communication software with a synthetic speech and this project has been undertaken in collaboration with IIT, Kharagpur.

Here are some of the following devices which may be used for children with hearing impairment:

Alerting Devices	Telecommunication Devices for Deaf
Audiometer	Automated Teaching System
Behind the Ear	Educational toys
Bone Conduction Receiver	Hansel Training System
Hearing Aid	Language Master
NUVOX Telephone Amplifier	Memory Remediation

NUVOX Telephone Coupler
Sound Lamp
Speech Trainer
Microcomputers
Self-feeding tray
Talking Typewriter
Touch-Tutor

Assistive Devices for the Mentally Handicapped

Persons with Mental handicap form the most heterogeneous group, and no two individuals of the same category are alike. Their profiles and current level of functioning are different. Hence the teaching – learning materials are to be prepared according to the needs of the individual. However certain T & L materials are provided by the NIMH in the forms of folders, hand-outs, brochures which are helpful to teachers/ parents and community workers to train the person with mental retardation to develop – skills that are socially accepted and age appropriate in the attainment of a dignified place in the society. Teaching and learning material could be procured from certain institutions like : (i) Ekalavya Institute, Bhopal, (ii) Ed-Craft, Hyderabad, (iii) THPI, Hyderabad, (iv) Life Help Centre for Handicapped, Madras.

Some of the following aids may be useful for children with mental retardation :

1. Pegs
   Aims: To teach general awareness (number skill through play-way method).
2. Dominoes
   Aim: To teach colour concept
3. Sensorial Appartus
   Aim: To teach size concept
4. Matching Cards
   Aim: To teach how to match various types of figures
5. Recreational Toys
   Aim: To teach motor ability

6. Geometrical Shapes
   Aim: To teach shape concept
7. Mathematical Signs
   Aim: To teach number skills
8. Model Clock
   Aim: To teach time concept
9. Alphabets/Digits
   Aim: To teach the child pre-reading.

In view of many advantages and computer revolutions, there is a need to provide trained manpower, suitable hardware and software to improve the quality of life of children with mental retardation in inclusive schools, special schools and rehabilitation centers (Goel 2002).

Computer programs can

- Generate instructional objectives
- Produce records of progress and report card
- Administer, score and interpret test performance
- Record and analyze classroom observations
- Generate instructional activities
- Manage meeting schedules
- Store information about community resources
- Enhance student interaction and motivation
- Provide immediate feedback
- Teach reading, spelling, arithmetic skills, communication skills, etc.
- Provide needed reinforcement
- Allow self paced instruction
- Store student's health, discipline and academic records
- Free the teacher to work with other students while some students work on the computer
- Help in systematic planning implementation, evaluation and documentation
- Increase cognitive skills, memory, and logic
- Develop joy and sense of achievement

Thus, the micro computer is extremely useful as a teaching aid . Initially it may seem expensive but it is a quite reliable and economical teaching aid for the children with mental retardation in the long run if the schools are able to procure appropriate hardware and software.

Assistive Devices for the Locomotor Handicapped

Mobility impairment refers to any condition that limits an individual's ability to navigate through their environment. Mobility assistive technology products and services for the physically challenged are used to ensure freedom of movement around the home or office. . A permanent or portable ramp can also help in this regard.

Devices for the Locomotor handicapped include wheel chairs, crutches, calipers, braces, modified shoes, artificial limbs, splints, walkers, etc. that promote their physical, social and psychological rehabilitation.

- A student having no upper limb can operate the computer having keyboard with key-guards with foot or by using an electronic head-pointer fixed on the forehead.
- A student having no upper and lower limb can use optically operated computer keyboard. The key is triggered by the passing by passing an optical light, ordinary light, infrared light or laser beam can be used.
- Information technology can be helpful to the students with orthopedic disability in following ways :
    - On-line education through computer mediated communication,
    - electronic lecture
    - collaborative learning,
    - tele-teaching,
    - online testing,
    - digital resource library,
    - virtual classroom,

- speech recognition
- synthesis based software

ALIMCO, Kanpur is the pioneering oranisation that manufactures and distributes to institutions registered under companies act, registered societies, trusts recognized by the Ministry of Social Justice and Empowerment.

Some of the following aids may be useful for children with orthopaedic disabilities:

Automatic Page Turner	Institutional Relaxation Chair
Bus Wheel Chair Lift	Leg Brace/Splint
Dorsal Feeding Splints	LS Brace
Drive Control Units	Stair Climbing Wheel Chair
Finger Shoulder Ladd	

Assistive Technology and Inclusion

Disablement, needless to say, significantly reduces the life quality of a person as it substantially diminishes their work ability. Assistive or adaptive technology, however, can bring back the individual's employability at an acceptable level.

Unfortunately, most people, even the disabled themselves, in the third world countries are not aware that assistive technology may become their real friend in assisting them in everyday life. I would like to highlight in this article some assistive technologies for different types of disabilities; before that it is worth mentioning what an assistive technology means.

There is no specific definition of Assistive Technology (AT). It simply denotes any item, piece of equipment, or system that is used to increase, maintain or improve functional capabilities of individuals with disabilities.

The definition does not necessarily imply that AT must include computers, or that it must be expensive, or that certain medical professionals can only prescribe it. Special educators, who support students in inclusive settings, are becoming more proficient at adapting core curriculum, infusing basic skills into daily activities, and scheduling staff, students and other resources to best meet students' needs. Although many educators are utilizing a range of "supplementary aids and services" necessary to educate students with disabilities with their non-disabled peers, many are not sufficiently familiar with assistive technology to use it effectively. There is a wealth of material on accessing assistive technology resources. However, these resources are often underutilized and will remain so until teachers and other school professionals learn the basics. There are a number of issues that need attention when considering the use of assistive technology.

1. **Involve the student with the disability in the process.**

Studies show that one of the main reasons individuals do not use assistive technology devices, even when they would be helpful, is because they were not involved in the selection of the equipment (Scherer, 1993)*. We all have priorities of color, style, and durability. Some students enjoy the attention that accompanies using a device with lots of bells and whistles; others have a difficult time with being the center of attention. Family members as well as peers are often helpful in determining such details. By involving families in the process, the likelihood of technology use at home is greater. By involving peers in the process, on-the-spot problem solving occurs on a regular basis. Such critical thinking skills can be incorporated into science and social studies lessons as students are introduced to the use of assistive technology. As an experiential component, they may then require the students to invent an item that could be used by an individual with a disability.

2. **Target a specific activity.**

It is extremely difficult to buy or design an adaptation if the end goal is not clear. Often professionals look for devices that are available and then try to "fit" them to the students. This is problematic because if the student's priorities are not considered, it is unlikely that the device will be utilized. A more productive approach is to identify the activity in which the student needs or wishes to participate so that the initial research into existing adaptations takes on a direction.

3. Look for people with "technical expertise" beyond the educational realm.

Teachers rarely consider identifying people who have specific skills in carpentry, electronics, mechanical engineering, computers, and general "fix-it" skills to help with the design and construction of adaptations. There are a number of programs across the country that use volunteers to help develop customized adaptations for individuals. Once activities and technology needs have been identified, tapping into service organizations for additional expertise and funding can bring remarkable results. Coordinating efforts with technical classes in high schools, community colleges and universities which require specific projects can provide mutual benefits.

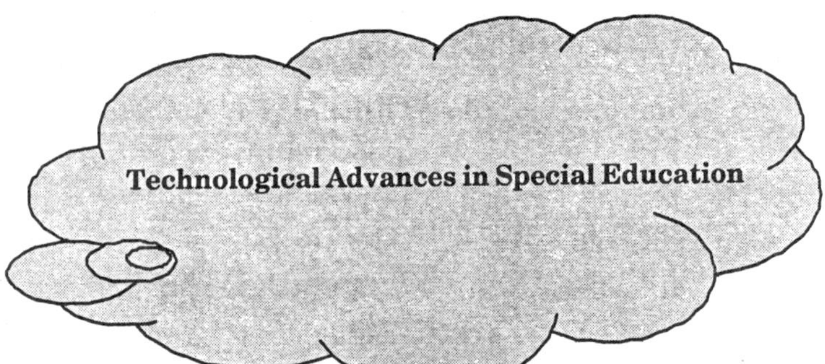

The following technological advances may be considered in the field of special education:

- Prevention of disabilities
- Developing the inherent capabilities of people with disabilities
- Manufacture & fabrication of aids & appliances
- Bringing about changes in the environment.

Criteria to use Technology

#	Feasibility	#	Simplicity
#	Acceptability	#	Flexibility
#	Interchangeability	#	Portability
#	Affordability	#	Durability
#-	Serviceability		

Aids and Appliances Serve Specific Purposes

- Aids for personal care
- Aids for household work
- Aids for location
- Aids for transportation
- Aids for communication
- Aids for vision
- Aids for learning
- Aids for leisure time

Technological inputs in Education

- To improve the efficiency of teachers
- To reduce the cost of education
- To improve the quality of education
- To decrease the duration in the realization of educational objectives
- To bring more children under the umbrella of education
- To develop the specific temper in the learner

Advantages of Microcomputers

- Enhancing student interaction and motivation
- Providing immediate feedback
- Providing record-keeping capabilities & IEP development
- Providing needed reinforcement
- Allowing self-paced instruction
- Freeing the teacher to work with other students while some students work on the computer.

General Rules in Procurement of Aids and Appliances for PWDs

- After thorough assessment and diagnostic evaluations – recommendations of aids and appliances for PWDs are from competent persons of the concerned discipline.
- ADIP scheme to be strictly followed which states – income below Rs.5000/- p.m. gets the aids/appliances free of cost. Income between Rs.5000/- to Rs.8000/- p.m. pays 50% of the cost of any particular aid and income above Rs.8000/- p.m. pays the full cost of the aid/appliance.
- Proof of the client in the form of two photographs and authentic income slip/ photocopy of ration card.
- Renewals of aids and appliances once in three years.

List of Manufacturers

1. Advance Engineering Works
   22 Lytton Road, Dehradun
2. Amar Enterprises, 99/101, Keshavji Naik Road, Bombay
3. Ambalal Munshi Nature Cure Hospital, Ambalal Munshi Foundation
   12/13 Boat Club Road, Pune
4. Anchor Industries, 185, Bombay Talkies Compound, Malad, Bombay-

5. Artificial Limbs Manufacturing Corporation
   G T Road, Kanpur
6. Asian Power Cyclopes
   Rochipura, PO : Majra, Dehradun
7. Bajaj Electricals Ltd. 45-47, Veer Nariman Road, Bombay
8. Baliwala and Homi Private Ltd.,
   614, Jagannath Shankersheth Marg, Dhobi Talao, Bombay
9. Bharat Graphics
   194, Industrial Area Phase-II, Chandigarh
10. Blind Boys Academy, Ramakrishna Mission Ashram
    PO : Narendrapur, 24, Paraganas (W.B.) – 743
11. Blind People's Association, Near Indian Institute of Management
    Dr. Vikram Sarabhai Road, Vastrapur, Ahmedabad – 380 015
12. Empire Industries Ltd, Empire House, 414
    Senapati Bapat Marg, Mumbai – 400 013
13. Fellowship of the Physically Handicapped
    F.P.H. Building, Lala Lajpatrai Marg, Hazi Ali, Bombay – 400
14. Gujarat Type Foundry, Gaiwadi, Giragaum, Bombay – 400 044
15. HES Limited, Patel Estate
    Jogeshwari (West), Mumbai - 400 102
16. Hind Optial Company, Kalbadevi Road, Bombay – 400 002.
17. Hindustan Machine Tools Ltd, Watch Marketing Division
    26/1, Levelle Road, Bangalore - 560 001
18. IDEM Thermoformers
    Wonderpack Industries, 72 I Floor, Shivlal Mansion
    Lamington Road, Near Mumbai Central, Mumbai – 400 008
19. Indian Communications Network Pvt. Ltd.
    306, Tulsiani Chambers, Nariman Point, Mumbai – 400 021
20. Indian Institute of Technology
    Hauz Khas, New Delhi – 110 016

21. Indian Telephone Industries Ltd., Western Region, Advent Building
Bhosale Marg, Bombay – 400 021.
22. J. Dutta & Co., Hadavkar Compound, Bhavani Shankar Cross Road,
Behind Jai, Gopal Industrial Estate, Dadar (W. Rly) – Bombay – 400 028
23. Latha Industries
89/1 Triplicane High Road, Triplicane, Chennai – 600 005
24. Mahavir Brothers, 202, Triveni House, Khetwadi Back Road
Opp. 13th Lane, Bombay – 400 004.
25. Mansukhlal Company, Optician, Kalbadevi Road, Bombay – 400 002.
26. M.M. Industries, Hampton Court, Nathalee Parekh Marg, Near Coloba PO., Mumbai – 400 006.
27. Minal Engineering Limited
214/A, Paradise Complex
Sayajigunj, Vadodara – 390 005, Gujarat
28. Moksha Enterprises
F-6, Nacharam Industrial Estate
Road No.18, Nacharam, Hyderabad – 500 076 (AP)
29. NAB Louis Braille Memorial Research Centre
Rustom Alpaiwala Complex
124-127, Cotton Depot, Cotton Green, Mumbai – 400 033
30. NAB Talking Book Studio, c/o The NAB Workshop for the Blind
11, Khan Abdul Gaffar Khan Road, Worli Seaface, Mumbai – 400 025
31. National Institute for the Visually Handicapped
116, Rajpur Road, Dehradun – 248 001 (UP)
32. National Rehabilitation Engineering Institute
Blind People's Association, Vastrapur, Ahmedabad – 380 015
33. National Scientific Company
1958, Pilanji Kotla, Mubarakpur, New Delhi – 110 003

34. Navjivan Textiles, 37, Jijabhai Dadabhai Lane,
    Behind Handloom House, Mumbai – 400 001
35. Photophones Ltd., 7, Saki Vihar Road, Bombay – 400 072
36. Pinball Manufacturing Co.
    147, GIDC Makarpura Industrial Estate, Vadodara
37. Pneumatic Controls
    35-B, Rama Road, New Delhi – 110 015

Conclusion

It is hoped that in the 21st century many web sites may be launched on the Internet by leading agencies for the benefit of the PWDs in India. Since the country is moving towards rapid development in IT sector, it is hoped that they will have a great future in the new millennium. We are living in democratic India. Democracy means transparency and transparency stands for right to information. With rapid industrialization, India is heading towards information revolution. IT is an agent of transformation of every aspect of human life. While education is creating a learning society, IT is making it knowledge-based. A new awareness is on the increase, so is its application in our social and economic life. It is fast penetrating into our rural areas. It is becoming increasingly important that millions of people with disabilities and rehabilitation practitioners do their own thinking to develop information-based rehabilitation and to use IT for formulating better plans and services. In this great noble and humanitarian task, we hope to continue our crusade against disability and look forward to a bright future for the disabled population of India.

References

- **Goel, S.K.** (1990) Education, training and rehabilitation of the handicapped in India: Retrospect and Prospect, Education and Society (Australia, 8(1), 21-29.
- **Goel, SK** (2000) Improving quality of life in India: Challenges and emerging concerns. In Robert L Schalock & Ken Keith (Eds)

Cross-Cultural Perspectives on Quality of Life. Washington" American Association on Mental Retardation, pp. 231-239.

- **Goel, SK** (2001) Information-based rehabilitation of visually handicapped in India: Challenges and emerging concerns. Paper presented in "Regional Level Technical Workshop for Professional Personnel Working for the Disability Rehabilitation" organized by SMRC, Bhubaneswar and RCI, Govt. of India held at Bhubaneshwar during 29-30 January.
- **Goel, SK** (2005) "An Orientation Guide For Promotion Of Vocational Education And Training Among Persons With Disabilities", Bhopal: PSSCIVE
- **Goel, SK** (2006) Report of the "Working Group Meeting for the Compendium of Scientific and Technological Developments for the Vocational Rehabilitation of Persons with Disabilities" held at PSSCIVE, Bhopal during Aug. 28- Sept. 01, 2006.
- **Goel, SK** (2009) "A Database of Vocational Education, Training And Rehabilitation Services for PWDs in India" Bhopal: Regional Institute of Education
- Mental Retardation. Paper presented at the 7th World Congress of the IASSMD at Vigyan Bhavan, New Delhi (India) during March 24-28.

18

Training of 'Adobe Photoshop' To Differentlyabled People

Dr. Rameshwari Pandya
Ms. Pooja Mistry

The computer technology is spreading all over the world! Could we have ever imagined back in the 80s that computers would play such a huge role in our lives? Computers have become an integral part of day to day life. They have become an integral part of the education system also. Having computers as a part of ones education can prove very helpful. Being good in studies and computers can secure better job prospects, in this age and time computer knowledge is a must.Computers have helped a lot in compiling a lot of data which used to be in hard records. One of the uses or benefits of computers is that they are able to provide and retrieve information so quickly so they have increased the pace of our work. The increase in the speed of work has helped us to do many things with less resource. Each day something new comes out which makes technology a better friend to humans - and a computer literate should at least be abreast with the information.

This is one use of computers in our lives other than that computers has helped us to work with machines which have the ability to produce the best quality of products with maximum speed and efficiency. In today's world it is necessary that to cater for such a heavy population things are made at the higher pace with best quality, so it is possible with the help of computer that we are able to cater the the need of quantity and quality of products required in daily life. Computer today is in every walk of life, and is helping us a lot in developing at a fast pace. Disability is an umbrella term, covering impairments, activity limitations, and participation restrictions. An impairment is a problem in body function or structure; an activity limitation

Differentlyabled in India

In our country about 16.15 Million people suffer from one or other types of disabilities. (e.g. visual, hearing, speech, and locomotors disabilities.) This covers 1.9% of our population. The rates of physical disabilities are 2% in the rural & 1.6% in the urban areas. (Source: Shubhanker Banerjee -1996) The physically handicapped is a valuable human resource which is often left untapped. This reservoir of human capabilities should be viewed from the perspective of employability if we are to help them achieve any measure of self- reliance .All aspects of placement, vocational training, job reservations, concessions, assistance and awards for physically handicapped persons should be considered.

After independence, various programs and schemes are being implemented to bring the disabled people of the society into mainstream. Ministry of welfare is the apex body for the rehabilitation of the handicapped in India acting directly or through the state welfare departments, voluntary organizations and international agencies. WHO the World health Organization defines Disability as follows: "Disabilities is an umbrella term, covering impairments, activity limitations, and participation restrictions. An impairment is a problem in body function or structure; an activity limitation is a difficulty encountered by an individual in executing a task or action; while a participation restriction is a problem experienced by an individual in involvement in life situations. Thus disability is a complex phenomenon, reflecting an interaction between features of a person's body and features of the society in which he or she lives". According to a directory of educational and vocational training institutes for the handicapped, there are around 458 institutions and agencies, both governmental and voluntary organizations are involved in the field of welfare and for the habilitation of the handicapped in India. Some national institutes are: National institute for visually handicapped National institute for the orthopaedically handicapped, National institute for the Hearing handicapped, National institute for mentally handicapped Most of them lead an isolated and lonely life. For the progress of the nation as a whole it is essential that this segment should also contribute its share in the process of socio - economic development.A disability may occur during a person's lifetime or may be present from birth. A physical impairment is any disability which limits the physical function of limbs or fine or gross motor ability.

Need of Computer Training for Differentlyabled

Computer training is the knowledge and ability to use computers and technology efficiently. Computer training can also refer to the comfort level someone has with using computer programes and other applications that are associated with computer.The basic purpose of computer training programs for handicapped people is that Computer work can be done easily. Computer knowledge coupled with certain other job skills increases one's chances of getting a job. Those with knowledge of computers are considered trainable for many kinds of jobs. As most of the jobs involve the use of computers, computer education is an eligibility criterion for almost all of the modern-day jobs. Higher education involving network administration, hardware maintenance or software skills open doors for brighter job opportunities.

Computer education helps one manage one's own business assets and personal finances. Computers serve as efficient means for management of information. Personal financial assets, medical records and important documents can be stored in an electronic format in a computer system. Today, banking transactions and payments of bills can be done over the Internet. Similarly, online shopping is becoming widely popular. To be in the race, it is very important to take computer education. The ability to use a personal computer and related technologies is rapidly becoming an absolute necessity for employment in virtually every industry. From the retail industry to the manufacturing industry to health care and insurance, computer literacy is becoming an important prerequisite to employment, and those who lack such training often find themselves left out in the cold when employment decisions are made. Even many jobs that previously did not require the use of a computer now do, and basic computer training is becoming an absolute necessity for those who need to gain these important skills.

In today's information driven world, computer skills and knowledge have rapidly become essential qualities for a person to possess. So, through computer training the handicapped people can do work on their own and most of work can be finished by computers, which has such a wide variety of applications, are indeed ruling society. To keep up the pace in this fast life of today, computer education is extremely important. Computers are an integral part of life and so is computer education. The differentlyabled persons have limitation of walking, standing but for computer work they are fit as they can perform their work in sitting posture.

About the Adobe Photoshop

Adobe Photoshop, or simply Photoshop, is a graphics editing program developed and published by Adobe Systems. It is image manipulation software. and is the flagship product of Adobe Systems. It has been described as "an industry standard for graphics professionals"It is widely used by professionals in a variety of disciplines, from motion graphics to web design to photography enhancement and beyond. 'Adobe Photoshop' is the leading image manipulation software for professional and advanced digital image makers. Photoshop has long been considered the standard of professional level graphics editing, and is popular for its number of tools, filters and visual effects.

It is Multimedia professionals like

- Photographers
- Designers
- Animators and
- Graphic producers.

Adobe Photoshop CS software delivers the broadest and most productive toolset available for web production, print production, and digital Photography. With Photoshop CS we can explore our creativity, Work at peak efficiency, and achieve the highest quality results across all media. It provides integrated tools for creating and outputting crisp, editable vector shapes and text. With these new tools, we can incorporate resolution-independent, vector – based graphics and type into pixel – based images to achieve an unparalleled range of design effects.

Adobe Photoshop CS's new features help us to customize keyboard shortcuts to suit our work. We can assign a new or existing shortcut to menu items, tools, and palette command. We can create PDF presentation with page transition by converting multiple files into a single, multi – page Adobe PDF document. The new filter gallery helps us to apply a series of filter to an image.

In Adobe Photoshop have different version First of all seven version -7 released after that version -8, version -9, version -10 .And other new version came that is CS, CS-2, CS-3 and CS-4 like that version was change and new tools and technique was come. New version is better than the old version because people do it her work easily through new version. As well as develop a new skill in different version.

In today's challenging business environment, Adobe Photoshop 7.0 helps you stay competitive with innovative tools that deliver new ways to express your creativity and work efficiently. With Photoshop 7.0, you can more easily produce exceptional imagery for print, the Web, wireless devices, and other media. The latest release of the world's leading image-editing solution. When opening graphics in Photoshop, Web designers will notice drastic colour shifts. The new colour management system in Photoshop reinterprets files by default. If you work with Web graphics, you need to turn this feature off. Go to File > Color Settings > Profile Setup. Under 'Embed Profiles', un-check 'RGB', and under assumed profiles, select 'None' from the RGB dropdown. Under 'Profile Mismatch Handling', select 'Ignore'.

Meet Every Challenge

Photoshop 7.0 rounds out its comprehensive toolset with new capabilities to meet any creative or production demand and to handle the widest variety of image-editing tasks in the most efficient way. The File Browser lets you quickly inspect images before opening them by viewing thumbnails and

Metadata such as color profile, date modified, and Exchangeable Image File (EXIF) information generated by digital cameras. With the new Healing Brush, you can effortlessly remove scratches and other flaws while

Preserving the image's shading, lighting, and texture. With enhanced Web features, you can instantly make Web page elements transparent simply by knocking out one or more colors; create dithered transparencies; manage Web page rollovers and animations; and create more sophisticated Web rollovers.

Stay Competitive

Powerful new tools help you explore your creativity without limits so you can more easily meet the multimedia demands of today's market. Simulate traditional painting techniques (including pastels and charcoal) with dry and wet brush effects and use brushes to add special effects. Adjust dozens of precise brush settings including size, shape, and tilt to create custom brushes that you can share with other Photoshop users. With the new Pattern Maker plug-in, you can select any area of an image and automatically generate a nearly endless assortment of background patterns. And the enhanced Liquify plug-in lets you distort images more easily and gain greater control over warping.

Work with Confidence

Photoshop 7.0 offers unparalleled precision and control so you can be confident you're achieving consistently superior output. New security features let you restrict access to your images with password protection. Using the enhanced Picture Package feature, you can quickly print a folder of images as customized pages, including multiple photos in different sizes on the same page. Create a sophisticated online showcase for your images with new Web Photo Gallery templates. Keep vector art and text looking crisp online by letting Image Ready automatically assign higher priority to those areas when optimizing for the Web.

Photoshop 7.0 is tightly integrated with other Adobe professional graphics programs for print, Web, paper and dynamic media, including Adobe Illustrator®, Adobe InDesign®, Adobe AlterCast™, Adobe GoLive™, Adobe Live Motion™, Adobe Premiere®, Adobe After Effects®, Adobe Acrobat®, and others. With Photoshop7.0, you can work with familiar, productive Adobe tools to create the highest quality graphics. Photoshop 7.0 also offers exciting enhancements and new features for Adobe Image Ready™ 7.0, which ships with Photoshop. Image Ready offers specialized features for accomplishing advanced Web-production tasks and creating highly sophisticated Web graphics and animations.

Meet Every Challenge

These days, graphics professionals are being called on to create images that work across a variety of media.You need a solution that lets you handle the widest variety of image-editing tasks and output images to multiplemedia—including print, the Web, wireless devices, and video—without having to learn a whole new set of tools. Photoshop 7.0 helps you work more efficiently than ever to meet the multimedia demands of today's Marketplace and make impossible deadlines possible.

Quickly Locate and Organize Images

The new File Browser lets you search for images visually rather than just by file name, saving time and effort. Using easy-to-view thumbnails, you can quickly organize and retrieve images from your hard drive, external drives, CDs, and disks directly within Photoshop. The File Browser provides metadata about the images displayed, such as date created, date modified, and EXIF (Exchangeable Image File) information from digital cameras. You can rotate, batch rename, rank, sort, and changes your files as well as manage image folders.

Use of Photoshop

Use of Photoshop as a image editing, for web designing, graphic designing, logo designing, and making a color ful photo.

Logo Stamp

If you have an image that you use over and over again, such as a logo or signature, you should make it into a brush. When creating custom brushes from image files, Photoshop saves the image on your 'Brushes' palette. Select the image, click on the Menu arrow on the 'Brushes' palette and select 'Define Brush'. The image now appears on the palette. You can use it just as you do with other brushes.

Save Photos As GIFs

Photoshop has improved its index colour conversions, which allows for higher quality 8-bit, 256-colour conversions from 24-bit images. Although photographs are normally saved as JPG images, the improved colour conversion will let you convert them to GIFs for Web use. This reduced file size will still retain image quality. To save an image as GIF, go to File > Export > GIF89a Export.

3D Transform

The new 3D Transform plugin lets you work with 2D images as if they were solid 3D objects, so you can adjust the perspective on an image from straight-on to various angles. Click on Filter > Render > 3D Transform. Draw a wire-frame over your image and use the Pan Camera and Trackball tools to manipulate the image perspective, and click OK.

Make It An Action Item

Actions automate routine tasks and save a lot of time. To create an 'Action', click on the 'Menu' arrow on the 'Action' palette and click on 'New Action'. Click 'Record' to start recording and carry out all the steps for the action you perform regularly. Once you're done, click on the 'Stop' button on the Action palette. To repeat the action, select it and click on the Play button on the palette.

Justification of the Project

Department of Extension and Communication, Faculty of Family and Community Sciences of The Maharaja Sayaji Rao University of Baroda has undertaken various action projects covering thrust areas like Moral value, Income generating activity, activity with blind girls, computer training etc. but this type of activity has not been done before.

The basic purpose of computer training programs on 'Adobe Photoshop' to guide the people that they can use the computer in their daily routine while doing their jobs and performing their tasks. The World Health Organization insists upon training must be performance oriented and job specific and it must not be expected to stand on its own. The training is basically one of the major tools for an organization through which it gains competent users and cream from the talent. Computer training classes give professionals edge in the ever changing business world. New software releases come out yearly and technology changes are seen. Yesterday's computer skills are obsolete and to stay ahead of the pack by taking the computer training class is the need of the hour. Computer is one of the technologies which is used by every one. The physically handicapped persons are no exception. They should not be ignored by the society. They also need the encouragement and support to live a dignified life. They have to learn and experience new technologies for the betterment of themselves as well as the society.

One of the reasons for their learning of computer 'Adobe Photoshop' is that a handicapped person can work on it's own. They do not have to move out as they can take order through e mail. Yet they can remain active, and independent. They are aware about new technology. There are practical demonstration showing that computer is the most viable avenue for providing employment opportunities for physically handicapped. Who can not move out freely because of their physical inabilities. In the modern concept of Global village, the physically handicapped boys and girls can work from their village home and can get proper instruction from their employer. As internet provides the necessary communication link this ensures better delivery system and right place for the neglected people of the society based on dignity of labour.

Now government is also providing bank loans for buying the computers and just one small room for doing work. Because of these reasons differentlyabled were selected as beneficiaries for the present project. Looking to the various benefits "An Action project on training of 'Adobe Photoshop' among Differentlyabled people of Vadodara city was taken up".

Objectives of the project

Broad Objective

To give training on computer 'Adobe Photoshop' amongst Differentlyabled people of Vadodara city.

Specific Objective

- To develop understanding regarding computer 'Adobe Photoshop' amongst selected Differentlyabled people of Vadodara city.
- To develop skills in utilization of computer 'Adobe Photoshop' amongst selected Differentlyabled people of Vadodara city.
- To study the reactions of the Differentlyabled people of Vadodara regarding the training on computer 'Adobe Photoshop'.

Methodology

To make any programme effective and successful the very first step is the drawing up of a plan of the action.It is necessary as systematic planning can provide guideline to implement the programme successfully.

Planning for Starting the Project

Before starting the project, a systematic planning was done, which was as follows:

Identify the Non Government Organization

In order to promote computer 'Adobe Photoshop' training for differentlyabled people it was important to identify an organization that could offer innovative efforts and help the project worker to meet the project objectives. Project worker visited The Society for Physically Handicapped. A detailed discussion about the project was held between the project worker and founder of the organization.The following pre-requisites were felt necessary to training of 'Adobe Photoshop' among differentlyabled people.Any centre with good infrastructure facilities like place, furniture, light, computer lab was required for smooth running of the project.Sufficient and suitable time for the training, allowing free of cost for training of computer 'Adobe Photoshop'.

Deciding the Venue, and Time for the Project

The project venue was computer laboratory of The Society for Physically Handicapped, E.M.E. Road, Majoor Mahajan Society Naka, Fathegunj, Vadodara- 390002, from Monday to Saturday from 6:00p.m. to 7:30p.m. for the training. There were five computers for the training as well as practice which they could spare for the project.

Getting Permission from the Founder of a The Society for Physically Handicapped.

The Project worker before conducting the training took written permission from the 'The Society for Physically Handicapped' to conduct Action Project on computer 'Adobe Photoshop' as the target group knew the basics of a computer and they were ready to learn 'Adobe Photoshop'.

Contacting Resource Person

The project worker contacted resource person and took help and guidance to person to teach computer 'Adobe Photoshop'. The project worker invited the resource person for their expert advice, Suggestions and to conducted expert talk and live Demonstration on computer. So that learners could easily understand the whole procedure.

Selection of the Content

The project worker discussed with to the experts regarding the project and its importance the objective of the project, the duration of course was one month, daily one and half hour except Sundays. Content was suitable in terms of ability of disabled people to learn new things, usage of computer and course were following:

- Importance of computer 'Adobe Photoshop'.
- Uses of Computer 'Adobe Photoshop'.
- Uses of Different toolbar.
- Uses of Different Menu bar.
- Small Animation.

Preparing Teaching Aids

Teaching Aids helps the learners to understand the concept easily several experiments have shown that Teaching Aids can be helpful in making any programme successful, project worker prepared teaching aids like charts, posters, and pamphlets for different lessons.

Execution of the Project

The project aimed at training of computer 'Adobe photoshop' was executed after the planning of all the aspects of this project. It was executed under the following steps.

Rapport Building with the Target Group

First time when project worker met them and she introduced her self and discussed with them about the project which she had in mind. Informally during discussion she foumd out their names and interest in learning 'Adobe Photoshop' gradually rapport was built. They also shard their experiences during the introduction class and it was good time for building rapport with them.

Traning session for 'Adobe Photoshop' with differently abled people

The Project worker took help from an expert to conduct the training programme. Expert is qualified person having two years experience in the field of computer 'Adobe Photoshop.' A session was conducted between the 'The Society for Physically Handicapped.' and the project worker to take care of their doubts and make them realize that the training in 'Adobe Photoshop' will have great value for differentlyabled people in future So, they understood the value of learning. At the end of the session differentlyabled people learnt computer 'Adobe Photoshop' and as well as were given practical experience which was helpful to them. Practical experience is quite useful for the success of final out come.

Motivational Activities

A motivational activity is necessary for every person. Student motivation naturally has to do with students' desire to participate in the learning process. But it also concerns the reasons or goals that underlie their involvement or non involvement in academic activities. Although students may be equally motivated to perform a task, the sources of their motivation may differ. The term Motivation to learn has a slightly different meaning. It is defined by one author as "the meaningfulness, value, and benefits of academic tasks to the learner-regardless of whether or not they are intrinsically interesting" (Hermine Marshall 1987). Motivation to learn is characterized by long-term, quality involvement in learning and commitment to the process of learning (Carole Ames 1990).

Physically present in the classroom but largely mentally absent; they fail to invest themselves fully in the experience of learning. Because of this motivational activity is necessary. In this action project on 'Adobe Photoshop' different types of activities like indoor games, devotional songs and sing song etc were planned while working with the disabled. Thus, it created interest, and they did not become a bored. Through motivational activity educators tried in reducing student apathy. As motivational activity is very useful for learners as well as for researcher they create interest and helps in understanding that's why motivational activity is important.

Valedictory Programme

Action project training was completed with successful valedictory function. Certificates were given to the differently abled people. At the end of training thanking note was delivered by the project worker. The project was a success as differentlyabled people were satisfied with the computer 'Adobe Photoshop' training

Finding Discussion

About the the Society for Physically Handicapped.

The society for physically handicapped E.M.E. road, Majoor Mahajan society naka, Fathegunj, Vadodara- 390002. ph.no: 0265-2792242.is a Vadodara based voluntary organization having premises of 11000sq.ft.with two floored infrastructure, registered under ' Persons with disability Act – 1996', devoting services for the welfare, betterment, upliftment and development of "Differentlyable community" all around Vadodara district, having more than 2000enrolled family members.

For realization of hopes and aspirations of persons with disabilities, The society for the physically handicapped helps them in discovering their ability, exposing their potentials and equipping them accordingly to achieve a new identify. Simultaneously it assists them to cross the world of the disability to a different ability and from sympathy to empathy – A world of new millennium. The society for the physically handicapped focuses on the components of early identification, awareness, and rehabilitation. Make interventions towards inclusion for the improved quality of life for the peoples with disabilities.

Highlights of the Activities Organized

- Take measures to create barrier free environment.
- Assist in accessibility of equal opportunity and protection of life.
- Providing Educational Aids.
- Organizing Medical camps, distribution of aids and appliances as per needs.
- Employment placement Services.
- Devising self employment and vocational training program and supplying aids.

- Upliftment of Social Status.
- Free Physiotherapy treatment to disabled.
- Dissemination of information about scholarship, concession loan etc.
- Organizing life partner selection mela and marriage counseling.
- Computer training centre.
- Conducting Survey for identification of differently able community as per the guidelines of Govt. of Gujarat under maharshi Asta Vakra Samudya Adharit Viklang Punervasan Yojna.

Over and above all these Activities, with complete devotion and dedication The society for the physically handicapped has played a dominant role in the upliftment of persons with disabilities in each & every sphere of his life ceaselessly since 1972. It has proved and history reveals that:

- Disabled prefer to work than to live on charity.
- Disabled are not job handicapped.
- Disabled can be productive.
- Disabled are not emotional liabilities to the Society.

The society for the physically handicapped is not content to rest on its laurels. It knows that much more needs to be done differently able persons need to be touched by its guiding spirit.

To meet the aspirations of the differently able community, The society for the physically handicapped has planned following:

- Training in Desktop Publishing, Computer Art, Graphics and animation.
- Apparels manufacturing unit and Tailoring Classes.
- Repairs of home appliances and electronic equipments.

Evaluation of the Project

In Action Project Evaluation and feedback is important. The Project worker can use the reactions of the trainees for the effectiveness and guide for the future programme.

Evaluation is one of the sources of information with the success of objective of the project. To know the effectiveness of the project Evaluation was conducted by the project worker.

Back Ground information

Table: 1 Percentage distribution of physically handicapped according to their age

N=17

Sr. No	*Age in years*	*Percentage (%)*
1	15-30	53
2	31-45	35
3	46-60	12

Table 1 reveals that 53%of handicapped were between 15-30 year of age where as 35% were between 31-45years where as 12% between 46-60 years.

Table:2 Percentage Distribution of physically handicapped according to their gender

N=17

Sr. No	*Gender*	*Percentage (%)*
1	Male	82
2	Female	18

It is also revealed from the table2 that 82%of handicapped were male & very few 18%were female.

Table: 3 Percentage distribution of physically handicapped according to their religion

N=17

Sr. No	*Religion*	*Percentage (%)*
1	Hindu	76
2	Muslim	6
3	Christian	12
4	Buddha	6

Table 3 shows that 76% of handicapped were Hindu and 12% were Christian and only 6% were Muslim and Budhist.

Table: 4 Percentage distribution of physically handicapped according to their Marital status

N=17

Sr. No	*Marriage*	*Percentage (%)*
1	Married	41
2	Unmarried	59

Table 4 reveals that 41% of handicapped were married 59% were unmarried.

Table: 5 Percentage distribution of physically handicapped according to their Educational level

N= 17

Sr. No	*Educational level*	*Percentage (%)*
1	Secondary	12
2	Higher secondary	47
3	Diploma	12
4	Graduate	23
5	Post graduate	6

Table 5 shows that47% handicapped were educated till higher secondary 23% were graduate further table reveals that 12% were diploma holders 6% were educated up to post graduation level.

Table: 6 Percentage distribution according to computer training taken by them

N=17

Sr. No	*Computer training*	*Percentage (%)*
1	Basic	94
2	Tally	-
3	Hardware	6
4	Software	-

It is shows that all handicapped people knew the basic of computers and six percent had taken traning of Computer Hardware.

Table: 7 Percentage distribution of physically handicapped according to their disability

N=17

Sr. No	*Disability*	*Percentage (%)*
1	Leg	17
2	Hand	

Table 7 shows that 100% of handicapped people had disability of the leg.

Table: 8 Percentage distribution according to their disability

N = 17

Sr. No	*How they became disabled*	*Percentage (%)*
1	Since birth	47
2	Through Accident	6
3	Polio	35
4	Any other	12

Table 8 reveals that 47% of them were handicap from the birth & 35% were because of polio &12% were having any other reason and 6% of people were disablled because of accident.

Table: 9 Percentage distribution according to the years of association with the institute

N=17

S.No	*Since how long*	*Percentage (%)*
1	1-5 years	41
2	6-10 years	41
3	11-15 years	18

Table 9 reveals that 41%of handicapped were coming to this institute since last 5 years and another 41% were coming since last 10years & very few 18% of people were coming since15 years.

Table: 10 Percentage distribution according to the mode of traveling

N = 17

Sr. No	*Mode of traveling*	*Percentage (%)*
1	Through tri Cycle	35
2	With other persons vehicle	24
3	Any other.	41

Table 10 shows that 35% handicapped came through tricycle 24%were coming with other persons vehicle & 41% were came by bus or autoriksha.

Table: 11 Percentage distribution according to the facility provided by the government

N=17

Sr. No	*Facility from Government*	*Percentage (%)*
1	Yes	82
2	No	18

Table 11 shows that 82% of people reported that they were provided government facility and only 18% of people reported that they did not get any facility.

Table: 12 Percentage distribution according to any facility provide by NGO's or Bank

N=17

Sr. No	*Facility*	*Percentage (%)*
1	Yes	47
2	No	53

Table 12 shows that 53% of handicapped were not getting any facility by NGO's or Bank, and 47%were getting some or the other facility.

Problems faced during the Project work

- The time allotted for the activities was very limited so, it became very difficult for the project worker to complete the work.
- Some students were irregular thus project worker found it difficult since she had to repeat the previous topics again.

Suggestions

- A Similar type of project can be taken up with other organization of Baroda city which are working with differently abled people.
- Other such type of course like data entry, designing can be taken up for the differentlyabled people

Bibliography

- **Banerjee, S.** (1996) Programme for disabled welfare, Social welfare, Vol.43 No.5 New Delhi.
- **Bender. M;** Valletutti.P; and Bender. R (1976) Teaching the Moderately and severely handicapped, library of congress cataloging in publication data, Maryland.
- **Buisch, C.A;** and J.L. Schulman (1969) Toyes and games for educationally Handicapped children.
- **Mohapatra, S.** (1995) Acceptance of the Disabled in society, Social welfare., vol. 41 No.10, New Delhi.
- **Prasad.** (1996) Consider their abilities not disability, Social welfare, Vol.43 No.5 New Delhi.
- **Verma, S.** (1997) The Handicapped Child-What is possible?, Social welfare, Vol. 44 No. 8-9 New Delhi.

Webliography

- http://www.cvtips.com
- www.helium.com
- www.blurtit.com
- encyclopedia.farlex.com

Index

In the next phase, a strategy was evolved and low-cost media messages were developed keeping in view the background information of the target community in general and their need saliency in particular, with regard to pre-natal care. The media materials like leaflets and posters were developed, pre-tested, finalized and distributed. Four social animators were selected from within the community and given orientation thoroughly in providing simulation, conducting focus group meetings and collecting feedback. The media messages were distributed in two phases. The posters were affixed in targeted places.

There was a gap of one month between both the phases of distribution of message materials. After the distribution of leaflets, focus group meetings were organized with selected members of the community to bring clarity to the messages. Finally, the evaluative assessment was worked out to draw a comparative conclusion between the base-line and end-line study. Critical ratio (CR) was computed to find out the significant difference between the base-line and end-line reports.

Discussion

Data analysis of background profile of the samples, as presented in Table – 1, reveals that the average monthly income of the samples of tribal and rural groups was Rs.1500 and Rs.2350/- respectively. Their educational background showed that more number of women were illiterate in tribal areas than rural areas, the level of education was better in rural areas than their counterparts in tribal settings.

Table – 1
Background profile

Particulars		*Tribal*	*Rural*
Family income per month (Average)		*Rs.1500.00*	*Rs.2350.00*
Education	Illiterate	67%	5%
	Primary	31%	72%
	Under Metric	2%	23%

U

V